Against

Romanticism

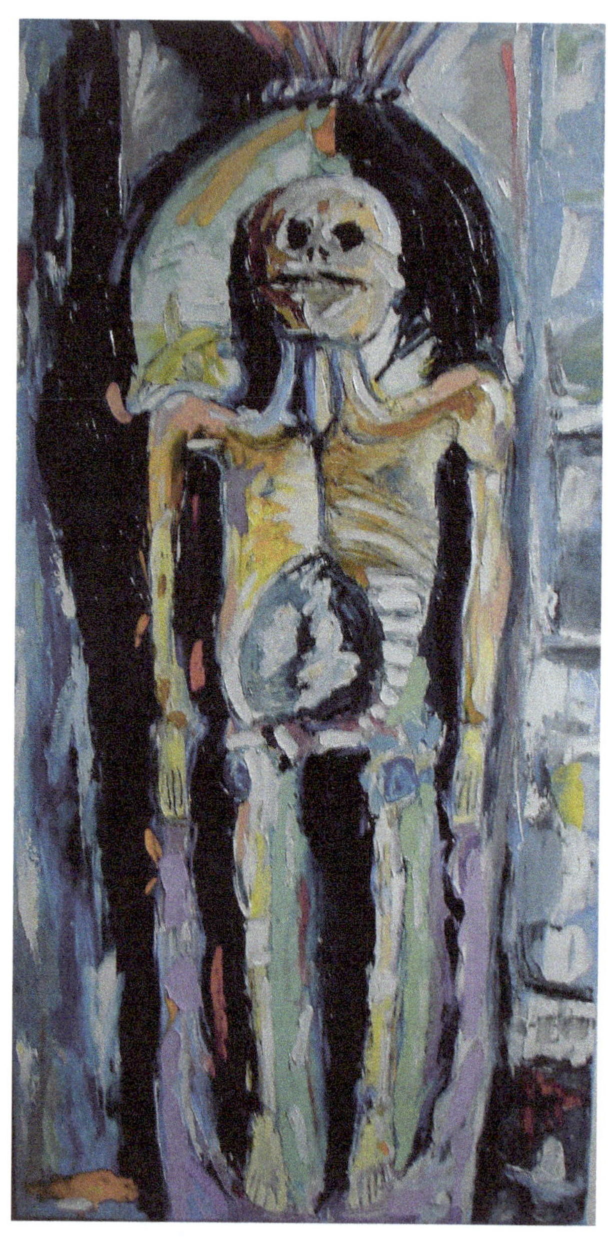

Allegory on Nationalism
(based on mid-fifteenth-century cadaver tombstone, Beaulieu
churchyard near Drogheda)
Oil on canvas / Ola ar chanbhás 40cm x 80cm
Painting by Caoimhghin Ó Croidheáin

Against Romanticism

From Enlightenment to Enfrightenment and the Culture of Slavery

Caoimhghin Ó Croidheáin

A Handbook for Cultural Practitioners

Colophon

Gaelart Publishing

Design: Ieva Grbacjana (https://igrbacjana.com/)
Cover photography: Philip O'Neill (https://www.philiponeillphotography.com/)
Cover painting: *Sapere Aude!* by Caoimhghin Ó Croidheáin (http://gaelart.net/)
Back cover: *Pallas and the Centaur* (Public domain / Wikimedia Commons)

Typeset in 12pt Cambria and 10pt Work Sans

Published in Dublin, Ireland

The greatest part of a writer's time is spent in reading, in order to write; a man will turn over half a library to make one book.
Samuel Johnson

To my nieces Sophie and Eva

**The rays of the sun
Drive away the night;
Destroyed is the hypocrite's
Surreptitious power.**
Wolfgang Amadeus Mozart
The Magic Flute

Contents

Acknowledgements

Against Romanticism: From Enlightenment to Enfrightenment and the Culture of Slavery is a compilation of fifteen articles published by globalresearch.ca, first appearing on June 22, 2018 and continuing until May 17, 2021. I expanded and edited the articles and added frontispieces to each chapter.

I would like to express my gratitude to Professor Michel Chossudovsky of The Centre for Research on Globalization (CRG), Montreal, Canada, and Editor of globalresearch.ca without whose support over the years this book would have never have come together. Professor Chossudovsky's insistence on publishing independent reports, research, and analysis on a variety of different social, political, economic, cultural, strategic and environmental issues, has been an inspiration for me and his many readers around the world.

In a similar vein, I would like to acknowledge my gratitude to Angie Tibbs, Editor of dissidentvoice.org and Dr. Kiyul Chung, Visiting Professor, Tsinghua University, Beijing, China, Editor in Chief of 21cir.com, both of whom have stood against the tide of growing conservatism and controls that are being exerted on many internet websites today. They have been great interlocutors and generous publishers of my articles over the years.

I would also like to thank Professor Michael Cronin, Dr Trish Van Bolderen, Dr David Denby, Roberto Quaglia, Brendan Bradley, Paul Cryan and Owen Brannigan for their encouraging discussions and support on the various topics covered in the book.

I would like to thank Ieva Grbacjana for her great advice and elegant layout skills.

For a hilarious evening staging the photographs for the cover painting, I would like to express my gratitude to Barbara Gomes and Ivan Rodrigues, two Brazilians always up for a bit of *craic*.

For company and encouraging words (especially during the lockdowns), my mother Veronica, my sisters Karen and Susan, and my nieces Sophie and Eva.

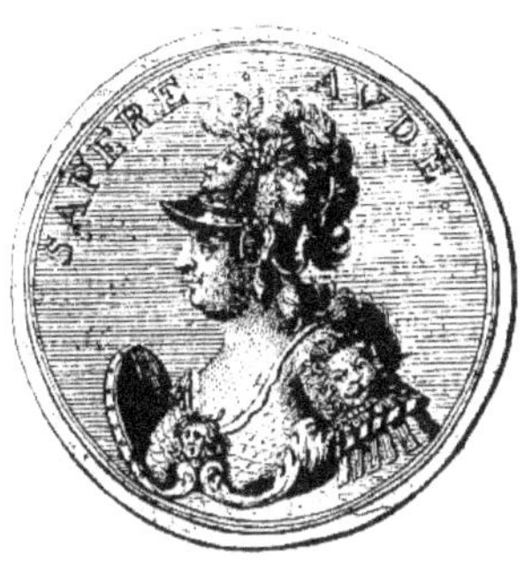

Sapere Aude **- 'Dare to Know'**

Medal of the Society of Truth-Lovers also Societas Alethophilorum (1740). Front with portrait of Minerva with the image of the philosophers Leibnitz and Wolff on the helmet. The aim of the society was the knowledge of the truth as the result of one's own conviction from sincere search and its defense. The primary task of the society was to help Christian Wolff's philosophy gain a higher presence.
(https://second.wiki/wiki/gesellschaft_der_wahrheitsliebenden)
(Image: Public Domain / Wikimedia Commons)

Christian Wolff (1679-1754) was a German polymath, lawyer and mathematician as well as one of the most important philosophers of the Enlightenment between Leibniz and Kant. His main achievement was a complete oeuvre on almost every scholarly subject of his time, displayed and unfolded according to his demonstrative-deductive, mathematical method, which perhaps represents the peak of Enlightenment rationality in Germany.
(https://en.wikipedia.org/wiki/Christian_Wolff_(philosopher)

Sapere aude is the Latin phrase meaning 'Dare to know'; and is also loosely translated as 'Dare to be wise', or even more loosely as 'Dare to think for yourself!' Originally used in the *Epistularum liber primus* (First Book of Letters) (20 BCE), by the Roman poet Horace, the phrase *Sapere aude* became associated with the Age of Enlightenment, during the 17th and 18th centuries, after Immanuel Kant used it in the essay, 'Answering the Question:
What Is Enlightenment?' (1784)
(https://en.wikipedia.org/wiki/Sapere_aude)

Introduction

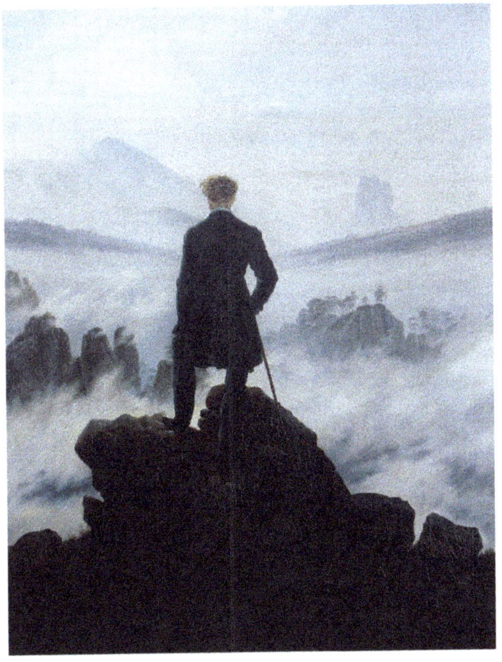

Caspar David Friedrich (1774–1840),
Wanderer above the Sea of Fog (1818), Kunsthalle Hamburg
(considered one of the masterpieces of Romanticism)
(Cybershot800i / Public Domain / Wikimedia Commons)

Alone we can do so little; together we can do so much.
Helen Keller

Ar scáth a chéile a mhaireann na daoine
(In the shadow of each other, we live)
Irish saying

What's the matter with Romanticism?

All artforms are in the service of the greatest of all arts:
the art of living.
Bertolt Brecht

We are all raised in a culture of Romanticism, an amorphous ideology that saturates cultural and political beliefs in society today. Romanticism is defined by its emphasis on subjectivity, emotion and individualism. It has pervaded all the arts, society and politics and its individualism is an essential aspect of ideologies such as Modernism, Postmodernism, Nationalism, and Neoliberalism. Romanticism arose as a reaction to the Age of Enlightenment, a period of time when intellectual and philosophical movements discussed and developed ideas on liberty, toleration, progress, separation of church and state, and constitutional government.

The early Romanticists appeared progressive in that they reacted to the extremes of the Industrial Revolution but then advocated a return to medieval ideas about society and production. However, the height of Romanticism coincided with the development and rise of socialist ideology. The socialists also criticized the Industrial Revolution but from a very different perspective. They were more concerned with the poverty and extremes of wealth inequality created by laissez faire capitalism, especially questioning individual control of the means of production.

Thus, it can be argued that the Romanticists wanted to see a move backwards to the individualist feudal ways of doing things rather than giving in to the potential of a collectivist future. In the arts Romanticism emphasized intense emotion, horror and awe of the beauty of nature in opposition to Enlightenment ideas derived from the naturalism of the Greek and Roman classics and empirical reason.

The Enlightenment philosophers also used rational thinking to fight the extreme forms of social injustice prevalent at the time. They opposed absolute monarchy, torture and the death penalty, questioned religious orthodoxy, while supporting concepts of free speech and thought, republicanism and revolution, separation of church and state, and a civil order based on natural law.

As Romanticism gave way to Realism a pattern emerged of Romanticist-influenced movements (Modernism, Postmodernism, Metamodernism) competing with Enlightenment-influenced movements (Realism, Social Realism, Socialist Realism). The descendants of the Romanticist movement all had in common the antirationalist rejection of Enlightenment thinking, while the descendants of the Enlightenment continued with ideas of liberty, exposing colonialism and working-class poverty, and depicting resistance to oppression.

Today, as in the past, there is still an ideological conflict in society between a diversionary, escapist culture (which is dominant, hegemonic and well-funded) and a culture of criticism and resistance (which is in the minority and barely funded, if at all).

Inside this diversionary, escapist culture we are led to believe that all is fine and we only need to work, relax and enjoy life while our politicians take care of any local, national and international issues. However, these 'background' issues are not steady, unchanging facets of life. They are dynamic, belligerent and dangerous.

We are sinking into a quicksand of Romanticism leaving elites free to carry out war agendas on a global scale. There is a gradually developing showdown between the current unipolar world and the fast-developing pressure for a multipolar world.

While it is considered that the history of Romanticism has been problematic, it is still perceived to be 'better' than the history of science, which, through the development of ever more sophisticated technology, is thought to be increasing and refining exploitation of human and natural resources, and therefore, ultimately destroying the planet.

However, is this true? This book attempts to reexamine the effects of Enlightenment and Romanticist ideas on society today while at the same time exploring their history and origins in the eighteenth and nineteenth centuries.

Chapter 1 looks at the original intentions of the Enlightenment philosophers showing that the main motivating force for their endeavors was not just to maintain the scholarly work of Renaissance humanism but to develop the ideas necessary for democratic institutions and the fight against social injustice in all its forms. Far from being cold rationalists, the Enlightenment philosophers were moved emotionally by the society around them to try and effect positive changes, thus explaining the use of the term Sentimentalism to describe the Enlightenment artforms that tried to expose the plight of the poor. The conservative and aristocratic nature of German Romanticism is examined as well as the working-class perspectives on Enlightenment and Romanticist philosophies, as analyzed by Marx and Engels, who saw a connection between Enlightenment ideas and socialism.

Chapter 2 shows the effects of Enlightenment and Romanticism on politics. Philosophers like Montesquieu wrote about concepts of citizenship and republican government that would replace one's status of being a subject under the absolute rule of monarchies. The Romanticist emphasis on cultural, linguistic and ethnic nationalism arose in opposition to the burgeoning liberal and socialist movements of the time. By the twentieth century competing nationalisms led to the tragedy of the Great War and then to the extreme ethnic nationalism of national socialism in Germany and the Second World War. Since then the influence of Romanticism can still be seen in the rise of supranational entities and postnationalism, from, for example, a 'German' national identity to a 'European' national identity (rather than international working-class solidarity).

Chapters 3 to 12 apply these ideas to various artforms: art, music, opera, dance, poetry, literature, theatre, architecture, cinema, and TV. The history of each form since Enlightenment times is examined and the effects of such ideas on form and content is contrasted with the form and content of Romanticist movements. As Romanticism pulled the arts in ethereal and escapist directions, resistance culture examined the plight of the oppressed using different forms such as naturalism, realism, social realism, as well as working-class socialist realism. In more difficult times these fundamentally different Enlightenment and Romanticist approaches to the arts came into conflict with each other and at other times one took over from the other depending on the changing socio-political circumstances. The overwhelming influence of Romanticist ideas today can be attributed as much to the repackaging and sale of mass suffering as catharsis, as to the massive financial support given them by global entities.

Chapter 13 summarizes these ideas into a general analysis of culture that goes in two opposite directions. One that diverts the attention of people away from exploitation (the culture of slavery) and another which aims to create awareness of how such exploitation operates (the culture of resistance). This chapter also shows that while science and technology are responsible for much exploitation of people and resources, modernity cannot be reduced to the domination of nature and human beings by science. Many progressive movements and changes were brought about by Enlightenment ideas and these ideas are an essential aspect of the different forms that the culture of resistance takes today.

On a broader level, the connection between Romanticism and the problematic history of irrationalism is discussed in the Conclusion and shows the continuing importance of rational thinking as the basis for future action.

Through developing an awareness of the socio-political fault lines in today's culture, cultural practitioners can create a new democratic spirit with an emphasis on the value of ordinary people, while at the same time making an important contribution to the fight against poverty, oppression, and injustice.

Chapter 1
Philosophy

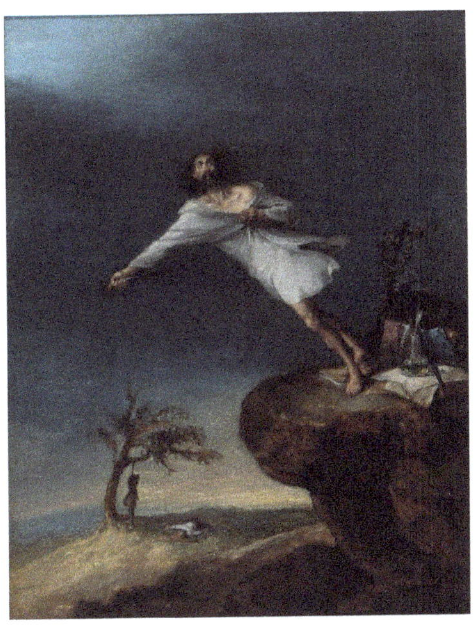

Satire on Romantic Suicide (1839) by Leonardo Alenza y Nieto (1807–1845)
(Public Domain / Wikimedia Commons)

We are slipping back from the age of reason into the mire of mystery, into a world of gods and devils, ghouls and angels. The difference this time is that we have chosen ignorance over knowledge, vapidity over insight, folly over realism. Consequently, we only have ourselves to blame when the rich and powerful take advantage of us.
Andrew Davenport

Re-Examining Emotion and Justice in Enlightenment Ideals

> *A man who desires to be solely head, is just as much a monster as one who desires to be only heart; the whole, healthy man is both. And that he is both, with each in its place, the heart not in the head and the head not in the heart, is precisely what makes him a human being.*
> Johann Gottfried Herder

What is Romanticism? And how does it affect us in the 21st century? The fact is that we are so immersed in Romanticism now that we cannot see the proverbial wood for the haunted-looking trees. Romanticism has so saturated our culture that we need to stand back and remind ourselves what it is, and examine how it has seeped into our thinking processes to the extent that we are not even aware of its presence anymore. Or why this is a problem. The Romanticist influence of intense emotion makes up a large part of modern culture, for example, in much pop music, cinema, TV and literature, e.g. genres such as Superheroes, Fantasy, Horror, Magical realism, Saga, Westerns.

Romanticism and the modern world

Romanticism arose out of the Enlightenment in the eighteenth century as a reaction to what was perceived as a rationalisation of life to the point of being anti-nature. The Romanticists were against the

Industrial Revolution, universalism and empiricism, emphasising instead heroic individualists and artists, and the individual imagination as a critical authority rather than classical ideals.

The Enlightenment had developed from the earlier Renaissance with a renewed interest in the classical traditions and ideals of harmony, symmetry, and order based on reason and science. On a political level the Enlightenment promoted republicanism in opposition to monarchy which ultimately led to the French revolution.

The worried conservatives of the time reacted to the progressive ideas of the Enlightenment and reason with a philosophy which was based on religious ideas and glorified the past (especially Medieval times and the 'Golden Age'). This philosophy became known as Romanticism and emphasised medieval ideas and society over the new ideas of democracy, capitalism and science.

Romanticism originated in Europe towards the end of the 18th century, and in most areas was at its peak in the approximate period from 1800 to 1890. It was initially marked by innovations in both content and literary style and by a preoccupation with the subconscious, the mystical, and the supernatural. This period was followed by the development of cultural nationalism and a new attention to national origins, an interest in native folklore, folk ballads and poetry, folk dance and music, and even previously ignored medieval and Renaissance works.

The Romantic movement "emphasized intense emotion as an authentic source of aesthetic experience, placing new emphasis on such emotions as apprehension, horror and terror, and awe—especially that experienced in confronting the new aesthetic categories of the sublimity and beauty of nature."[1] The importance of the medieval lay in the pre-capitalist significance of its individual crafts and tradesmen, as well as its feudal peasants and serfs.

Thus, Romanticism was a reaction to the birth of the modern world: urbanisation, secularisation, industrialisation, and consumerism. Romanticism emphasised intense emotion and feelings which over the centuries came to be seen as one of its most important characteristics, in opposition to the 'cold', 'unfeeling' Enlightenment rationalism that had resulted in widespread industrialization.

---

[1] https://en.wikipedia.org/wiki/Romanticism

Origins of Enlightenment emotion

However, this 'cold', 'unfeeling' scenario is actually very far from the truth. In fact, the Enlightenment itself had its origins in emotion. Enlightenment philosophers of the eighteenth century tried to create a philosophy of feeling that would allow them to solve the problem of the injustice in the unfeeling world they saw all around them.

Anthony Ashley Cooper, 3rd Earl of Shaftesbury (1671 – 1713) believed that all human beings had a 'natural affection' or natural sociability which bound them together, Francis Hutcheson (1694 – 1746) wrote that "All Men have the same Affections and Senses", probably best summed up in his question: "Whence this secret Chain between each Person and Mankind? How is my Interest connected with the most distant Parts of it?"[2]

David Hume (1711 – 1776) believed that human beings extend their "imaginative identification with the feelings of others" when it is required. Similarly, Adam Smith (1723 – 1790), the writer of *Wealth of Nations*, believed in the power of the imagination to inform us and help us understand the suffering of others.[3] In Italy, Cesare Beccaria (1738 – 1794) wrote his famous treatise *On Crimes and Punishments* (1764), which "condemned torture and the death penalty, and was a founding work in the field of penology and the Classical School of criminology."[4]

Voltaire (1694 – 1778) was so incensed at the trial, torture and execution of Jean Calas (for the murder of his son) despite his protestations of innocence, that he wrote his *Treatise on Tolerance on the Occasion of the Death of Jean Calas from the Judgment Rendered in Toulouse* (*Traité sur la tolérance*) in which he railed against religious intolerance and fanaticism. Hugo Grotius (1583–1645) believed[5] that individuals, both individual persons and individual groups of persons, are bearers of rights. His masterpiece *De Jure Belli ac Pacis* (1625; *On the Law of War and Peace*) is considered one

---

[2] Francis Hutcheson, An Inquiry into the Original of our Ideas of *Beauty and Virtue* (1726, 2004) https://oll.libertyfund.org/title/leidhold-an-inquiry-into-the-original-of-our-ideas-of-beauty-and-virtue-1726-2004

[3] Anthony Pagden, *The Enlightenment: And Why it Still Matters* (Oxford Uni Press, 2015) p72/73

[4] https://en.wikipedia.org/wiki/Cesare_Beccaria

[5] https://plato.stanford.edu/entries/grotius/

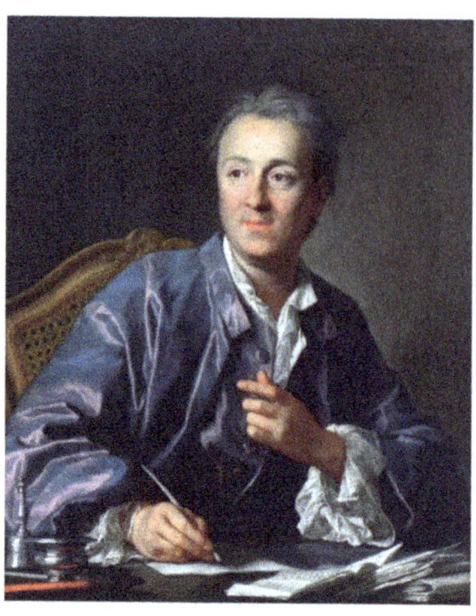

Portrait of Denis Diderot (1713-1784) (1767)
by Louis-Michel van Loo (1707–1771)
(Public Domain / Wikimedia Commons)

of the greatest contributions to the development of international law which Grotius wrote with the aim of minimizing bloodshed.[6]

For the Enlightenment philosophers the relationship between feeling and reason was of absolute importance. To develop ideas that would progress society for the better, a sense of morality was essential. Denis Diderot (1713–1784) a prominent French philosopher of the Enlightenment in France, for example, had strong views on the importance of the passions. Henry Martyn Lloyd writes:

Diderot did believe in the utility of reason in the pursuit of truth – but he had an acute enthusiasm for the passions, particularly when it came to morality and aesthetics. With many of the key figures in the Scottish Enlightenment, such as David Hume, he believed that morality was grounded in sense-experience. Ethical judgment was closely aligned with, even indistinguishable from, aesthetic judgments, he claimed. We judge the beauty of a painting, a landscape or our lover's face just as we judge the morality of a character in a novel, a play or our own lives – that is, we judge the good

---

[6] https://www.britannica.com/biography/Hugo-Grotius

and the beautiful directly and without the need of reason. For Diderot, then, eliminating the passions could produce only an abomination. A person without the ability to be affected, either because of the absence of passions or the absence of senses, would be morally monstrous.[7]

As Diderot wrote in a letter to Sophie Volland:

If the spectacle of injustice sometimes rouses me to so much indignation that I lose my judgement over it, and that I'd kill, I'd destroy, during this delirium; so the spectacle of equity fills me with a sweetness, inflames me with such ardor and enthusiasm that life would mean nothing to me if I had to yield it up.[8]

Moreover, to remove the passions from science would lead to inhuman approaches and methods that would divert and alienate science from its ultimate goal of serving humanity, as Lloyd writes:

That the Enlightenment celebrated sensibility and feeling didn't entail a rejection of science, however. Quite the opposite: the most sensitive individual – the person with the greatest sensibility – was considered to be the most acute observer of nature. The archetypical example here was a doctor, attuned to the bodily rhythms of patients and their particular symptoms. Instead, it was the speculative system-builder who was the enemy of scientific progress – the Cartesian physician who saw the body as a mere machine, or those who learned medicine by reading Aristotle but not by observing the ill. So the philosophical suspicion of reason was not a rejection of rationality per se; it was only a rejection of reason in isolation from the senses, and alienated from the impassioned body.[9]

---

[7] https://aeon.co/ideas/why-the-enlightenment-was-not-the-age-of-reason

[8] https://dokumen.pub/the-enlightenment-an-interpretation-vol-1-the-rise-of-modern- pagan-ism-1.html

[9] https://aeon.co/ideas/why-the-enlightenment-was-not-the-age-of-reason

Michael L. Frazer describes the importance of Enlightenment justice and sympathy in his book *The Enlightenment of Sympathy*. He writes:

> Reflective sentimentalists recognize our commitment to justice as an outgrowth of our sympathy for others. After our sympathetic sentiments undergo reflective self-correction, the sympathy that emerges for all those who suffer injustice poses no insult to those for whom it is felt. We do not see their suffering as mere pain to be soothed away when and if we happen to share it. Instead under Hume's account, we condemn injustice as a violation of rules that are vitally important to us all. And under Smith's account, we condemn the sufferings of the victims of injustice as injustice because we sympathetically share the resentment that they feel toward their oppressors, endorsing such feelings as warranted and acknowledging those who feel them deserve better treatment.[10]

Cooper, Hume and Smith were living in times, not only devoid of empathy, but also even of basic sympathy. Robert C. Solomon writes of society then in *A Passion for Justice*:

> There have always been the very rich. And of course there have always been the very poor. But even as late as the civilized and sentimental eighteenth century, this disparity was not yet a cause for public embarrassment or a cry of injustice. [...] Poverty was considered just one more 'act of God,' impervious to any solution except mollification through individual charity and government poorhouses to keep the poor off the streets and away from crime.[11]

Enlightenment emotion eventually gave rise to social trends that emphasised humanism and the heightened value of human

---

[10] Michael L Frazer, *The Enlightenment of Sympathy: Justice and the Moral Sentiments in the Eighteenth Century and Today* (Oxford Uni Press, 2010) p126/127

[11] Robert C Solomon, *A Passion for Justice: Emotions and the Origins of the Social Contract* (Rowman and Littlefield Pub., 1995) p13

life. These trends had their complement in art, creating what became known as the 'sentimental novel'. While today sentimentalism evokes maudlin self-pity, in the eighteenth century it was revolutionary as sentimental literature:

focused on weaker members of society, such as orphans and condemned criminals, and allowed readers to identify and sympathize with them. This translated to growing sentimentalism within society, and led to social movements calling for change, such as the abolition of the death penalty and of slavery. Instead of the death penalty, popular sentiment called for the rehabilitation of criminals, rather than harsh punishment. Frederick Douglass himself was inspired to stand against his own bondage and slavery in general in his famous *Narrative* by the speech by the sentimentalist playwright Sheridan in *The Columbian Orator* detailing a fictional dialogue between a master and slave.[12]

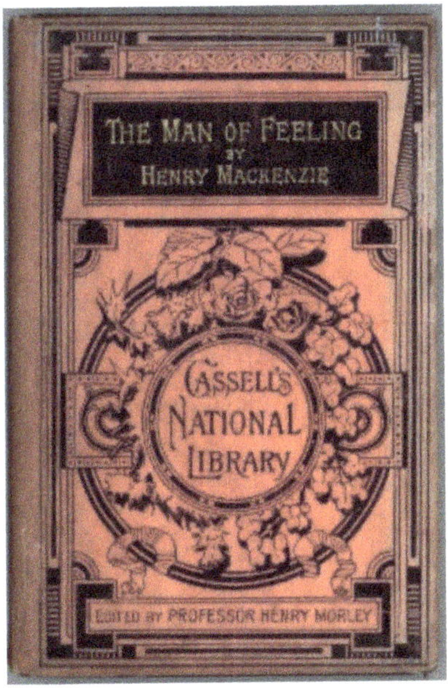

Cassell & Company edition by David Price (1886)
(Public Domain / Project Gutenberg)

---

[12] https://en.wikipedia.org/wiki/Sentimental_novel

As Solomon notes: "What distinguishes us not just from animals but from machines are our passions, and foremost among them our passion for justice. Justice is, in a word, that set of passions, not mere theories, that bind us and make us part of the social world."[13]

Writers such as the Scottish author Henry Mackenzie tried to highlight many things that he perceived were wrong during his time and showed how many of the wrongs were ultimately caused by the established pillars of society. In his book, *The Man of Feeling* (1771), he has no qualms about showing how these pillars of society had, for example, abused an intelligent woman causing her to become a prostitute (p44/45), destroyed a school because it blocked the landowner's view (p72), and hired assassins to remove a man who had refused to hand over his wife (p91), etc.[14] Mackenzie shows again and again the injustices of British military and colonial policy, and who is responsible. As Marilyn Butler writes:

> Henry Mackenzie's *The Man of Feeling* (1771), is pointedly topical when it criticizes the consequences of a war policy - press-ganging, conscription, the military punishment of flogging, and inadequate pensions - and when, like the same author's *Julia de Roubigné* (1777), it attacks the principle of colonialism. An interest in such causes was the logical outcome of art's frequently reiterated dedication to humanity. It was a period when the cast of villains was drawn from the proud men representing authority, downwards from the House of Lords, the bench of bishops, judges, local magistrates, attorneys, to the stern father; when readers were invited to empathize with life's victims.[15]

It took a long time for the ideas of sentimentalism (emotions against injustice) to filter down to the Realism (using facts to depict ordinary everyday experiences) that Dickens used in the nineteenth century to finally evoke some kind of empathy for people

---

[13] Robert C Solomon, *A Passion for Justice: Emotions and the Origins of the Social Contract* (Rowman and Littlefield Pub., 1995) p45

[14] Henry Mackenzie, *The Man of Feeling* (Oxford World's Classics Oxford Uni Press, 2009)

[15] Marilyn Butler, *Romantics, Rebels and Reactionaries: English Literature and its Background 1760-1830* (Oxford Uni Press, 1981) p31

impoverished by society. As Solomon notes:

> It wasn't until the late nineteenth century that Dickens shook the conscience of his compatriots with his riveting descriptions of poverty and cruelty in contemporary London, [...] that the problem of poverty and resistance to its solutions [e.g. poorhouses] has become the central question of justice.[16]

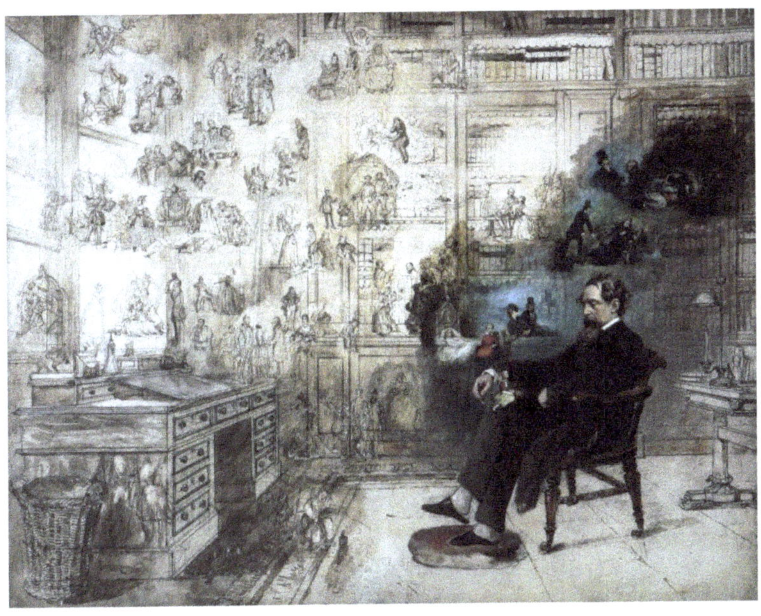

Dickens's Dream by Robert William Buss, portraying Dickens at his desk at Gads Hill Place surrounded by many of his characters
(Public Domain / Wikimedia Commons)

European literary sentimentalism arose during the Enlightenment, and partly as a response to sentimentalism in philosophy. In England the period 1750–1798 became known as the Age of Sensibility as the sentimental novel or the novel of sensibility became popular.

---

[16] Robert C Solomon, *A Passion for Justice: Emotions and the Origins of the Social Contract* (Rowman and Littlefield Pub., 1995) p13

Romanticist emotionalism: the opposite of Enlightenment sentimentalism

However, sensibility in an Enlightenment sense was very different from the Romanticist understanding, as Butler notes: "It is, in fact, in a key respect almost the opposite of Romanticism. Sensibility, like its near-synonym sentiment, echoes eighteenth-century philosophy and psychology in focusing upon the mental process by which impressions are received by the senses. But the sentimental writer's interest in how the mind works and in how people behave is very different from the Romantic writer's inwardness."[17]

She writes that 'neither Neoclassical theory nor contemporary practice in various styles and genres put much emphasis on the individuality of the artist' (p29). This is a far cry from the apolitical, inward-looking, self-centered Romantic artists who saw themselves outside of a society that they had little interest in participating in, let alone changing for the better. Butler again:

> Romantic rebelliousness is more outrageous and total, the individual rejecting not just his own society but the very principle of living in society - which means that the Romantic and post Romantic often dismisses political activity of any kind, as external to the self, literal and commonplace. Since it is relatively uncommon for the eighteenth-century artist to complain directly on his own behalf, he seldom achieves such emotional force as his nineteenth-century successor. He is, on the other hand, much more inclined than the Romantic to express sympathy for certain, well-defined social groups. Humanitarian feeling for the real-life underdog is a strong vein from the 1760s to the 1790s, often echoing real-life campaigns for reform.[18]

Thus, Enlightenment and Neoclassical ideas put less stress on the artist as an individual and such writers emphasized the expe-

---

[17] Marilyn Butler, *Romantics, Rebels and Reactionaries: English Literature and its Background 1760-1830* (Oxford Uni Press, 1981) p29/30

[18] Marilyn Butler, *Romantics, Rebels and Reactionaries: English Literature and its Background 1760-1830* (Oxford Uni Press, 1981) p30/31

riences of downtrodden groups. Exposing such experiences has always been the artist's form of resistance to overwhelming power. However, the movement over time towards the Romanticist inward-looking conception of emotion and feelings has had knock-on negative effects on society's ability to defend itself from elite oppression (through what could be called cultural styles of self-absorption, escapism and diversion rather than exposure, criticism and resistance), and retarded 'art's frequently reiterated dedication to humanity'. Solomon describes this process:

> What has come about in the past two centuries or so is the dramatic rise of what Robert Stone has called "affective individualism," this new celebration of the passions and other feelings of the autonomous individual. Yet, ironically, it is an attitude that has become even further removed from our sense of justice during that same period of time. We seem to have more inner feelings and pay more attention to them, but we seem to have fewer feelings about others and the state of the world and pay less attention to them.[19]

Thus, while Enlightenment sentimentalism "depicted individuals as social beings whose sensibility was stimulated and defined by their interactions with others", the Romantic movement that followed it "tended to privilege individual autonomy and subjectivity over sociability".[20]

Romanticism as a philosophical movement of the nineteenth century had a profound influence on culture which can still be seen right up to today. Its main characteristics are the emphasis on the personal, dramatic contrasts, emotional excess, a focus on the nocturnal, the ghostly and the frightful, spontaneity, and extreme subjectivism. Romanticism in culture implies a turning inward and encourages introspection. Romantic literature put more emphasis on themes of isolation, loneliness, tragic events and the power of nature. A heroic view of history and myth became the basis of much

---

[19] Robert C Solomon, *A Passion for Justice: Emotions and the Origins of the Social Contract* (Rowman and Littlefield Pub., 1995) p37

[20] https://www.cambridge.org/core/books/cambridge-companion-to-the-scottish-enlightenment/literature-and-sentimentalism/A0E80265553C8CB60B97667365724940

Romantic literature.

It was in Germany that Romanticism took shape as a political ideology. The German Romanticists felt threatened by the French Revolution and were forced to move from inward-looking ideas to formulate conservative political answers needed to oppose Enlightenment and republican ideals. According to Eugene N. Anderson:

> In the succeeding years the danger became acutely political, and the German Romanticists were compelled to subordinate their preoccupation with the widening of art and the enrichment of individual experience to social and political ideas and actions, particularly as formulated in nationalism and conservatism. These three cultural ideals, Romanticism, nationalism and conservatism, shared qualities evoked by the common situation of crisis. [...] The Germans had to maintain against rationalism and the French a culture which in its institutional structure was that of the *ancien régime*. German Romanticism accepted it, wished to reform it somewhat, idealized it, and defended the idealization as the supreme culture of the world. This was the German counter-revolution. [...] They endowed their culture with universal validity and asserted that it enjoyed the devotion of nature and God, that if it were destroyed humanity would be vitally wounded.[21]

The reactionary nature of German Romanticism was demonstrated in its hierarchical views of society, its chauvinist nationalism, and extreme conservatism which would have serious implications for future generations of the German populace.

Indeed, on May 29th 1945, the German author Thomas Mann (1875-1955), Nobel Prize laureate in Literature, gave a lecture at the Library of Congress titled "Germany and the Germans" in which he stated:

> German Romanticism, what is it but an expression of this fin-

---

[21] Eugene N. Anderson, 'German Romanticism as an Ideology of Cultural Crisis', p301-312. Source: *Journal of the History of Ideas*, Jun., 1941, Vol. 2, No. 3 (Jun., 1941), pp. 301-317. Published by: University of Pennsylvania Press. Stable URL: http://www.jstor.com/stable/2707133

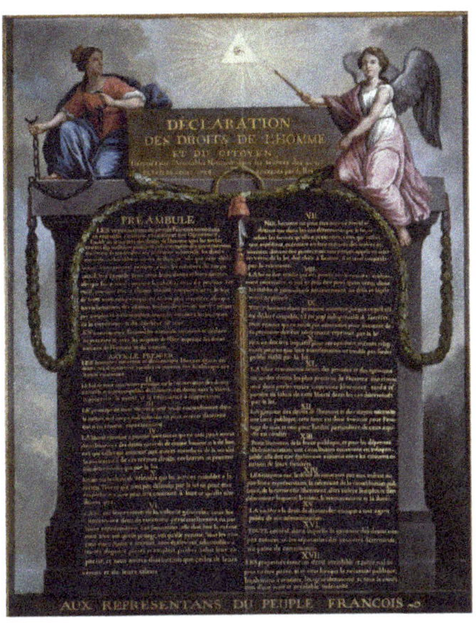

Declaration of the Rights of Man and of the Citizen, painted by
Jean-Jacques-François Le Barbier (1738–1826)
(Public Domain / Wikimedia Commons)

est German quality, German inwardness? Much that is long-
ingly pensive, fantastically spectral, and deeply scurrilous, a
high artistic refinement and all-pervading irony combine in
the concept of Romanticism. But these are not the things I
think of primarily when I speak of Romanticism. It is rather a
certain dark richness and piousness - I might say: antiquar-
ianism-of soul that feels very close to the chthonian, irrational, and demonic forces of life, that is to say, the true sources of life; and it resists the purely rationalistic approach on
the ground of its deeper knowledge, its deeper alliance with
the holy. The Germans are the people of the romantic count-
er-revolution against the philosophical intellectualism and
rationalism of enlightenment—a revolt of music against literature, of mysticism against clarity.[22]

As Anderson writes on German Romanticism:

---

[22] 'Germany and the Germans' [by] Thomas Mann. https://babel.hathitrust.org/cgi/pt?id=uc1.
b4153667&view=1up&seq=7

The low estimate of rationalism and the exaltation of custom, tradition, and feeling, the conception of society as an alliance of the generations, the belief in the abiding character of ideas as contrasted with the ephemeral nature of concepts, these and many other romantic views bolstered up the existing culture. The concern with relations led the Romanticists to praise the hierarchical order of the Ständestaat and to regard everything and every-one as an intermediary. The acceptance of the fact of inequality harmonized with that of the ideals of service, duty, faithfulness, order, sacrifice - admirable traits for serf or subject or soldier.[23]

Anderson also believes that the Romanticists remained swinging "between individual freedom and initiative and group compulsion and authority" and as such could not have brought in fundamental reforms, because: "By reverencing tradition, they preserved the power of the backward-looking royalty and aristocracy."[24]

Thus, Romanticist self-centredness in philosophy translated into the most conservative forms for maintaining the status quo in politics. Individual freedoms were matched by authoritarianism for the masses. The individual was king alright, as long as you weren't a 'serf or subject or soldier'.

Beyond morality: Working Class perspectives on Reason and Romanticism

We have never intended to enlighten shoemakers and servants—this is up to apostles.
Voltaire (1694–1778)

---

[23] Eugene N. Anderson, *'German Romanticism as an Ideology of Cultural Crisis'*, p313/314 Source: *Journal of the History of Ideas*, Jun., 1941, Vol. 2, No. 3 (Jun., 1941), pp. 301-317. Published by: University of Pennsylvania Press. Stable URL: http://www.jstor.com/stable/2707133

[24] Eugene N. Anderson, *'German Romanticism as an Ideology of Cultural Crisis'*. p316. Source: *Journal of the History of Ideas*, Jun., 1941, Vol. 2, No. 3 (Jun., 1941), pp. 301-317. Published by: University of Pennsylvania Press. Stable URL: http://www.jstor.com/stable/2707133

In France, the growth of the new middle class put pressure on the aristocratic status-quo. The new bourgeoisie wanted 'liberty' and 'equality' - freedom for the new entrepreneurs to trade and a desire to have political control of the economy:

> The middle class, bitterly resentful of the privileges of the aristocracy in law and property, sought to rise to equality of status with the landed nobility; and to this end it advocated, with passion, the doctrines of natural law and universal rights. With few exceptions, however, the members of the bourgeoisie did not want the lower classes to rise to equality with themselves.[25]

The French Enlightenment writer, historian, and philosopher, Voltaire (1694–1778), was an important representative of the new era, taking progressive stances on many issues such as separation of church and state, and freedom of speech. He was a fearless advocate of civil liberties and he satirized the intolerance and religious dogmas of his day. Yet, there were still limits to his thinking:

> Voltaire saw it as a prerogative of the educated classes: the rights to speak freely, to publish, to hold property, and to be protected by the law. None of these rights, he thought, had much to do with the working classes, who were generally too 'stupid and brutal' even to be aware of such matters.[26]

It would take the theoretical and practical work of two Germans to bring Enlightenment ideas onto a truly universal stage, one that encompassed both peasants and workers. Around the same time of the early period of Romanticism, Karl Heinrich Marx (1818–1883) and Friedrich Engels (1820–1895) were born. They grew up in a very different Germany. Capitalism had become established and was creating an even more polarised society between the extremely rich and the extremely poor as factory owners pushed their work

---

[25] Thomas H. Greer, *A Brief History of Western Man* (New York: Harcourt, Brace, Jovanovich, 1972) p348

[26] Thomas H. Greer, *A Brief History of Western Man* (New York: Harcourt, Brace, Jovanovich, 1972) p347

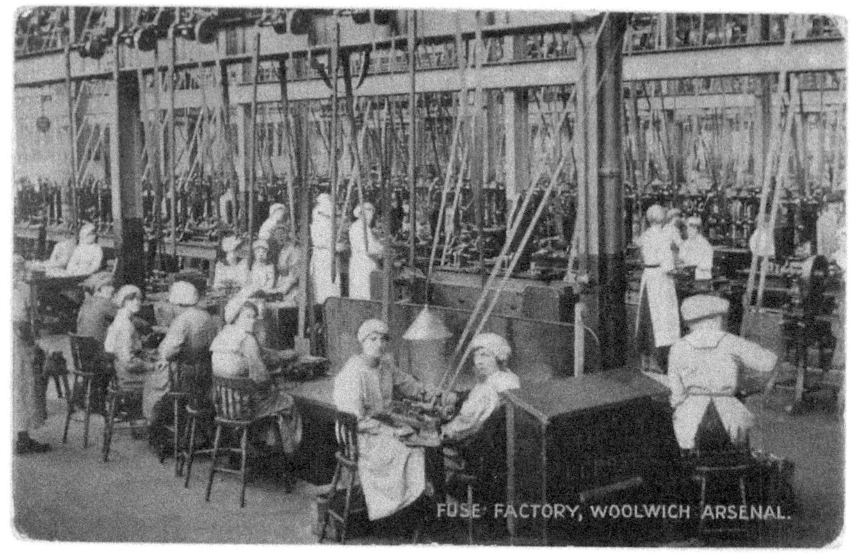

Workers in the fuse factory, Woolwich Arsenal late 1800s
(Unknown author / Wikimedia Commons)

ers to their physical limits.

The Romanticists reaction to such exploitation was to look backwards to medievalism instead of forward to proletarian revolution. Rather than questioning the organisation of society and who should own and control the new means of production in the 'dark, satanic mills' they chose to revere an ideal that society could return to peasant culture (which, of course, was safely hierarchical and not collectivist like working-class trade unions). The Enlightenment attitude to mechanization, as Michael Cronin notes, was more open: "the Enlightenment response of thinkers like Diderot to the arrival of the machine was not rejection but accommodation: 'The enlightened way to use a machine is to judge its powers, fashion its uses, in light of our own limits rather than the machine's potential. We should not compete against the machine'."[27]

On his way to work at his father's firm in Manchester, Engels called into the offices of a paper he wrote for in Cologne and met the editor, Marx, for the first time in 1842. They formed a friend-

---

[27] Michael Cronin, *Eco-Translation: Translation and Ecology in the Age of the Anthropocene* (2017) p119 quoting from Richard Sennett, *The Craftsman* (2009) p145

ship based on shared values and beliefs regarding the working class and socialist ideas. They saw a connection between the earlier Enlightenment ideas and socialism. For example, as Engels writes in *Anti-Duhring*: "in its theoretical form, modern socialism originally appears ostensibly as a more logical extension of the principles laid down by the great French philosophers of the eighteenth century. Like every new theory, modern socialism had, at first, to connect itself with the intellectual stock-in-trade ready to its hand, however deeply its roots lay in economic facts."[28]

They were also critical of Romanticism. In a 'Letter from Marx to Engels In Manchester' Marx criticises the Romanticist obsessions with Medievalism and the 'Golden Age'. He writes: "The first reaction against the French Revolution and the period of Enlightenment bound up with it was naturally to see everything as mediaeval and romantic [...]. The second reaction is to look beyond the Middle Ages into the primitive age of each nation".[29]

However, once Marx and Engels had connected themselves to the Enlightenment they soon saw the limitations of Enlightenment concepts of reason and sentiment. As B. Krylov wrote in his Preface to Marx and Engels' *On Literature and Art*:

Marx and Engels stripped away the romantic idealisation of the Middle Ages and, at the same time, demonstrated the inconsistency of the abstract view held by the Enlighteners that this was merely an age of social and cultural regression. They pointed out that the transition from slave-owning to feudal society was historically inevitable and showed that the establishment of the feudal mode of production was a step forward in the development of human society, compared to the reign of slavery which had preceded it. This enabled Marx and Engels to form a new approach to medieval culture and art and point out those features in them which reflected the progressive course of historical development.[30]

---

[28] Marx and Engels, *On Literature and Art* (Progress Publishers: Moscow, 1978) p.270

[29] Letter from Marx to Engels In Manchester
https://www.marxists.org/archive/marx/works/1868/letters/68_03_25-abs.htm

[30] https://www.marxists.org/archive/marx/works/subject/art/preface.htm

Marx and Engels analysed West European Romanticism in a way that gave credit for any progressive aspects despite its limitations, as Krylov writes:

> Considering romanticism a reflection of the age beginning after the Great French Revolution, of all its inherent social contradictions, they distinguished between revolutionary romanticism, which rejected capitalism and was striving towards the future, and romantic criticism of capitalism from the point of view of the past. They also differentiated between the romantic writers who idealised the pre-bourgeois social system: they valued those whose works concealed democratic and critical elements under a veneer of reactionary utopias and naive petty-bourgeois ideals, and criticised the reactionary romantics, whose sympathies for the past amounted to a defence of the interests of the nobility.[31]

Similarly, Krylov notes how Marx and Engels could see elements of class struggle in Enlightenment writing:

> Marx and Engels held in high esteem the heritage of the English and French 18th-century Enlighteners including their fiction and works on aesthetics. Their comprehensive analysis of the activity of the Enlighteners explains its close links with the life of society and the class struggle during the preparation for the French bourgeois revolution and draws a line between the moderately bourgeois and the democratic elements in their heritage.[32]

However, Marx and Engels realised that the new bourgeois rulers would be limited by their conceptions of property, justice, and equality, which basically meant they only applied universality to themselves and their own property. The new rulers were buoyed up by the victory of their ideological fight over the aristocracy but incapable of applying the same ideas to the masses who helped them

---

[31] https://www.marxists.org/archive/marx/works/subject/art/preface.htm
[32] https://www.marxists.org/archive/marx/works/subject/art/preface.htm

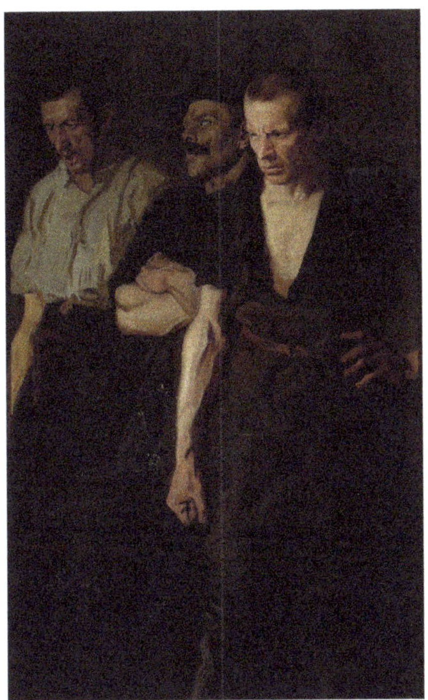

Strike (1910) by Stanisław Lentz (1861–1920),
National Museum in Warsaw
(Public Domain / Wikimedia Commons)

to victory. Thus, Marx and Engels viewed the struggle for reason as important but limited to the new ruling class' world view, just like the aristocracy before them, as they wrote:

Every form of society and government then existing, every old traditional notion was flung into the lumber room as irrational; the world had hitherto allowed itself to be led solely by prejudices; everything in the past deserved only pity and contempt. Now, for the first time, appeared the light of day, henceforth superstition, injustice, privilege, oppression, were to be superseded by eternal truth, eternal Right, equality based on nature and the inalienable rights of man. We know today that this kingdom of reason was nothing more than the idealised kingdom of the bourgeoisie; that this eternal Right found its realisation in bourgeois justice; that this equality reduced itself to bourgeois equality before the law; that bourgeois property was proclaimed as one of the essential rights of man; and that the government of reason, the Contrat Social of Rousseau, came into being, and only could come into being, as a democratic bourgeois republic. The great thinkers of the eighteenth century could, no more than their predecessors, go beyond the limits imposed upon them by their epoch.[33]

As for sentiment, they were well aware of the Realist critical nature of modern writers (the Realist movement rejected Romanticism) and indeed praised them (e.g. G. Sand, E. Sue, and Boz [Dickens]), but limited themselves to offering some advice. While recognising that progressive literature had a mainly middle-class audience (and were happy enough with these authors just 'shaking the optimism' of their audience), they knew that this was not by any means a socialist literature and were well aware of sentimentalist limitations. Engels states:

I think however that the purpose must become manifest from the situation and the action themselves without being expressly pointed out and that the author does not have to serve the reader on a platter — the future historical resolution of the social conflicts which he describes. To this must be added that under our conditions novels are mostly addressed to readers from bourgeois circles, i.e., circles which are not directly ours. Thus the socialist problem novel in my opinion fully carries out its mission if by a faithful portrayal of the real conditions it dispels the dominant conventional illusions concerning them, shakes the optimism of the bourgeois world, and inevitably instills doubt as to the eternal validity of that which exists, without itself offering a direct solution of the problem involved, even without at times ostensibly taking sides.[34]

---

[33] Marx and Engels, *On Literature and Art* (Progress Publishers: Moscow, 1978) p271
[34] Marx and Engels, *On Literature and Art* (Progress Publishers: Moscow, 1978) p88

Sentimental literature focused on individual misfortune, and constant repetition of such themes certainly appeared to universalise such suffering, so that, as David Denby writes, "In this weeping mother, this suffering father, we are to read also the sufferings of humanity." Thus, "individualism and universalism appear to be two sides of the same coin". Sentimental literature gives the reader the 'spectacle of misfortune' and a representation of the reaction of a 'sentient and sensible observer' who tries to help with 'alms, sympathy or indeed narrative intervention.' Furthermore, the literature of sentiment "mirrors eighteenth-century theories of sympathy, in which a spontaneous reaction to the spectacle of suffering is gradually developed, by a process of generalisation and combination of ideas, into broader and more abstract notions of humanity, benevolence, justice."[35]

This brings us then to the problem of interpretation, as Denby suggests: "should the sentimental portrayal of the poor and of action in their favour be read as an attempt to give a voice to the voiceless, to include the hitherto excluded? Or, alternatively, is the sentimentalisation of the poor to be interpreted, more cynically, as a discursive strategy through which the enlightened bourgeoisie states its commitment to values of humanity and justice, and thereby seeks to strengthen its claims to universal domination?"[36]

While such ideas of giving a 'voice to the voiceless' was a far cry from monarchical times, and claims of commitment to humanity and justice were laudable, the concept of universality had a fundamental flaw, for example: "The universal claims of the French Revolution are opposed to a [aristocratic] society based on distinctions of birth: it is in the name of humanity that the Revolution challenges the established order. But for Sartre this does not change the fact that the universal is a myth, an ideological construct, and an obfuscation, since it articulates a notion of man which eliminates social conflict and disguises the interests of a class behind a facade of universal reference."[37]

---

[35] David J. Denby, 'Individual, universal, national: a French revolutionary trilogy?' (*Studies of Voltaire and the Eighteenth Century*, 335, Voltaire Foundation, 1996) p28/29

[36] David J. Denby, *Sentimental Narrative and the Social Order in France, 1760–1820* (Cambridge Studies in French, 1994) p117

[37] David J. Denby, 'Individual, universal, national: a French revolutionary trilogy?' (*Studies of Voltaire and the Eighteenth Century*, 335, Voltaire Foundation, 1996) p27

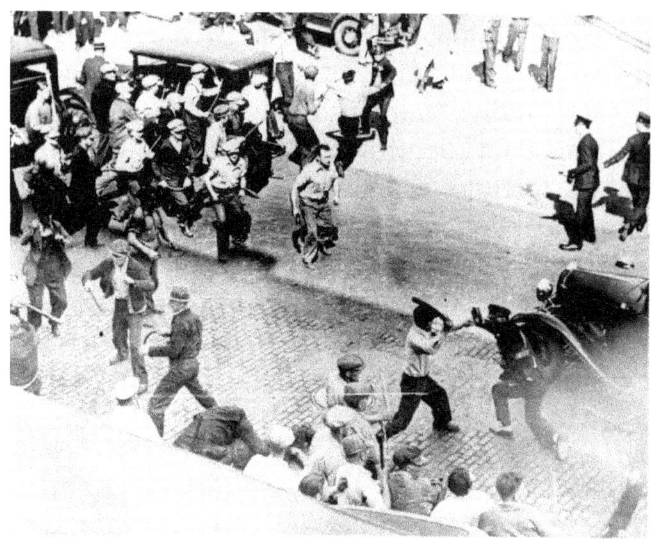

Striking teamsters battling police on the streets of Minneapolis,
Minnesota, June 1934
(Public domain / Wikimedia Commons)

Thus, for Marx and Engels defining concepts such as good and evil, right and wrong, virtue and vice, justice and crime, that is, a universal moral theory, could not be achieved while society is divided into classes:

We maintain [...] that all moral theories have been hitherto the product, in the last analysis, of the economic conditions of society obtaining at the time. And as society has hitherto moved in class antagonisms, morality has always been class morality; it has either justified the domination and the interests of the ruling class, or ever since the oppressed class became powerful enough, it has represented its indignation against this domination and the future interests of the oppressed. That in this process there has on the whole been progress in morality, as in all other branches of human knowledge, no one will doubt. But we have not yet passed beyond class morality. A really human morality which stands above class antagonisms and above any recollection of them becomes possible only at a stage of society which has not only overcome class antagonisms but has even forgotten them in practical life.[38]

Marx and Engels worked towards that morality through their activism with working class movements and culture. Their critical writing also formed an essential part of working-class ideology and culture of resistance and has remained influential in resistance movements the world over.

The culture of resistance today still uses realism, documentary, and histories of oppression to show the harsh realities of globalisation. Like during the Enlightenment, empathy for those suffering injustice forms its foundation. And unlike Romanticism, reason and science are deemed to be important tools in its struggle for social emancipation and progress.

There is no doubt that the influence of Romanticism has become ever stronger in twentieth and twenty-first century culture. Romanticist-influenced TV shows on Netflix are watched worldwide. Love songs dominate the pop industry and superheroes are now the mainstay of cinema. Even Romanticist nationalism is making a comeback. Now and then calls for a new Enlightenment are heard, but like the original advocates of the Enlightenment, they are limited to the conservative world view of those making the call, and whose view of the Enlightenment could be compared to a form of Third Way politics, that is, they avoid the issue of class conflict.

---

[38] Frederick Engels, *Anti-Dühring* (1877), Part I: Philosophy IX. Morality and Law. Eternal Truths
https://www.marxists.org/archive/marx/works/1877/anti-duhring/ch07.htm

Chapter 2

Politics

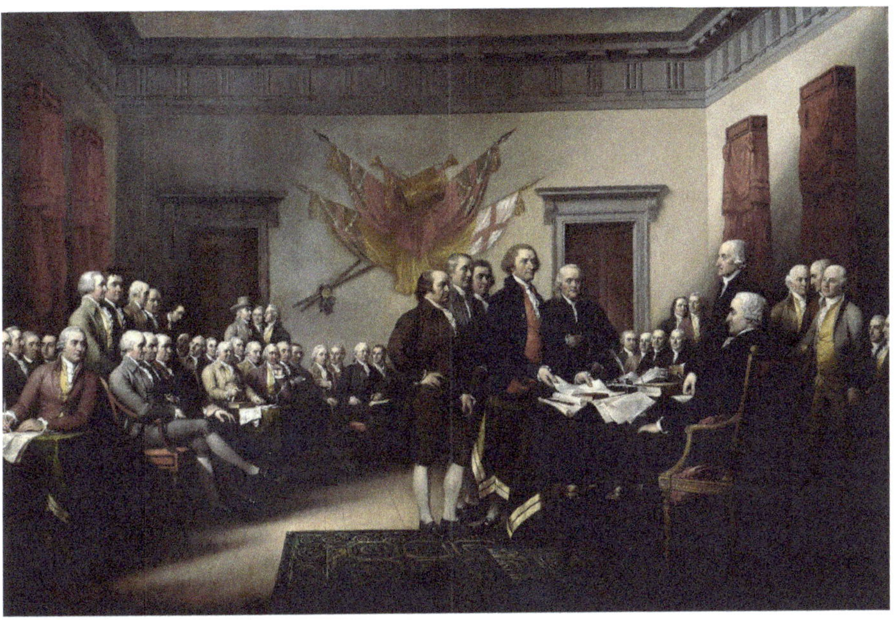

John Trumbull's (1844–1930) *Declaration of Independence* imagines
the drafting committee presenting its work to the Congress
(Public Domain / Wikimedia Commons)

*Ignorance has always been the weapon of tyrants;
enlightenment the salvation of the free.*

Bill Richardson

Romanticism as a Tool for Elite Agendas

Civil government, so far as it is instituted for the security of property, is in reality instituted for the defense of the rich against the poor, or of those who have some property against those who have none at all.
Adam Smith

The oppressed are allowed once every few years to decide which particular representatives of the oppressing class are to represent and repress them.
Karl Marx

Romanticism as an eighteenth century artistic, literary, musical and intellectual movement emerged as a reaction to Enlightenment ideas of science, reason and human progress. The effect of Romanticism on politics was to reassert conservative ideas about society based on hierarchy and individualism as the Romanticists looked back to medieval times and monarchism for inspiration. Enlightenment ideas, however, focused on the laws as a counter to monarchical privilege and looked to concepts of citizenship and republicanism as the way forward, ideas which were taken up by workers movements the world over. However, Romanticist ideas of the exclusivist nation are coming to the fore again in a world altered by the positive and negative effects of international worker mobility, immigration and desperate refugees.

The Enlightenment and politics – 'You were, crucially, a citizen, not a subject'

In the early eighteenth-century in Europe the power of the monarchical system began to wane and Enlightenment ideas about the running and ruling of society began to take hold. Enlightenment liberalism freed the individual, as Isaac Kramnick writes, "to place at the heart of politics the sacredness of each separate individual's own quest for happiness and the good life,"[39] in reaction to the religious perspective that "a virtuous person lived a life of self-denial and privation."[40] However, this new-found individual freedom could be constricted for the 'common good', as Kramnick states:

> The political universe was demystified, as the magical power of thrones, scepters, and crowns was replaced by rational acts of consent. The individual (understood, of course, in the Enlightenment as male and property-owning) did not receive government and authority from a God who had given his secular sword to princes and magistrates to rule by his divine right. Nor did the individual keep any longer to his subordinate place in a divinely inspired hierarchy, in which kings and noblemen had been placed above him as 'your highnesses' who were society's natural governors. Government was voluntarily established by free individuals through a willful act of contract. Individuals rationally consented to limit their own freedom and to obey civil authority in order to have public protection of their natural rights. Government's purpose was to serve self-interest, to enable individuals to enjoy peacefully their rights to life, liberty, and property, not to serve the glory of God or dynasties, and certainly not to dictate moral or religious truth.[41]

Enlightenment ideas on politics focused on the idea of the '*patrie*' or patria, a word derived from *pater* (father) from ancient Rome

---

[39] Isaac Kramnick, (ed.) (1995) *The Portable Enlightenment Reader*, New York Penguin. pxv
[40] Isaac Kramnick, (ed.) (1995) *The Portable Enlightenment Reader*, New York Penguin. pxiv
[41] Isaac Kramnick, (ed.) (1995) *The Portable Enlightenment Reader*, New York Penguin. pxvi

and would later be equated with republicanism. Chevalier Louis de Jaucourt (1704–1779) (the biographer of Leibniz) wrote in the *Encyclopédie* that *patrie* "represents a father and children, and consequently that it expresses the meaning we attach to that of family, of society, of a free state, of which we are members, and whose laws assure our liberties and our well-being."[42] This new emphasis was based on equality of all before the law rather than on the narrow definitions of ethnicity used in definitions of the nation.

In the pre-modern polity, society was made up of separate feudal sovereignties that were at the same time local power centres. Different ethnic groups lived in insular, heterogeneous communities with local and agrarian independent economies. The economy developed as kingdoms expanded into other ethnic areas. The transition from ethnicity to nationhood happened when the members of different ethnic groups developed a common culture making them into a 'nation'.

However, as Anthony Pagden writes: "Unlike the nation, the patria was a community, a group. You owed it your love and your life, but you were also a part of it. You were, crucially, a citizen, not a subject."[43]

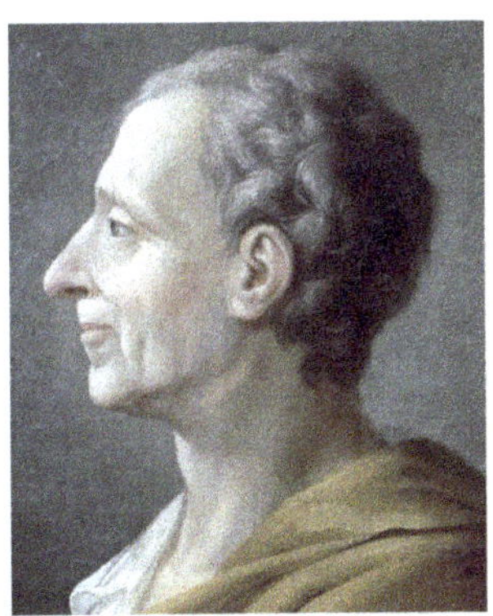

Charles-Louis de Secondat, Baron de La Brède et de Montesquieu (1689–1755), Portrait by an anonymous artist. Generally referred to as simply Montesquieu, was a French judge, man of letters, and political philosopher
(After Jacques-Antoine Dassier / Public domain / Wikimedia Commons)

---

[42] *The Enlightenment: And Why it Still Matters* by Anthony Pagden (Oxford Uni Press, 2015) p259
[43] *The Enlightenment: And Why it Still Matters* by Anthony Pagden (Oxford Uni Press, 2015) p259

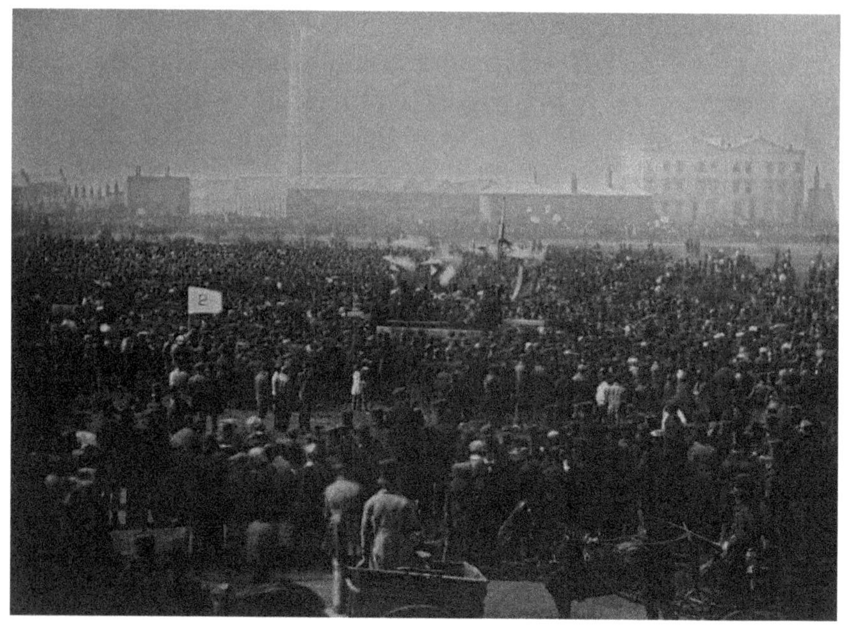

Photograph of the Great Chartist Meeting on Kennington Common,
London in 1848
(Royal Collection / Public domain / Wikimedia Commons)

The patria was loosely connected to the concept of a republican government where the citizen, as Charles-Louis de Secondat (Montesquieu) (1689-1755) wrote, would be asked to love the laws and the homeland (*patrie*) and that this love would require "continuing preference of the public interest over one's own."[44] These ideas about the *patrie* have "come to be called modern civic patriotism. It was benign, generous, outward-looking, and in principle at least excluded no one".[45] They can be seen as universal in that they described a form of politics, republicanism, that was not concerned with language, religion or ethnicity but with the idea that all were citizens and equal before the law.

Equality before the law is the principle that each person must be treated equally by the law (principle of isonomy) and that all are subject to the same laws of justice (due process). This principle

[44] *The Enlightenment: And Why it Still Matters* by Anthony Pagden (Oxford Uni Press, 2015) p260
[45] *The Enlightenment: And Why it Still Matters* by Anthony Pagden (Oxford Uni Press, 2015) p261

arose out of the discontent that prevailed under monarchical rule whereby the king or queen was above the law, so that equality guaranteed that no one or group of individuals could be privileged or discriminated against by the rulers. Much later, in Paris (in 1948), this principle was enshrined in Article 7 of the Universal Declaration of Human Rights (UDHR) which states that: "All are equal before the law and are entitled without any discrimination to equal protection of the law".[46]

Equality before the law is a basic principle of legal documents like the Irish Constitution (1937), for example:

All citizens shall be held equal before the law (Article 40 of the Constitution). This means that the State cannot unjustly, unreasonably or arbitrarily discriminate between citizens. You cannot be treated as inferior or superior to any other person in society simply because of your human attributes or your ethnic, racial, social or religious background.[47]

The universal aspect of such principles is an important aspect in that universalism accepts universal principles of most religions and is inclusive of others regardless of other persons ethnic, religious or racial background.

As an approach to ethnic difference in society, universalism is similar to 'instrumentalist' approaches which accepts a minimal set of qualifications for membership of a community, unlike the 'primordialism' of conservative nationalism which tries to fix exclusivist kinship, historical traditions and homeland of the 'nation'.

The Romantic reaction – 'from patriotism to tribalism'

It was in Germany that nationalism came to emphasise the ethnic basis of the nation with the ancient origins of the German language symbolising the German Volk stretching back into pre-history. In his essay *On the Origin of Language* [1772], Johann Gottfried von

---

[46] https://en.wikipedia.org/wiki/Equality_before_the_law

[47] https://www.citizensinformation.ie/en/government_in_ireland/irish_constitution_1/constitution_fundamental_rights.html

Herder (1744–1803) argued for the national origin of language. He wrote,

> [i]t [the urge to express] is alive in all unpolished languages, though, to be sure, according to the degree of each nation's culture and the specific character of its way of thinking.[48]

Herder was a German philosopher (who hated absolutism and Prussian nationalism) and advocated republicanism and democracy. Herder's influence could be seen in the widespread cultural and linguistic movements that swept Europe from the 1780s to the 1840s. Influenced by the Romantic Movement, the cultural nationalists emphasised the *volksgeist* of the peasantry as the true basis of the nation. However, it is important to note that while it is true that Herder insisted on respecting, preserving, and advancing national groupings, he did it for much more benign reasons than the later Romantic Nationalists, particularly his rejection of national chauvinism:

> (1) For Herder, this is emphatically something that must be done for all national groupings equally—not just or especially Germany! (In the Letters for the Advancement he emphatically rejects any such notion of a "favorite people [*Favoritvolk*]", as he puts it.) (2) The "nation" in question is not racial but linguistic and cultural (in the Ideas and elsewhere Herder indeed criticizes and rejects the very concept of race). (3) Herder does not seek to seal off nations from each other's influence or to keep them static; he regards inter-linguistic and -cultural exchange and linguistic-cultural development as normal and welcomes them. (4) Nor does his commitment to national groupings involve a centralized, militarized state (in the Ideas and elsewhere he strongly advocates the disappearance of such a state and its replacement by loosely federated local governments with minimal instruments of force). (5) In addition, his insistence on respecting national

---

[48] *On the Origin of Language: Two Essays by Jean-Jacques Rousseau and Johann Gottfried Herder* (Chicago: University of Chicago Press, 1986) p149.

groupings is accompanied by the strongest denunciations of military conflict, colonial exploitation, and all other forms of harm between nations; a demand that nations instead peacefully cooperate and compete in trade and intellectual endeavors for their mutual benefit; and a plea that they should indeed actively work to help each other.[49]

However, as nationalism as a political ideology took hold, language became the target and the site for conflicting political ideologies and definitions of the nation were formed on ethno-linguistic grounds.

At the same time during the early nineteenth century the industrial revolution had caused a profound change in the social and economic make up of society internally. These changes resulted in the creation of self-conscious (and internationalist) classes and heightened class antagonism that saw the rise of workers movements such as the Saint-Simonians and Fourierists in France and the Chartists and Owenites in the United Kingdom.

Thus, the workers movements took Enlightenment ideas of equality to their logical conclusion in the form of class struggle and social revolution, while the Romanticists looked to the peasantry for their ideal, reasserting the primacy of the older 'vertical' structure of society (i.e. containing all classes). The rise of nationalism saw the growth of exceptionalism as ethnic exclusivity became the norm. Under the influence of Romanticism and ideas of ethnic purity, and in parallel with the rise of the centralised nation state, the ethnic homogenisation of the populace meant the (near) destruction of indigenous local languages and local foreign language communities.

For example, in France there existed about thirty patois or popular Romance languages. In *A Cultural History of the French Revolution*, Emmet Kennedy describes a report to the Convention on 16 prairial Year II (4 June 1794) where the Abbé Grégoire lists the extensive range of patois, dialects and languages in France as "Bas-Breton, Bourguinon, Bressan, Lyonnais, Dauphinois, Auvergnat, Poitevin, Limousin, Picard, Provençal, Languedocien, Velayen,

---

[49] https://plato.stanford.edu/entries/herder/

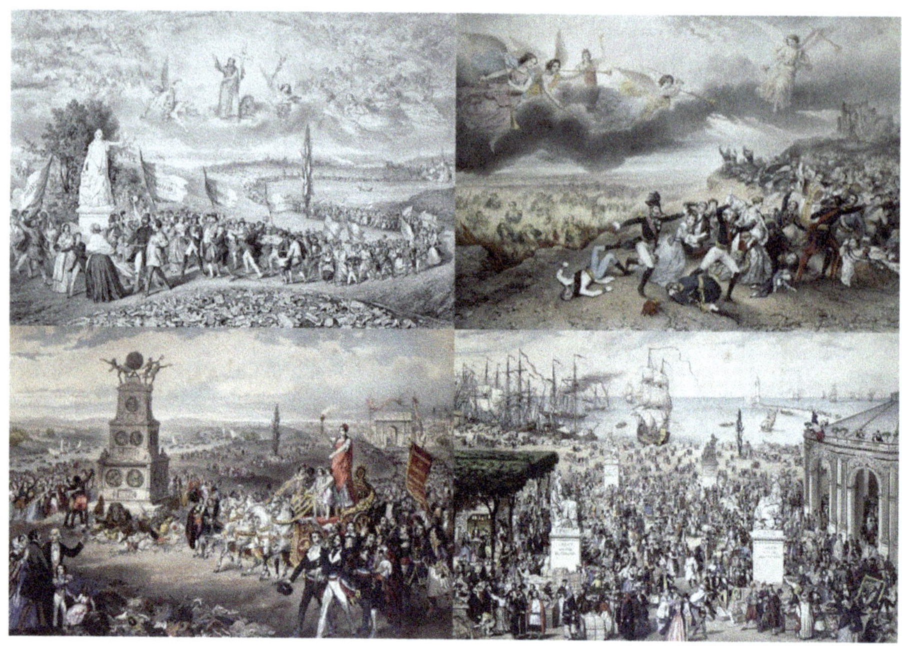

La République universelle démocratique et sociale, painted by
Frédéric Sorrieu (1807-1887) in 1848. Top left: *Le Pacte*, Top right:
Le Prologue, Bottom left: *Le Triomphe*, Bottom right: *Le Marché*. He
was notable for his works testifying the liberal and nationalist
revolutions in France and in Europe
(Public domain / Wikimedia Commons)

Catalan, Béarnais, Basque, Rouergat, and Gascon." According to Kennedy, "[o]nly about a sixth (fifteen) of the departments around Paris spoke French exclusively. Elsewhere bilingualism was common."[50]

Yet, in another report to the Convention in 1794, Barère links the areas where "foreign" languages are to be found, such as Basque, German, Flamand and Breton, with the areas of insurrection and counterrevolution. Barère writes,

[f]ederalism and superstition speak Bas-Breton; emigration and hatred of the Republic speak German; counterrevolution

---

[50] *A Cultural History of the French Revolution* by Emmet Kennedy (New Haven: Yale University Press, 1989) 325-6. See also *Peasants into Frenchmen: The Modernization of Rural France, 1870-1914* by Eugen Weber (London, Chatto & Windus, 1979) p326, and *Language from Below: The Irish Language, Ideology and Power in 20th Century Ireland* by Caoimhghin Ó Croidheáin p.107

speaks Italian, and fanaticism speaks Basque. Let us break these harmful instruments of terror.[51]

In post-revolutionary France linguistic redefinition took on serious political overtones as the question of self/other was redrawn along linguistic lines. Already the interests of the state were taking precedence over the rhetoric of the democratic nation.

Johann Gottlieb Fichte (1762 – 1814), took exceptionalist and chauvinist ideas of the nation even further. He wrote:

the German, if only he makes use of all his advantages, can always be superior to the foreigner and understand him fully, even better than the foreigner understands himself, and can translate the foreigner to the fullest extent. On the other hand, the foreigner can never understand the true German without a thorough and extremely laborious study of the German language, and there is no doubt that he will leave what is genuinely German untranslated.[52]

Fichte (like Herder, but with a chauvinistic bias) shifted cultural value from the elites to the common people (*volk*). According to Tim Blanning in *The Romantic Revolution*:

Folk art, folk dancing and folk songs were not to be despised for their roughness but treasured for their authenticity. They were the 'archives of a nationality', the 'national soul' and 'the living voice of the nationalities, even of humanity itself'.[53]

---

[51] *A Cultural History of the French Revolution* by Emmet Kennedy (New Haven: Yale University Press, 1989) 325-6. See also *Peasants into Frenchmen: The Modernization of Rural France, 1870-1914* by Eugen Weber (London, Chatto & Windus, 1979) p326 , and *Language from Below: The Irish Language, Ideology and Power in 20th Century Ireland* by Caoimhghin Ó Croidheáin p.107

[52] *Addresses to the German Nation* [1808] by Johann Gottlieb Fichte, trans. R.F. Jones and G.H. Turnbull (Chicago and London: The Open Court Publishing Company, 1922) p130. Also, "Concerning international politics, Herder has often been classified as a "nationalist" or (perhaps even worse) a "German nationalist" (for example, by R.R. Ergang in *Herder and the Foundations of German Nationalism* [1931] and K.R. Popper in *The Open Society and its Enemies* [1945]). Some other philosophers from the period deserve such a characterization (for instance, Fichte). But where Herder is concerned it is deeply misleading and unjust." https://plato.stanford.edu/entries/herder/

[53] *The Romantic Revolution* by Tim Blanning (Phoenix, Great Britain, 2010) p119

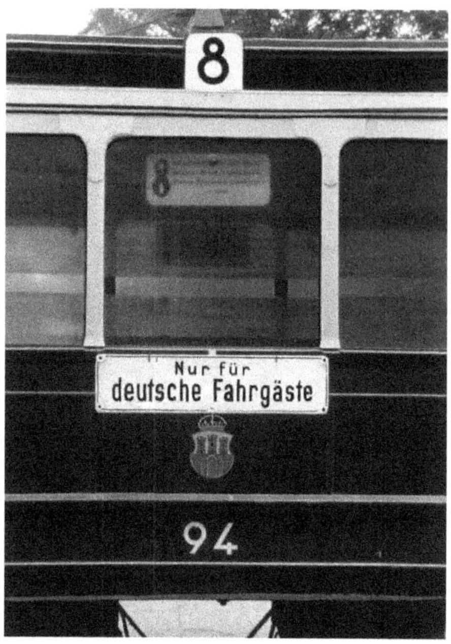

'Nur für Deutsche' (Eng. 'Only for Germans') on the tram number 8 in
occupied Kraków
(Theuergarten Ewald / Public domain / Wikimedia Commons)

The Romanticists promoted popular ballads which had been
seen as "the dregs of fairy-tales, superstitions, songs, and crude
speech".[54] Of particular note was the Ossian cycle of epic poems
published by the Scottish poet James Macpherson from 1760. The
work was an international success and was translated into all the
literary languages of Europe. Even though Ossian was soon realised
to be a creation of its author, and not from ancient sources, it was
highly influential both in the development of the Romantic movement and the Gaelic revival.

As in other forms of culture the Romanticists emphasised all
that was backward-looking and medieval in opposition to Enlightenment figures who had tried to create a new culture based on reason and science. Moreover, Romantic folk culture was very different
from working class culture which developed during the Industrial

---

[54] *The Romantic Revolution* by Tim Blanning (Phoenix, Great Britain, 2010) p12

Revolution. With the influence of socialist ideas and movements over the following decades, working class authors and poets produced many fine poems, ballads and novels about the struggles of ordinary people.

It is interesting to note that in the late seventeenth century and the early eighteenth century, the cultural elites of Europe were actually more interested in French than their own languages, and went on the Grand Tour of Europe to broaden their horizons and learn about language, architecture, geography, and culture demonstrating the elite switch from Enlightenment learning to Romanticist mythology as elites move from progressive universalism to nationalist 'crowd control' out of fear of the spread of working-class consciousness.

Also, it is ironic that the thrill of Romanticism often came from the safety of modernity (in the form of Enlightenment science) as the development of steamboats and railway systems allowed the new middle classes to experience the 'sublime' in the beauty of dramatic landscapes like the Alps.

Nationalism – 'countering the worst excesses of neoliberalism'

The influence of Romanticism on politics shifted revolutionary thinking from burgeoning socialist movements to nationalism instead. Nationalism is the perfect class conciliatory ideology in that it retains the full social order/hierarchy (i.e. it includes the elites) and homogenises the people by excluding other national languages and foreign communities while putting the elites into positions of leadership and control.

Using divide and rule tactics and stirring up xenophobic attitudes and fears, the new elites ran the new homogenised nations and used them for their old purposes: war. Modern global power struggles of the twentieth century started with nation set against nation in the First World War.

Similarly, Romanticism was an important aspect of right-wing ideology in Germany before and during the Second World War. For example, Ernst Jünger (1895–1998) a German author and philosopher, advocated a change from Romanticist folk culture (Kultur) to a Modernist urban soldier/worker culture instead. Jünger believed that "faith in the land is the faith of a declining existence" and that the modern working class would not have the same Romanticist ideas of rural existence.[55] Jünger wrote that:

> The country and the nation ... must come to terms with the following necessity: We must penetrate and enter into the power of the metropolis, into the forces of our time - the machine, the masses and the worker. For it is in them that the potential energy so crucial for tomorrow's national spectacle resides. All of the people of Europe are at work to use these powers. We will try to put aside the objections of a misguided romanticism which views the machine as in conflict with Kultur.[56]

According to Jeffrey Herf in *Reactionary Modernism*, Jünger "was not rejecting romanticism, only one of its favourite themes. In place of pastoral escape, he promised his readers that the battlefield and the metropolis could fulfill the romantic yearnings of antibourgeois youth", thus demonstrating the flexibility of Romanticism to change from rural fantasy to war fantasy, and to vacillate from peasantism to workerism as the elite agenda required. Herf notes, in a different essay, "Jünger explicitly set out to demonstrate that acceptance of technological modernity did not entail the embrace of a more all-encompassing view of the modern world that would include liberalism, Marxism, rationalism, or individual liberty" and that the people could "be won over to the 'new nationalism'."[57]

The widespread acceptance of these ideas in Germany led to the tragic 'national spectacle' of the complete destruction of Germany during the Second World War. This 'warning from the past' did not lead to the end of chauvinistic Romanticist nationalism but again showed its flexibility by taking on new forms.

---

[55] Jeffrey Herf, *Reactionary Modernism: Technology, culture, and politics in Weimar and the Third Reich* (2008) p86

[56] Jeffrey Herf, *Reactionary Modernism: Technology, culture, and politics in Weimar and the Third Reich* (2008) p86

[57] Jeffrey Herf, *Reactionary Modernism: Technology, culture, and politics in Weimar and the Third Reich* (2008) p87

Throughout the twentieth century the rise of globalism and neoliberalism led to a breakdown in nationalist ideology as the world became more and more economically and politically interconnected leading some to believe that we had moved on to an era of postnationalism. However, postnationalism is an internationalistic process whereby power is partially transferred from national authorities to supernational entities like the European Union. Thus, power is handed over from local elites to the super elite of the European Commission.

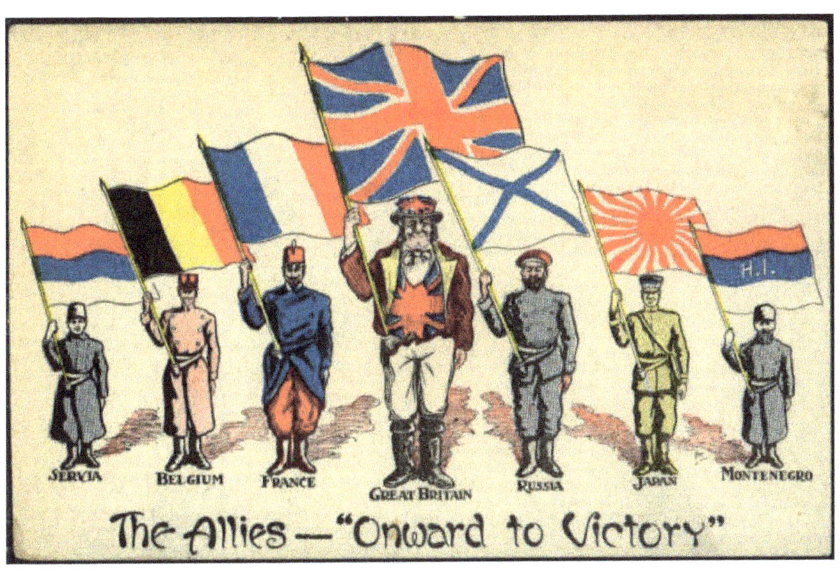

A postcard from 1916 showing national personifications of some of the Allies of World War I, each holding a national flag
(Public domain)

Nationalist sentiments are still used to allow elites to consolidate power and new nationalist movements have risen in many parts of the world as people turn to local elites to try and counter the worst excesses of neoliberalism. This has led to Hindu nationalism in India, Trump's "Make America Great Again" and "America First" campaigns, the United Kingdom's Brexit, anti-immigration rhetoric in Hungary, Germany's Pegida, France's National Front, and the UK Independence Party.

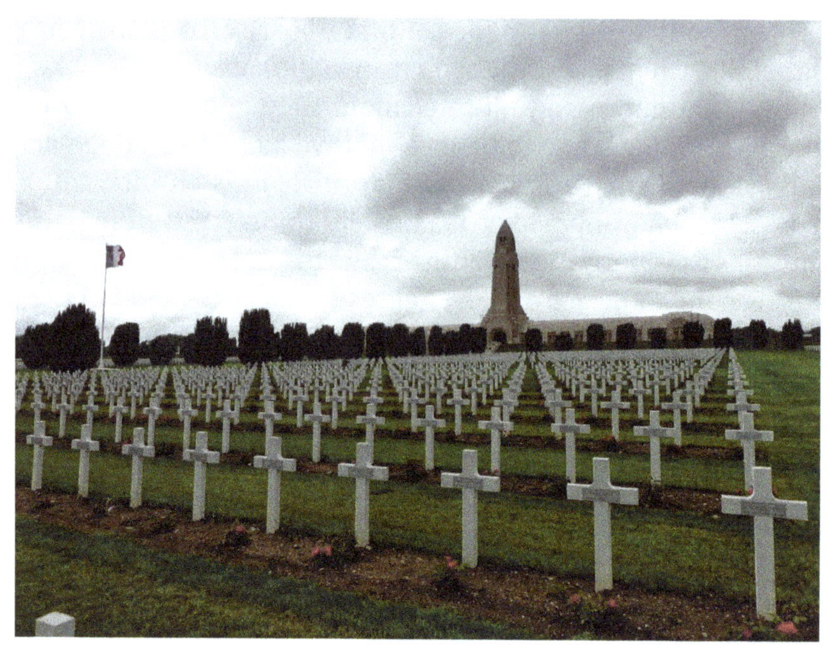

Ossuaire de Douaumont et Nécropole nationale
de Fleury-devant-Douaumont
(Paul Arps from The Netherlands / CC BY 2.0 / Wikimedia Commons)

Romanticist sentiments are still used and manipulated to keep the masses on board with the agendas of the elites, diverting people away from questioning the social and political systems under which they live and work. As the global economic and financial crises deepen there is the worrying possibility that more and more people will be dragged into these national and international power struggles rather than examining and fighting for their own social, economic and political interests, i.e. a revival of political and social consciousness.

Chapter 3

Art

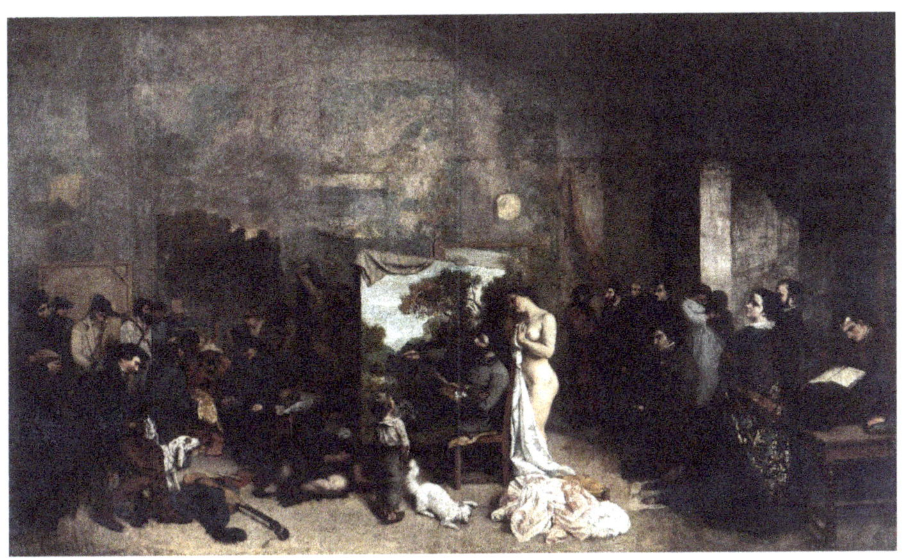

Gustave Courbet (1819–1877) *The Artist's Studio (L'Atelier du peintre):
A Real Allegory of a Seven Year Phase in my Artistic and Moral Life*
(1855), 359 cm × 598 cm (141 in × 235 in), oil on canvas,
Musée d'Orsay, Paris

*To be able to translate the customs, ideas and appearance
of my times as I see them - in a word, to create a living art -
this has been my aim.*
Gustave Courbet

Art Movements and the People's Movement

The whole exuberance, anarchy and violence of modern art ... its unrestrained, unsparing exhibitionism, is derived from [Romanticism]. And this subjective, egocentric attitude has become so much a matter of course for us ... that we find it impossible to reproduce even an abstract train of thought without talking about our feelings.

Arnold Hauser

Ever since the achievements of Renaissance humanism and the triumph of art over nature, with the development of new artistic techniques (the optics of perspective, the structure of anatomy, the mixing of pigments, and the development of movement) art was strengthened and, combined with the scientific explorations and achievements of the Enlightenment, led to the idea that Man could become stronger and better and hold an optimistic view of the future. He could improve his well-being and even take control of nature to create a better life for all.

This view continued through the decades and was associated with social revolutions and political activity which connected progressive ideas about society to artistic forms of expression which would illustrate and advance the hopes and desires of the masses for a better life and future. These artistic movements changed and developed from the Enlightenment to Realism to Social Realism and even Socialist Realism as artists both inspired and reflected the people's progressive movements the world over.

However, at every juncture, oppositional movements also stepped in and opposed progressive change and revolution by the people: from the Romantic movement in Revolutionary France to the Modernist movement to Postmodernism and now Metamodernism. These movements have derided every aspect of the progressive forces, from the quietist "l'art pour l'art" of Romanticism to the attack on artistic form by Modernism, to the later attack on ideological content by Postmodernism, and now the 'oscillation' between the two (form and content) of Metamodernism, a movement caught between self-obsession and the pressing desire of the masses for ideas and culture that would deal with climate change, financial crises, terror attacks and the neo-liberal squeeze on the social welfare system.

These two movements, Romanticism and the Enlightenment, have their basis in attitudes towards and beliefs in the efficacy of the burgeoning scientific movement. Romanticism, at its peak from 1800 to 1850, formed the basis of an anti-scientific strand in culture over the last two hundred years while the Enlightenment formed the basis of a scientific strand during the seventeenth and eighteenth centuries. Both strands have been in opposition ever since, their ideas reflected through various cultural movements which sprang up in different countries and at different times, some revolutionary and some reactionary.

The Anti-Scientific Strand

Romanticism

Romanticism is one of the most important historical movements in culture today as it still has a strong anti-science influence. Romanticism was characterized by its emphasis on emotion and individualism and glorified the past and nature, putting emphasis on the medieval rather than the classical traditions of ideals of harmony, symmetry, and order. The Romanticists rejected the norms of the Age of Enlightenment and the scientific rationalization of nature: both important aspects of modernity. Isaiah Berlin believed that the Romanticists opposed classic traditions of rationality and its basis in moral absolutes and agreed values which led "to something like the melting away of the very notion of objective truth".

Objective truth and reason were elevated by the artists and philosophers of the Enlightenment as a way to understand the universe and solve the pressing problems of the world. The Romanticists, however, were distrustful of the human world, and tended to strive for a close connection with nature to escape elements of modernity such as urbanisation, industrialisation and population growth, which therefore also allowed them to avoid questions centred around the growing working class, such as alienation, the ownership of the means of production, living conditions and conditions of employment.

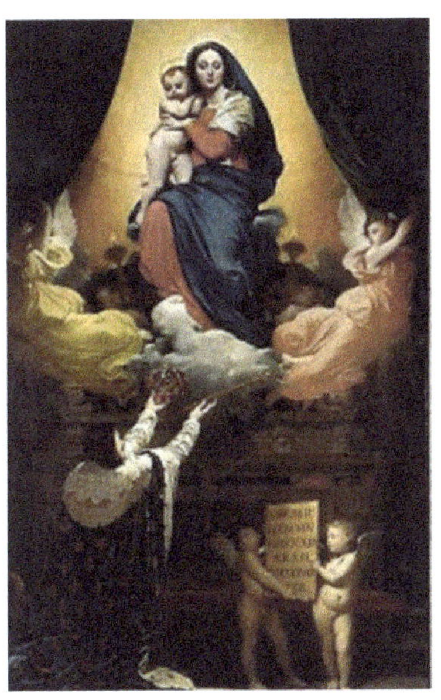
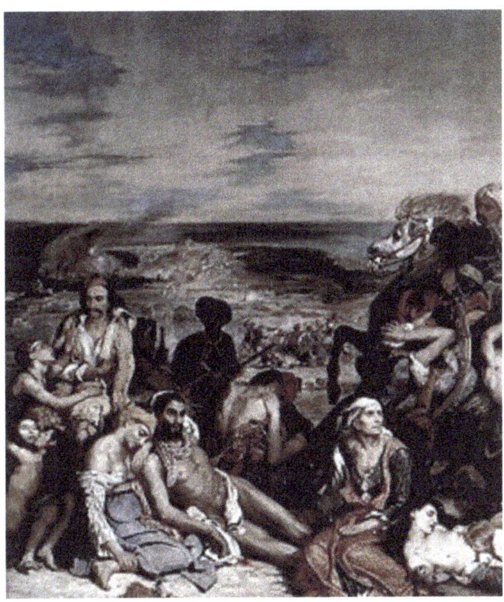

When Classicism met Romanticism. In the Salon of 1824 *The Vow of Louis XIII* by Jean-Auguste-Dominique Ingres (left) hung in the same room as *The Massacre at Chios* by Delacroix (right)
(Jean Auguste Dominique Ingres / Public domain / Wikimedia Commons, Eugène Delacroix / Public domain / Wikimedia Commons)

An early example of the clash between Classicism and Romanticism happened at the Salon of 1824 in Paris when *The Vow of Louis XIII* by Jean-Auguste-Dominique Ingres was hung in same room as *The Massacre at Chios* by Delacroix. As Elizabeth Prettejohn writes:

Ingres's *The Vow of Louis XIII* is pious and patriotic ... Delacroix's Scenes from the Massacres of Chios, on the other hand, is modern and activist ... In every aspect of pictorial style, too, the two pictures are starkly contrasted. Symmetry, simplicity, balance of complementary colors, and precision in drawing all contribute to the sense of hushed contemplation in the Ingres; complicated figure groupings, contorted poses, scattered accents of color, and energetic brushwork convey the disarray and sheer horror of Delacroix's massacre. Thus in both subject-matter and style the two pictures represent the battle between Classicism and Romanticism [in the French Academy], at the heady moment of its emergence.[58]

It is interesting to note that *The Massacre at Chios* was bought by the director of the royal museums without the King's official approval, an "irregular and politically risky procedure"[59] that demonstrated the strengthening politicised aspects of Romanticism. The Romanticists pursued the idea of "l'art pour l'art" (art for art's sake) believing that art did not need moral justification and could be morally neutral. According to Arnold Hauser in *The Social History of Art*:

Revolutionary France quite ingeniously enlists the services of art to assist her in this struggle; the nineteenth century is the first to conceive the idea of *"l'art pour l'art"* which forbids such a practice. The principle of "pure", absolutely "useless" art first results from the opposition of the romantic movement to the revolutionary period as a whole, and the demand that the artists should be passive derives from the ruling class's fear of losing its influence on art.[60]

This position (art for art's sake) originated with the elites in the nineteenth century and serves the same function today, Romanticism being the main influence on culture now.

---

[58] Elizabeth Prettejohn, *Beauty and Art* (Oxford: Oxford University Press, 2005), 78-9.

[59] https://en.m.wikipedia.org/wiki/The_Massacre_at_Chios

[60] Arnold Hauser, *The Social History of Art*, Vol 3 (Vintage Books, 1958) p147

Modernism

By the beginning of the 20th century, the Modernist movement was generally referred to as the "avant-garde" until the word "Modernism" became more popular. Modernism was the rejection of tradition, and the creation of new forms using reprise, incorporation, rewriting, recapitulation, revision and parody. The Modernist 'rejection of tradition', like with Romanticism, is the rejection of classical notions of form in art (harmony, symmetry, and order). Modernism (like Romanticism) also rejected the certainty of Enlightenment thinking. Modernism emphasised form over political content and rejected the ideology of Realism and Enlightenment thinking on liberty and progress.

While the Realist movement began in the mid-nineteenth century as a reaction to Romanticism, Modernism was a revolt against the 'traditional' values of Realism. Realist painters used common laborers and ordinary people in ordinary surroundings engaged in real activities as subjects for their works. However, Modernism rejected traditional forms which over time became less and less ´real´, more abstract and conceptualized, and ranged over many artforms.

As Peter Gay writes, 'the path to a modern romantic psychology was now open':

As modernists they argued that the true source of their inspiration was internal. Modernist painters looked for their subject matter not in nature but in strictly private motives; modernist novelists rejected (or severely modified) the age-old ideal of mimesis, the truthful imitation of the natural world; modernist composers disregarded the equally long-lived wish for a naturalistic copying of natural sounds. Modernist painters did canvases of abstract shapes, and Piet Mondrian went so far as to declare nature to be an enemy to art. Thus the modernist standard became a deeply private affair. Hence the romantics aim at art for art's sake - or even better, of art for artists' sake – was rarely mentioned but grew into the ideal for all artists.[61]

---

[61] Peter Gay, *Why the Romantics Matter* (Why X Matters Series) (2015) p29/30

The Great War brought about more disillusionment with Enlightenment ideals of progress among the Modernists who turned inwards and attacked art forms, instead of war-mongering capitalism.

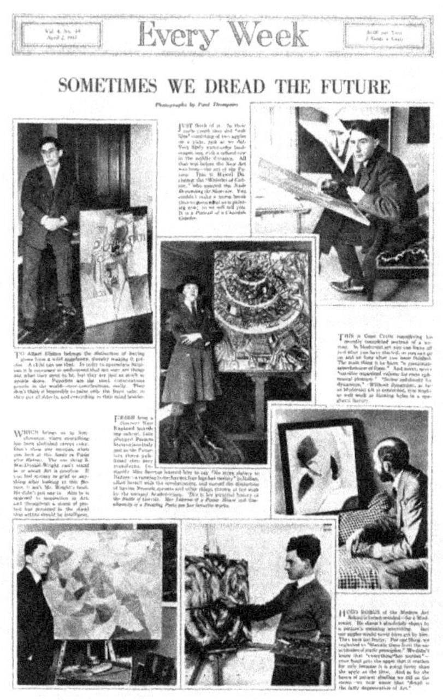

Albert Gleizes (with Chal Post, 1915); Marcel Duchamp (with his brother Jacques Villon's Portrait de M. J. B. peintre (Jacques Bon) 1914); Jean Crotti; Hugo Robus; Stanton MacDonald-Wright; and Frances Simpson Stevens with Battle of Gorizia (center), Sometimes we dread the future, *Every Week*, Vol. 4, No. 14, April 2, 1917, p. 14 (Every Week / Public domain / Wikimedia Commons)

The Romantic continuity in Modernism produced individual, horrified reactions to war but were ultimately no threat to the ruling elites. Like an angry child smashing his own toys, the Modernist attacked his own particular cultural forms. What was left was atonalism and abandonment of traditional rhythmic strictures in music, the departure from traditional realist styles in art, and the prioritisation of the individual and the interior mind, and abandonment of the fixed point of view in literature. The Dada movement, for example, was developed in reaction to the Great War by 'avant-garde' artists who rejected the logic, reason, and aestheticism of modern capitalist society but then only to respond with nonsense and irrationality in their art works.

Thus, the Romanticist Modernist movement failed the masses and stood outside the people's movement, turning in on itself and attacked reason instead of uniting with the progressive forces against war. In the end it was mainly the political movements of James Connolly in Ireland and V.I. Lenin in Russia (the two geographical ends of Europe) who mainly organised the working classes against the war.

David Alfaro Siqueiros (1896-1974), the revolutionary artist and founder of the Mexican Mural Movement, had this to say about the Modernist 'avant-garde':

If we look closely at their work it is the most reactionary movement in the history of culture. It has not developed anything new in composition or perspective and has lost much of that which has been accumulated over twenty centuries. It is based on the hysteria of novelty for the sake of novelty, in order to satisfy a parasitic plutocracy. The artist who changes his style every 24 hours is the best-known artist. When he has exhausted all the solutions, the others become his followers and sink into repetitious imitation.[62]

The allusion here, presumably to Picasso (1881–1973), famous for changing his style many times, is interesting in relation to Joaquín Sorolla (1863–1923) the Spanish artist whose depictions of ordinary Spanish people in monumental works of social and historical themes were overshadowed by Picasso until relatively recently. Picasso was credited with inventing Cubism, an art style produced in Paris during the 1910s and 1920s, and depicted the subject from differing viewpoints at the same time within the same painting. It was also a style that conflicted with the representational system in art that had prevailed since the Renaissance.

---

[62] D. Anthony White, *Siqueiros: Biography of a Revolutionary Artist* (Booksurge.com, 2008) p413

Many pseudo-scientific explanations were given to explain Cubism such as the effect on art of modern society, new scientific developments, photography taking over art's representational role, etc. but even Picasso himself ridiculed this:

Mathematics, trigonometry, chemistry, psychoanalysis, music and whatnot, have been related to cubism to give it an easier interpretation. All this has been pure literature, not to say nonsense, which brought bad results, blinding people with theories.[63]

Indeed, Cubism is probably the most parodied of all forms of Modernist art.

Other Modernist forms such as Expressionism have been seen to be at least critical of capitalism and war (e.g. Max Beckmann (1884–1950), Otto Dix (1891–1969), George Grosz (1893–1959), but according to Lotte H. Eisner who quotes a 'fervent theorist of this style', Kasimir Edschmid:

The Expressionist does not see, he has 'visions'. According to Edschmid. "the chain of facts: factories, houses, illness, prostitutes, screams, hunger' does not exist; only the interior vision they provoke exists.[64]

Therefore, the external reality of life and death for ordinary people is ignored for the ecstasy of 'interior visions'. For Eisner, writing in *The Haunted Screen*, German Expressionist cinema is another example of the visual manifestation of Romantic ideals. She writes:

Poverty and constant insecurity help to explain the enthusiasm with which German artists embraced this movement [Expressionism] which, as early as 1910, had tended to sweep aside all the principles which had formed the basis of art until then.[65]

---

[63] https://picasso.shsu.edu/mallen/VISUAL-GRAMMAR-REVIEW-2.html
[64] https://monoskop.org/images/f/fd/Eisner_Lotte_H_The_Haunted_Screen.pdf (p10)
[65] https://monoskop.org/images/f/fd/Eisner_Lotte_H_The_Haunted_Screen.pdf (p9-10)

Richard Murphy also notes:

> one of the central means by which expressionism identifies itself as an avant-garde movement, and by which it marks its distance to traditions and the cultural institution as a whole is through its relationship to realism and the dominant conventions of representation.[66]

Expressionists rejected the ideology of realism, and Expressionist art, in common with Romanticism, reacted to the dehumanizing effect of industrialization and the growth of cities with extreme individualism and emotionalism, not collective social empathy and political change.

After the Great War and the Russian Revolution, in the 1920s and 1930s, the idea of depicting ordinary people in art spread to many countries in Realist and Social Realist forms especially as a reaction to the exaggerated ego encouraged by Romanticism. In the United States the Ashcan School was well known for works portraying scenes of daily life in New York city's poorer neighborhoods. However, the unsettling depictions of the darker side of capitalism by the Ashcan School was soon displaced with Modernism in the Armory Show of 1913 and the opening of more galleries in the 1910s that promoted the Modernist artwork of Cubists, Fauves, and Expressionists.

This takeover by Modernism in New York continued into the 1940s and 1950s with the development of Abstract Expressionism, an art form which was soon promoted globally as a counterweight to the Socialist Realism style developed in the Soviet Union, especially during the Cold War. The loose, splashing and dripping of paint in the work of Jackson Pollack became used as a symbol of the ideology of freedom and free enterprise in the United States. The victory of Modernism in the United States served two purposes: national and international. It dampened down the critical dissent of the Ashcan School while at the same time serving as a useful tool of foreign policy.

---

[66] Richard Murphy, *Theorizing the Avant-Garde: Modernism, Expressionism, and the Problem of Postmodernity* (Cambridge, Cambridge University Press,1999) p43

According to Frances Stonor Saunders in *The Cultural Cold War: The CIA and the World of Arts and Letters*, Abstract Expressionism was "Non-figurative and politically silent, it was the very antithesis to socialist realism. It was precisely the kind of art the Soviets loved to hate."[67] This was Modernism at its zenith as the wealthiest of art investors and the most influential art critics promoted Abstract Expressionism as "independent, self-reliant, a true expression of the national will, spirit and character."[68] However, the size of the confidence trick being perpetrated on the unsuspecting public became unsettling. According to Saunders:

> It was this very stylistic conformity, prescribed by MoMA and the broader social contract of which it was a part, that brought Abstract Expressionism to the verge of kitsch. 'It was like the emperor's clothes,' said Jason Epstein. 'You parade it down the street and you say, "This is great art," and the people along the parade route will agree with you. Who's going to stand up to Clem Greenberg and later to the Rockefellers who were buying it for their bank lobbies and say, "This stuff is terrible"?'[69]

The imposition of Modern Art on the public was also noted by the journalist, Tom Wolfe, who wrote about the 1960s and 1970s art scene in New York in *The Painted Word*:

> The notion that the public accepts or rejects anything in Modern Art, the notion that the public scorns, ignores, fails to comprehend, allows to wither, crushes the spirit of, or commits any other crime against Art or any individual artist is merely a romantic fiction, a bittersweet Trilby sentiment. The game is completed and the trophies distributed long before the public knows what has happened. [...] We can now

---

[67] Frances Stonor Saunders, *The Cultural Cold War: The CIA and the World of Arts and Letters* (The New Press, 1999) p254

[68] Frances Stonor Saunders, *The Cultural Cold War: The CIA and the World of Arts and Letters* (The New Press, 1999) p254

[69] Frances Stonor Saunders, *The Cultural Cold War: The CIA and the World of Arts and Letters* (The New Press, 1999) p275

also begin to see that Modern Art enjoyed all the glories of the Consummation stage after the First World War not because it was 'finally understood' or 'finally appreciated' but rather because a few fashionable people discovered their own uses for it.[70]

It was also in the early 1970s that the Irish artist Seán Keating (1889–1977), a Realist painter who painted images of the Irish War of Independence, the early industrialization of Ireland and many portraits of the people of the Aran Islands, was brought face to face with Modernism. In a well-known televised interview, Keating, now in his 60s, was brought around the ROSC'71 exhibition and asked to give his opinion on the exhibits. As Eimear O'Connor writes:

> When confronted by *The Table*, made by German artist Eva Aeppli (b.1925), Keating said it was 'downright horrible perversity, nightmare stuff ... an old lady who had gone completely mad and is dangerous ... I think it is morose ... vengeful against the human race...'[71]

This baiting of a famous Irish humanist whose love of the Irish people and progress, displayed the new confidence of the Irish elites who had jumped on the Modernist bandwagon as a symbol of fashionability and of final acceptance by the European elites who would allow Ireland to join the EEC (EU) in 1973.

Postmodernism

In the meantime, Postmodernism was also gaining strength. Some features of Postmodernism in general can be found as early as the 1940s but it would compete with Modernism in the late 1950s and became predominant by the 1960s. Postmodernism is defined as follows:

Postmodernism, also spelled post-modernism, in Western

---

[70] Tom Wolfe, *The Painted Word* (Bantam Books, 1987) p26/7
[71] Eimear O'Connor and Virginia Teehan, *Sean Keating: In Focus* (Hunt Museum, 2009) p33

philosophy, a late 20th-century movement characterized by broad skepticism, subjectivism, or relativism; a general suspicion of reason; and an acute sensitivity to the role of ideology in asserting and maintaining political and economic power. Postmodernism as a philosophical movement is largely a reaction against the philosophical assumptions and values of the modern period of Western (specifically European) history—i.e., the period from about the time of the scientific revolution of the 16th and 17th centuries to the mid-20th century. Indeed, many of the doctrines characteristically associated with postmodernism can fairly be described as the straightforward denial of general philosophical viewpoints that were taken for granted during the 18th-century Enlightenment, though they were not unique to that period.[72]

In other words, Postmodernism had a direct line of descent from Modernism, and Romanticism before that. The same Romanticist characteristics show up again – the suspicion of reason, subjectivism and denial of the ideas of the Enlightenment. Once again cynicism towards the idea of progress and working-class improvement is the mainstay. Every technique and trick of avoidance of the important issues facing the people's movements is used in Postmodernism: "common targets of postmodern critique include universalist notions of objective reality, morality, truth, human nature, reason, language, and social progress" and "postmodern thought is broadly characterized by tendencies to self-referentiality, epistemological and moral relativism, pluralism, subjectivism, and irreverence."[73]

Postmodernist artists decided that past styles (once criticised by Modernists for being 'traditional') were now usable in a parodic way along with appropriation and popular culture. The Postmodernist critique of universalist ideas of objective reality and social progress (otherwise known as Grand Narratives), has particular implications for the working classes and popular political movements as their liberatory philosophy and ideologies are based on them – whatever their supposed successes or failures in the past.

---

[72] https://www.britannica.com/topic/postmodernism-philosophy
[73] https://en.wikipedia.org/wiki/Postmodern_art

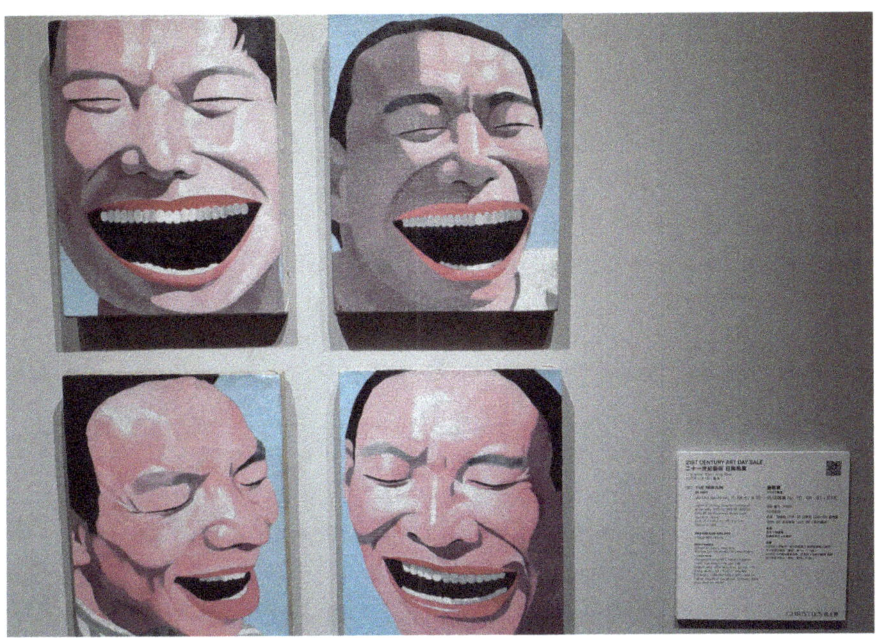

Yue Minjun, *Idol Series*
(DTAICHWOM SIMLOOA / CC BY-SA 4.0 / Wikimedia Commons)

To take them away is to fall back on the neo-liberal philosophy of the end-of-history and more of the same globalised capitalism *ad infinitum*. After the attack on Form in Modernism, we now get an assault on Content in Postmodernism.

When applied to the people's movement itself, such as the French Revolution, Postmodernist historiography, for example, all but wipes out its historic relevance and importance. As Richard J. Evans writes in *In Defence of History*, Simon Schama's book *Citizens: A Chronicle of the French Revolution* over-emphasises the bloody and violent nature of the revolution as if the politically-conscious people taking their lives into their own hands were irrational beings exploding with an animal lust for violence. Evans comments:

In *Citizens*, indeed, the French Revolution of 1789-94 becomes almost meaningless in the larger sense, and is reduced to a kind of theatre of the absurd; the social and economic misery of the masses, an essential driving force behind their involvement in the revolutionary events, is barely mentioned; and the lasting significance of the Revolution's many political theories and doctrines for modern European and world history more or less disappears.[74]

The opaquer forms of relativistic Postmodernist writing and thinking were exposed when Alan Sokal refused to get into line and exposed the French Postmodernists in a hoax essay published in *Social Text* in 1996. According to Francis Wheen in *How Mumbo Jumbo Conquered the World*:

As a socialist who had taught in Nicaragua after the Sandinista revolution, he [Sokal] felt doubly indignant that much of the new mystificatory folly emanated from the self-proclaimed left. For two centuries, progressives had championed science against obscurantism. The sudden lurch of academic humanists and social scientists towards epistemic relativism not only betrayed this heritage but jeopardised 'the already fragile prospects for a progressive social critique', since it was impossible to combat bogus ideas if all notions of truth and falsity ceased to have any validity.[75]

The obvious contradictions and cul-de-sacs of Postmodernism eventually brought it into decline and soon doors opened for a new obfuscatory philosophy to buttress increasingly crisis-ridden globalised capitalism – Metamodernism.

Metamodernism

According to Timotheus Vermeulen and Robin van den Akker in 'Notes on Metamodernism':

The postmodern years of plenty, pastiche, and parataxis are

---

[74] Richard J. Evans, *In Defence of History* (Granta Books, 2000) p245

[75] Francis Wheen, *How Mumbo Jumbo Conquered the World* (Harper Perennial, 2004) p89/90

over. In fact, if we are to believe the many academics, critics, and pundits whose books and essays describe the decline and demise of the postmodern, they have been over for quite a while now. But if these commentators agree the postmodern condition has been abandoned, they appear less in accord as to what to make of the state it has been abandoned for. In this essay, we will outline the contours of this discourse by looking at recent developments in architecture, art, and film. We will call this discourse, oscillating between a modern enthusiasm and a postmodern irony, metamodernism. We argue that the metamodern is most clearly, yet not exclusively, expressed by the neoromantic turn of late.[76]

So, there you have it – this is the best that Metamodernism can offer – a return to Romanticism! We have now come full circle as "the metamodern is most clearly, yet not exclusively, expressed by the neoromantic turn of late". And where is this pressure coming from, to allow a little reality back into the arts? Vermeulen and van den Akker write:

Some argue the postmodern has been put to an abrupt end by material events like climate change, financial crises, terror attacks, and digital revolutions [...] have necessitated a reform of the economic system ('un nouveau monde, un nouveau capitalisme', but also the transition from a white collar to a green collar economy).[77]

The contemporary crises of capitalism and climate change are finally impinging on the disintegrating Postmodern artistic consciousness, and the answer is reformism and 'new capitalism'. However, Metamodernism is "Like a donkey it chases a carrot that it never manages to eat because the carrot is always just beyond its reach. But precisely because it never manages to eat the carrot, it never ends its chase".[78] So, with a little bit of progressive critique, the Metamodern artist can regain credibility but without ever really

---

[76] https://www.tandfonline.com/doi/full/10.3402/jac.v2i0.5677

[77] https://www.tandfonline.com/doi/full/10.3402/jac.v2i0.5677

[78] https://www.tandfonline.com/doi/full/10.3402/jac.v2i0.5677

challenging the status quo.

From all of the above we can see the common threads tying Romanticism, Modernism, Postmodernism and Metamodernism together: individualism, art for art's sake, suspicion of reason, subjectivism and denial of the ideas of the Enlightenment. All are individualist movements that oppose the idea of collectivist ideology and action. Movements that ultimately serve the status quo and the ruling elites. Yet some of these same elites were involved in the development of the concepts of the Enlightenment in the beginning. What happened to them?

The Scientific Strand

The Enlightenment

The Enlightenment dominated the world of ideas in Europe during the 18th century. Enlightenment thinkers believed in the importance of rationality and science. They believed that the natural world and even human behavior could be explained scientifically. They felt that they could use the scientific method to improve human society. For the artists and philosophers of the Enlightenment, the ideal life was one governed by reason. Artists and poets strove for ideals of harmony, symmetry, and order, valuing meticulous craftsmanship and the classical tradition. Among philosophers, truth was discovered by a combination of reason and empirical research.

Neoclassicism

In art, the Enlightenment affected the revival of the many styles and spirit of classic antiquity inspired directly from the classical period which became known as Neoclassicism. The movement originated largely due to the writings of Johann Joachim Winckelmann (1717–1768), a German art historian and archaeologist who was a Hellenist and who first articulated the difference between Greek,

Greco-Roman and Roman art. His writings had a major influence on archaeology, art history, Western painting, sculpture, literature and philosophy.

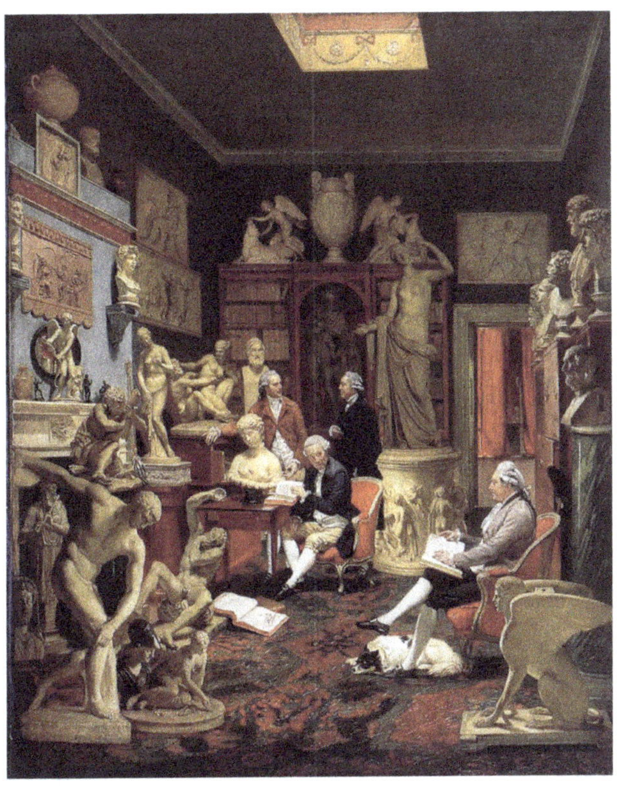

Charles Towneley in his sculpture gallery (1782) by Johann Zoffany (1733–1810) Oil on canvas, 127 cm x 102 cm, Towneley Hall Art Gallery and Museum, *Burnley, UK* (Public domain / Wikimedia Commons)

Neoclassicism was also a reaction to the aristocratic, excessively extravagant and superficial Rococo style of the eighteenth century. On a broader level, for example, in 1767 Diderot "deplored the way in which artists were still expected to consider the whims of individuals instead of the interests of the nation as a whole."[79] In France the artist Jacques Louis David (1748–1825) connected neoclassical art with the ideas of duty, honor, and patriotism in his paintings

---

[79] Hugh Honour, *Neoclassicism* (Penguin, 1991) p89/44

Oath of the Horatii and *The Death of Socrates*, for example:

> By using classical examples as models and guides, neoclassical art is characterized by its sense of order, logic, clarity, and to an extent, realism. Duty to a higher cause, such as one's country or its ruler, as well as the sense of decorum and appropriateness are emphasized. These qualities are seen in the increased 'naturalism' of landscapes (such as those of Canaletto and Bellotto) and in the fact that classical models inspired the new changes in landscape painting. In portraiture, artists such as Sir Joshua Reynolds attempted to elevate the genre by infusing it with the heroic influences of the 'Grand Style.' By incorporating the depth of the historical paintings into portraiture, artists sought to make portraits more than simply representations of 'likenesses.'[80]

The intellectual middle-class showed its Enlightenment interest in science by founding societies such as the Birmingham Lunar Society (1770s-1780s). The members' interest in art and science was evident in their discussions on philosophy, politics and the arts as well as conducting scientific experiments. The artist Joseph Wright of Derby, for example, combined an interest in science with the effects of light on the subjects he depicted. One of his paintings is his *Experiment with the Air Pump* (1768) which not only depicted the effect of oxygen deprivation on a bird but how the light fell on the observers in the composition. As Hugh Honour notes, Wright "was also, just as characteristically, a man of feeling. Even when painting a scientific experiment, he introduced the figure of a girl weeping" at the fate of the bird.[81]

In the field of political philosophy, the English philosopher Thomas Hobbes, for example, developed some of the fundamentals of European liberal thought: the right of the individual, the natural equality of all men and the idea that legitimate political power must be "representative" and based on the consent of the people. Therefore, the Enlightenment popularised the idea that with the

---

[80] http://theatreforall.weebly.com/neo-classicism.html
[81] Hugh Honour, *Neoclassicism*, (Penguin, 1991) p98

use of reason and logic social development and progress would be the norm for the masses and science and technology would be the instruments of human progress.

The ideas of the Enlightenment paved the way for the political revolutions of the eighteenth and nineteenth centuries as it under-

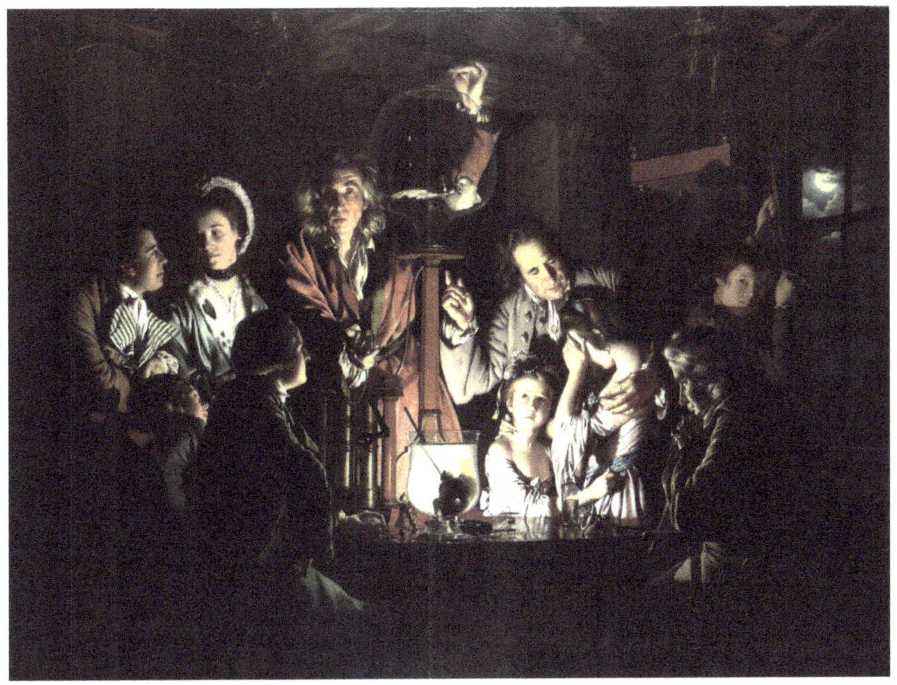

Experiment with the Air Pump (1768) by Joseph Wright of Derby (1734–1797) Oil on canvas, 183 cm × 244 cm (72 in × 94 1⁄2 in), National Gallery, London
(Public domain / Wikimedia Commons)

mined the authority of the monarchy and the Church. The French Revolution become the first main conflict between the men of the Enlightenment and the aristocracy. Within the arts this conflict arose between those who believed that art had a role to play and those who believed in 'art for art's sake'. As Hauser notes:

It is only with the Revolution that art becomes a confession of political faith, and it is now emphasized for the first time that it has to be no 'mere ornament on the social structure,' but 'a part of its foundations.' It is now declared that art must not be an idle pastime, a mere tickling of the nerves, a privilege of the rich and the leisured, but it must teach and improve, spur on to action and set an example. It must be pure, true, inspired and inspiring, contribute to the happiness of the general public and become the possession of the whole nation.[82]

However, the rising bourgeoisie who advocated the ideas of the Enlightenment realised that their objectives and those of the revolutionary public were not the same:

Yet as soon as the bourgeoisie had achieved its aims, it left its former comrades in arms in the lurch and wanted to enjoy the fruits of the common victory alone. [...] Hardly had the Revolution ended, than a boundless disillusion seized men's souls and not a trace remained of the optimistic philosophy of the enlightenment.[83]

Thus, began the conflict between the new rulers, the bourgeoisie, who wanted to set limits on progress, and the interests of the toiling masses who had not yet achieved one of the most basic concepts of Enlightenment philosophy: the natural equality of all men. This struggle for political and social freedom took different forms over the next century or so but had as one of its principles the idea that the arts would play a role.

Realism

As the bourgeoisie stepped up its development of capitalist society by building factories and markets, the Realist movement reacted to Romanticist escapism in favor of depictions of 'real' life, emphasizing the mundane, ugly and sordid: the somber side of exploitation.

The Realist artists used common laborers and ordinary people

---

[82] Arnold Hauser, *The Social History of Art*, Vol 3 (Vintage Books, 1958) p147
[83] Arnold Hauser, *The Social History of Art*, Vol 3 (Vintage Books, 1958) p157

in their normal work environments as the main subjects for their paintings. Its chief exponents were Gustave Courbet (1819–1877), Jean-François Millet (1814–1875), Honoré Daumier (1808–1879), and Jean-Baptiste-Camille Corot (1796–1875). Courbet hated the aristocracy and royalty, and advocated political and social change.

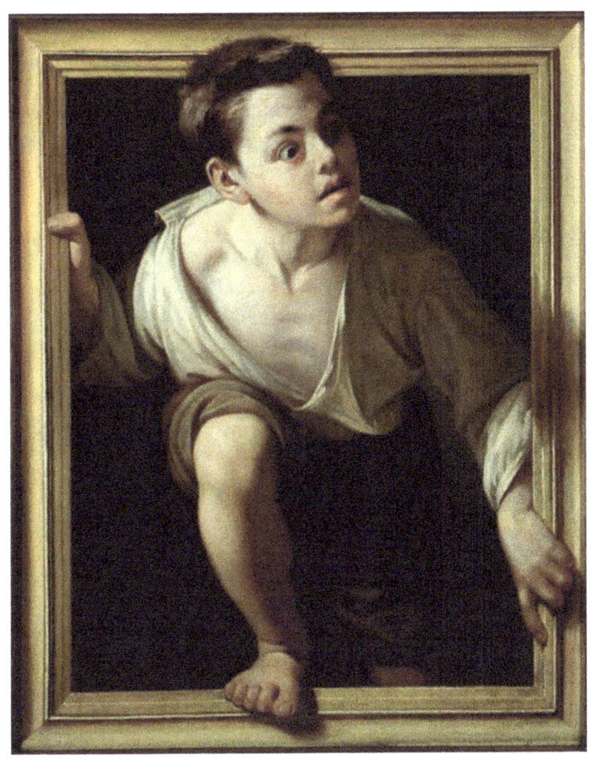

Escaping criticism (1874) by Pere Borrell del Caso (1835–1910)
Collection Banco de España, Madrid
(Public domain / Wikimedia Commons)

He painted ordinary people and on canvas sizes usually reserved for gods and heroes. Realist movements, like the Peredvizhniki or Wanderers group (1870–1890) in Russia, the Macchiaioli Art Movement (c.1855-80) in Italy, and the Barbizon School of Landscape Art (1830-75) in France, were founded in many Western countries.

In Spain, the artist Pere Borrell del Caso (1835–1910) was critical of the Romanticist style that dominated local art education. Borrell "rejected the idealization and insincerity that, in his eyes, were so typical of Romantic art and chose to change to the novel style of Realism."[84] He set up his own art academy, the Sociedad de Bellas Artes, where he encouraged his students to work *en plein air* [in the open air]. His painting, *Escaping criticism* (1874) is believed to be symbolic of his attitude to the styles of the time.

Social Realism

Meanwhile, as the Industrial Revolution grew in Britain, concern for the factory workers led to a major change in the ideology of the working class organisations seeking better conditions. While the Romanticists believed that the Industrial Revolution and its exploitative extremes in the factories was the result of science, the Marxists instead questioned the ownership of the factories, and who benefited from the greatly increased power of the new means of production, means that could benefit society as a whole. Therefore, while the Romanticists looked back to the medieval artisans and peasants, the Marxists saw science creating new possibilities for a better future for everybody.

Social Realism grew out of these changes as Social Realist artists drew attention to the everyday conditions of the working class and the poor and criticised the social structures which maintained these conditions.

In the twentieth century the Mexican and Russian revolutions gave a fillip to the Social Realist movement which reached its height of popularity during the 1920s and 1930s when capitalism was under severe pressure from the global economic depression.The Ashcan School in the USA and the Mexican muralist movement were two groups who exerted a huge influence at the time and many of the artists involved at the time were supporters of political working-class movements. While contemporary Social Realism has been kept in the background it is still a popular style with progressive artists.

---

[84] http://rijksmuseumamsterdam.blogspot.com/2012/01/pere-borrell-del-caso-escaping.html

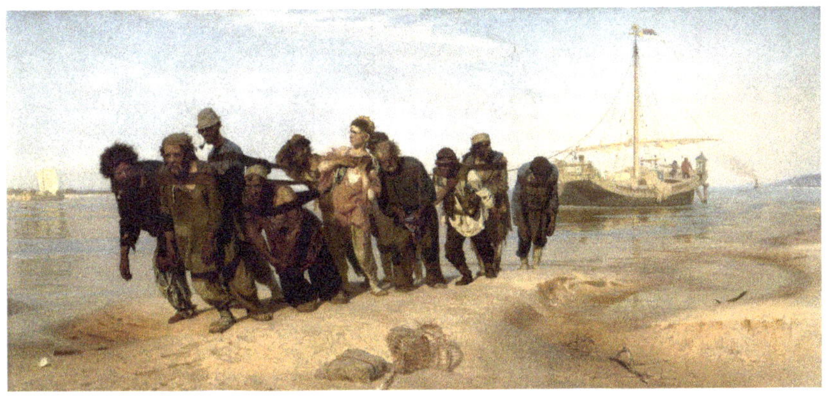

Ilya Repin, (1844–1930) *Barge Haulers on the Volga* (1870–1873)
(Public domain / Wikimedia Commons)

Socialist Realism

As nationalist struggles of the nineteenth century changed into socialist struggles during the twentieth century, the style and form of the art changed too as ordinary people were now depicted as subjects with dignity and power. This style became known as Socialist Realism. It was pronounced state policy at the Soviet Writers' Congress in 1934 in the Soviet Union and became a dominant style in other socialist countries.

Like Social Realism, Socialist Realism also met with fierce denunciations and controversy. However, despite its caricature as a style that depicts people as naïve, happy, joyous ciphers, its originators condemned any attempt to portray people living in an idyllic paradise as the work of shallow artists who would never be taken seriously by the populace:

An artist who tried to represent the birth of socialism as an idyll, who tried to represent the socialist system, which is being born in hard-fought battles, as a paradise populated by ideal people – such an artist would not be a realist, would not be able to convince anyone by his works. The artist should show how socialism is built out of the bricks of the past, out of the material which the past has left us, out of the material which we ourselves create in the sweat of our brow, in the blood of our toil and struggle, in, the hard battles of classes and in the hard toil of man to remold himself.[85]

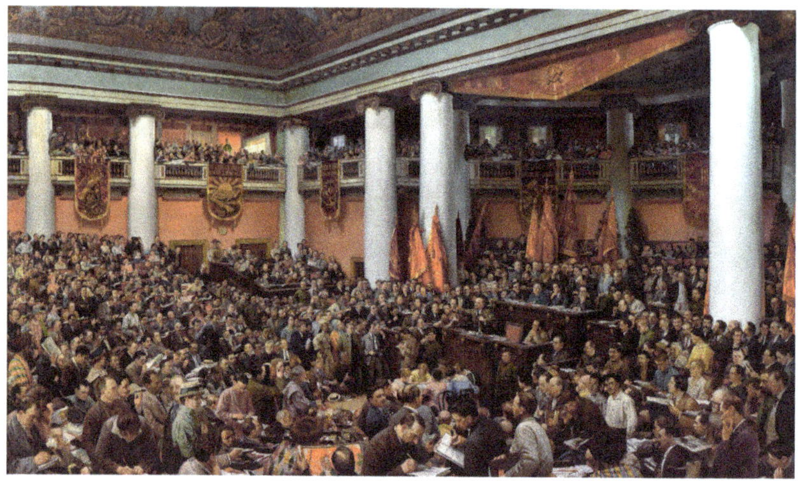

Isaak Brodsky, (1884–1939) *Lenin's speech on the 2nd World Congress of the Comintern (1924)* State Historical Museum
(Public domain / Wikimedia Commons)

Socialist Realism went into decline in the 1960s as the Soviet Union itself went from crisis to crisis until its end in 1991. Today it is a style which is still much criticised. Why is Socialist Realism such a taboo? Because Socialist Realism is a quadruple whammy – it contains four elements that elites don't like:

1. Anything to do with the Soviet Union (then) or Russia (today)

2. Any depictions of the working class anywhere (which are not subservient)

3. Any discussion of socialism or socialist ideology (past, present or future)

4. Any realist depiction of opposition to capitalism (that could influence others)

---

[85] https://www.marxists.org/archive/radek/1934/sovietwritercongress.htm

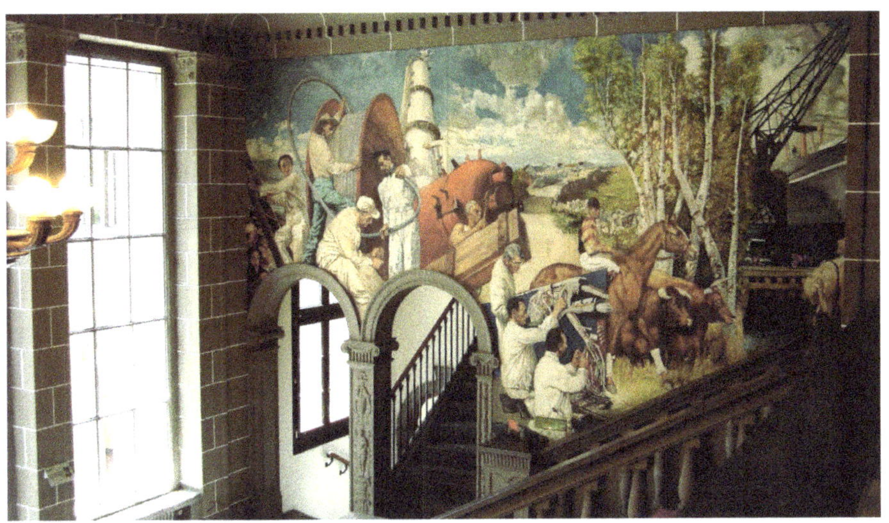

Irish Industrial Development (oil on wood panels) (1961)
by Seán Keating (1889–1977)
International Labour Offices (ILO) Geneva, Switzerland
(BiiJii / CC BY-SA 3.0 / Wikimedia Commons)
Positive images of Irish workers by Irish artist in Geneva – must be Socialist Realism!

If one looks at 'history of Western art' books it becomes apparent that there are very few positive images of the working class but plenty of images glorifying monarchs, aristocrats, the middle classes and Noble Peasants (the useful idiots of nationalism). Representations of peasants usually take the form of non-threatening genre paintings, and any Socialist Realist art is excluded.

The fact is that Romanticism in its different forms has made sure to keep the working classes out of the picture, and the only response of the peoples' movements should be to keep Romanticist influences at arm's length. Romanticism has become the capitalist art *par excellence*. Romanticism vacillates between cultures of despair and Nihilism. It is opposed to logic and reason and its extreme individualism ensures a divisive effect on any collectivist organisation.

Romanticism pervades most mass culture today and sells egoism and impotence back to the very people who turn to it for solace from desperation.

The long conflict between Romanticism and Enlightenment ideas contained in art movements over the last two centuries is set to continue as new responses to the contemporary crises of capitalism try to ameliorate the situation or fundamentally change the system underpinning it. What is needed are new national debates on the role and function of art in maintaining or changing the structure of society.

Debates similar to those described by an eyewitness to the Paris Commune, Villiers de l'Isle-Adam, who wrote: "a whole population is discussing serious matters, and for the first time workers can be heard exchanging their views on problems which up until now have been broached only by philosophers."[86]

---

[86] Villiers de l'Isle-Adam, in Le Tribun du Peuple, May 10, 1871, quoted in Stewart Edwards, *The Paris Commune 1871* (Quadrangle, 1977) p283

Chapter 4

Music

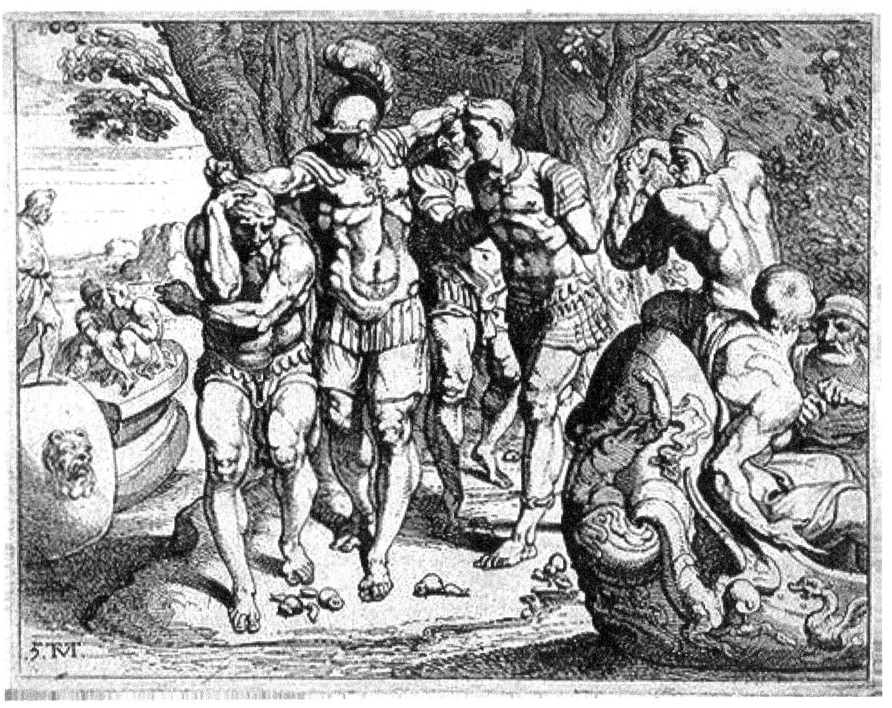

Theodoor van Thulden (1606–1669)
18th-century French engraving of Odysseus (Ulysses)
removing his men from the company of the lotus-eaters
(Public domain / Wikimedia Commons)

*Narcotic: drug that produces analgesia (pain relief),
narcosis (state of stupor or sleep), and addiction (physical dependence on the drug). In some people narcotics
also produce euphoria (a feeling of great elation).*
britannica.com

The Conversion of Music into a Mass Narcotic

People worry about kids playing with guns, and teenagers watching violent videos; we are scared that some sort of culture of violence will take them over. Nobody worries about kids listening to thousands - literally thousands - of songs about broken hearts and rejection and pain and misery and loss.

Nick Hornby

Romanticism as a philosophical movement of the nineteenth century had a profound influence on music which can still be seen right up to today. Its main characteristics in music are the emphasis on the personal, dramatic contrasts, emotional excess, a focus on the nocturnal, the ghostly and the frightful, and extreme subjectivism. Romanticism in culture implied a turning inward and encouraged introspection. As Hegel wrote: "The entire content [of romantic art] is therefore concentrated on the inner life of the spirit".[87]

Romanticist-influenced music increased its audience dramatically from the early theatres of the nineteenth century to the mass pop concerts of the modern era. Romanticism changed music from being a progressive force in society to being a narcotic and self-indulgent individualist experience. In modern times it has been industrialised and commercialised and sells individualism and political impotence to the very people who turn to it for relief from desperation in a highly alienated society.

The most regrettable aspect of this alienation is that music has

---

[87] https://www.marxists.org/reference/archive/hegel/works/ae/part2-section3.htm#s1

become more and more distant from people's movements for progressive change. Historically, progressive music, i.e. music which was in tune with the history of people's political struggles, tended to come from the people themselves, in the form of ballads or music from progressive composers and lyricists. With the commercialising of the pop music industry in the twentieth century, music became something to be consumed on a mass basis rather than produced by people on a local basis – by writing, playing or singing, as it was in the past with balladeers, choirs and progressive composers.

Here we will look at the influence of the Enlightenment on composers as they moved away from the earlier Baroque style, and the later effect of Romanticism on music from the Classical period in the eighteenth and nineteenth centuries, through to the development of the pop music industry in the twentieth century. Also examined will be composers and singers who resisted the pressure of the Romanticist influence and wrote and played music that was rooted in hardship and struggle and an awareness of international issues and crises as they affected the ordinary people of those countries.

Classical Music – 'structures should be well-founded'

While classical music in general has a broad meaning the Classical period was an era of classical music between roughly 1730 and 1820. Enlightenment respect for the politics, aesthetics and philosophy of classical antiquity (Classicism) combined with the development of 'natural philosophy' (the precursor of the natural sciences) had a profound effect on music: "Newton's physics was taken as a paradigm: structures should be well-founded in axioms and be both well-articulated and orderly."[88] The earlier Baroque music was highly ornamented and performers were expected to be good at improvising and elaborating by interweaving *mordents*, *trills*, *acciaccaturas* and *appoggiaturas* into their performances.[89] The complexity of Baroque music was criticized by Rousseau:

---

[88] https://en.wikipedia.org/wiki/Classical_period_(music)
[89] https://www.cmuse.org/differences-between-baroque-and-classical-music/

Jean-Jacques Rousseau, who was a musician and composer as well as philosopher, wrote in 1768 in the Encyclopédie: 'Baroque music is that in which the harmony is confused, and loaded with modulations and dissonances. The singing is harsh and unnatural, the intonation difficult, and the movement limited. It appears that term comes from the word 'baroco' used by logicians.' Rousseau was referring to the philosophical term *baroco*, in use since the 13th century to describe a type of elaborate and, for some, unnecessarily complicated academic argument.[90]

The effect of the Enlightenment ideas of Classical music on Baroque was to mark a change to a lighter, clearer texture. At the same time technical developments in musical instruments and the increase in size and standardisation of orchestras changed the way music was played. The major composers of this time were Wolfgang Amadeus Mozart (1756–1791), Ludwig van Beethoven (1770–1827), Joseph Haydn (1732–1809), Christoph Willibald Gluck (1714–1787), Johann Christian Bach (1735–1782), Luigi Boccherini (1743–1805), Carl Philipp Emanuel Bach (1714–1788), Muzio Clementi (1752–1832), Antonio Salieri (1750–1825), and Johann Nepomuk Hummel (1778–1837).

Various changes marked the transition from Baroque to Classical, for example, the piano ("fortepiano," literally "loud soft") replaced the harpsicord, and the size of orchestras increased as wind instruments were added to the strings. Musical forms were created like the symphony, or changed as the solo concerto gradually replaced the concerto grosso (a concerto for more than one musician).

Over time the growth of the middle classes throughout western Europe allowed composers and musicians to live and work independently of the nobility as organisations for teaching, performance and the preservation of music were founded.[91]

---

[90] https://en.wikipedia.org/wiki/Baroque_music

[91] https://en.wikipedia.org/wiki/Classical_music

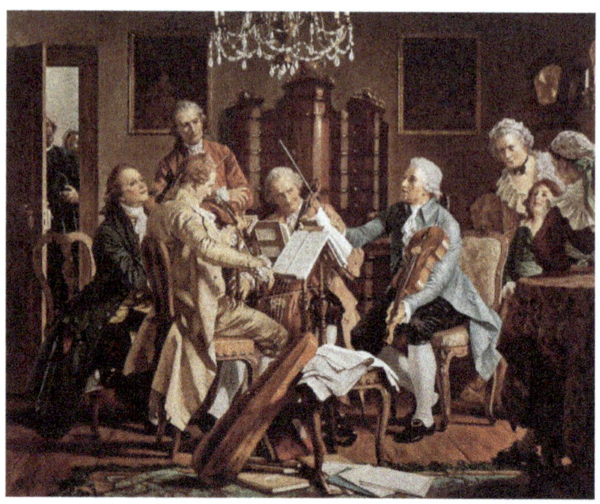

Joseph Haydn Playing Quartets, Anonymous - painting from the
StaatsMuseum, Vienna
(Public domain / Wikimedia Commons)

Romantic Music – 'more explicitly expressive and programmatic'

Romanticism originated at the end to the 18th century mainly as a reaction to the Age of Enlightenment and the Industrial Revolution which were perceived to be using science to destroy nature and man's traditional way of life. The Romanticist emphasis on feeling was in direct contrast with Enlightenment ideas of progress with reason and science being the primary source of knowledge. The philosophers and scientists of the Enlightenment had desired to move away from the Feudalism and Scholasticism of the religiously dominated Middle Ages. Unfortunately, the Romanticist artists, composers and poets took a new interest in aspects of medievalism that the Enlightenment philosophers had tried to defeat. Enlightenment ideas were also taken up by the new elites who used science in the exploitative ways so hated by the Romanticists.

The Romanticist reaction towards Classical music and the ideals of the Enlightenment in one sense was not surprising given the failure of those ideas ultimately in the French Revolution. As Friedrich Engels wrote in *Anti-Dühring* in 1877:

the French philosophers of the eighteenth century, the fore-runners of the Revolution, appealed to reason as the sole judge of all that is. A rational government, rational society, were to be founded; everything that ran counter to eternal reason was to be remorselessly done away with. We saw also that this eternal reason was in reality nothing but the idealised understanding of the eighteenth century citizen, just then evolving into the bourgeois. The French Revolution had realised this rational society and government. But, the new order of things, rational enough as compared with earlier conditions, turned out to be by no means absolutely rational. The state based upon reason completely collapsed.[92]

As Engels notes this resulted in the Reign of Terror and then Napoleonic despotism. The ideals of the Enlightenment philosophers were destroyed by an intensification of competition. He writes:

The promised eternal peace was turned into an endless war of conquest. The society based upon reason had fared no better. The antagonism between rich and poor, instead of dissolving into general prosperity, had become intensified by the removal of the guild and other privileges, which had to some extent bridged it over, and by the removal of the charitable institutions of the Church. The development of industry upon a capitalistic basis made poverty and misery of the working masses conditions of existence of society.[93]

How is it then that it is the Romanticists that are more associated with the revolutionary ideas of the time? Why were they seen by later critics and historians as reactionary or even politically irrelevant? According to Max Blechman in *Revolutionary Romanticism*:

The early romantics were revolutionaries: not because they believed in a political insurrection in their homeland [...] but because through public expression they hoped to redefine

---

[92] https://www.marxists.org/archive/marx/works/1877/anti-duhring/ch23.htm
[93] https://www.marxists.org/archive/marx/works/1877/anti-duhring/ch23.htm

the meaning of progress and revolutionize the values of modern civilisation." [...] Romanticism in Germany (as in France and England) was a protean [ever changing] movement, and the writings of formative romantics were contradicted by those of late romantics, some of whom broke with the early romantics' idealism for various forms of conservatism.[94]

The Romanticists, instead of questioning the class basis of society which was becoming more and more sharply delineated, sought inspiration from the simpler life, religiosity and culture of the Middle Ages. The idea of chivalrous heroes, the mystic and supernatural, untouched nature and the security of spiritual beliefs formed the basis of a new culture of individuals and heroes battling against crass modernity. Romanticist composers put much more emphasis on showing their innermost thoughts and feelings about love, hate and death through powerful expressions of emotion. Romanticist music developed "the use of new or previously not so common musical structures like the song cycle, nocturne, concert etude, arabesque [notably decorative music] and rhapsody, alongside the traditional classical genres."[95]

In general, Romanticist music was "more explicitly expressive and programmatic"[96] and public concerts were held for the urban middle class compared to earlier periods when they were mainly the domain of aristocrats. The string section was enlarged and the piano took over from the harpsichord as an accompaniment to songs (lieder) such as Schubert's *Winter Journey*. The main composers in the Romanticist style were Franz Schubert (1797–1828), Johannes Brahms (1833–1897), Louis-Hector Berlioz (1803–1869), Pyotr Ilyich Tchaikovsky (1840–1893), Felix Mendelssohn (1809–1847), Antonín Leopold Dvořák (1841–1904), Frédéric François Chopin (1810–1849), Edvard Hagerup Grieg (1843–1907), Robert Schumann (1810–1856), Nikolai Rimsky-Korsakov (1844–1908), Franz Liszt (1811–1886), Edward Elgar (1857–1934) and Richard Wagner (1813–1883).

---

[94] *Revolutionary Romanticism: A Drunken Boat Anthology* by Max Blechman (City Lights Books, 1999) p5

[95] https://en.wikipedia.org/wiki/Romantic_music

[96] https://en.wikipedia.org/wiki/Romantic_music

Many of these composers were also associated with that great combination of Romanticism and politics – Nationalism – and composed music using folk tunes, dance rhythms and local legends for this purpose. As nationalist leaders developed ideas of race and a unified nation (often based on territories containing many different ethnic and cultural groups) composers created the musical soundtrack to the burgeoning centralisation and homogenisation of modern states. One of the most negative aspects of nationalist political structures was the First World War, where the peoples of these relatively new states were set against each other in the style of the earlier feudal monarchies: in the interests solely of their leaders.

The Enlightenment progressive tradition in music

While Romanticism reached its peak during the period of 1800 to 1850, its influence continued on throughout the twentieth century. However, Enlightenment values of criticism and progressive change also developed in song and music movements concurrently with Romanticist escapist music. At different points in the twentieth century artists arose to challenge the status quo through critical lyrics and different musical forms such as, for example, Hanns Eisler (1898-1962) in Germany, Woody Guthrie (1912–1967) in the USA, and Violeta Parra (1917–1967) in Chile.

Hanns Eisler – 'One cannot always write optimistic songs'

Hanns Eisler (1898-1962) was an Austrian composer who fought in a Hungarian regiment during the First World War, resisted the debilitating effects of Romanticism in his music. After the war he became more and more radicalised and threw himself into the class politics of the day. Eisler had a long artistic association with Bertolt Brecht:

> Eisler wrote music for several Brecht plays, including *The Decision* (*Die Maßnahme*) (1930), *The Mother* (1932) and

Schweik in the Second World War (1957). They also collaborated on protest songs that celebrated, and contributed to, the political turmoil of Weimar Germany in the early 1930s. Their Solidarity Song became a popular militant anthem sung in street protests and public meetings throughout Europe, and their Ballad of Paragraph 218 was the world's first song protesting laws against abortion. Brecht-Eisler songs of this period tended to look at life from "below" — from the perspective of prostitutes, hustlers, the unemployed and the working poor. In 1931–32 he collaborated with Brecht and director Slatan Dudow on the working-class film *Kuhle Wampe*.[97]

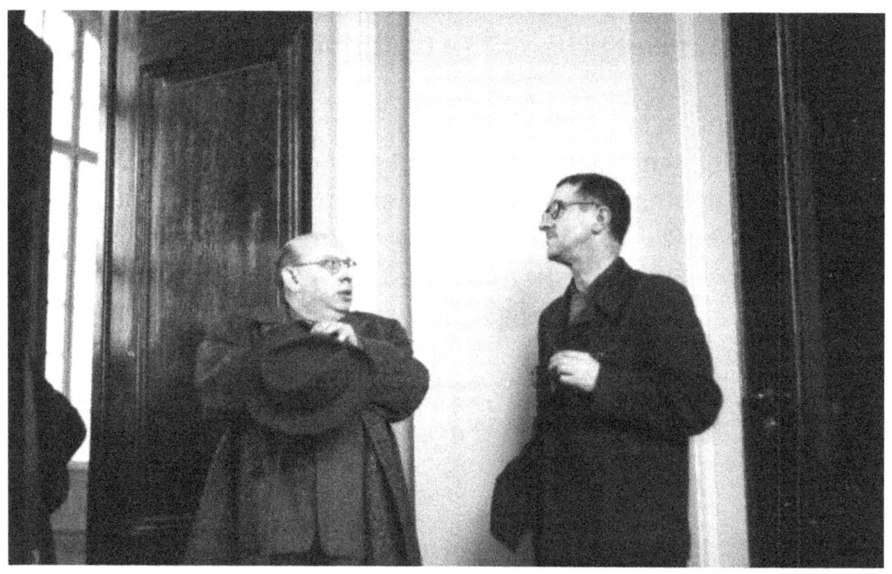

Hanns Eisler (left) and Bertolt Brecht, his close friend and collaborator, East Berlin, 1950
(Bundesarchiv / Bild 183-19204-2132 / CC-BY-SA 3.0, CC BY-SA 3.0 DE / Wikimedia Commons)

Eisler's connection with the class politics and struggles of the people are demonstrated in his awareness of the problems of composing in difficult times. He stated: "It is: consciousness-reflection-depression-revival-and again consciousness ... It must be done

---

[97] https://en.wikipedia.org/wiki/Hanns_Eisler

that way, otherwise it is not good. One cannot always write optimistic songs ... one must describe the up and down of actual situations, sing about it and comment on it."98 The dialectics of the process of consciousness and reflection helped him to work with ideas that are sorrowful without falling into a state of resignation. In one of his song series 'Ernste Gesänge' for baritone solo and string orchestra, Albrecht Betz notes:

The third song, 'Verweiflung' [Despair], is a fragment from Leopardi's famous poem 'A se stesso'; Eisler has condensed it and freed it of all its features of Romantic discontent. Sorrow, as well as occasional anger, is sublimated in the composition'.99

Similarly, in music practice, Eisler also avoided the Romanticist element: "I am always horrified to hear a group of union workers, toughened by many class struggles singing, "La, la, la, la, la, la, laaaa, aaaa," or "I am so lonesome when I remember you."100 In this sense Eisler and Brecht had a lot in common. Both had "an anti-romantic attitude" and "a rejection of the psychological and the autobiographical". Betz writes:

Both had in view the 'avoidance of the narcotic effects' of art, the aim to conduct experiments so as to bring it to the height of rationality which would correspond to the scientific age in which they lived, and above all to arm it with a theory which would rationalize the functions of this art.101

---

98 Hanns Eisler *Vokalsinfonik* - Vocal Symphonic Music Berlin Classics CD, Sleeve notes p24

99 *Hanns Eisler Political Musician* by Albrecht Betz [Trans Bill Hopkins] (Cambridge Uni Press: Cambridge, 1982) p235/7

100 *Hanns Eisler: A Rebel in Music: Selected Writings by Hanns Eisler* (Author), M. Grabs (Editor) (Kahn and Averill, London, 1999) p143

101 *Hanns Eisler Political Musician* by Albrecht Betz [Trans Bill Hopkins] (Cambridge Uni Press: Cambridge, 1982) p92

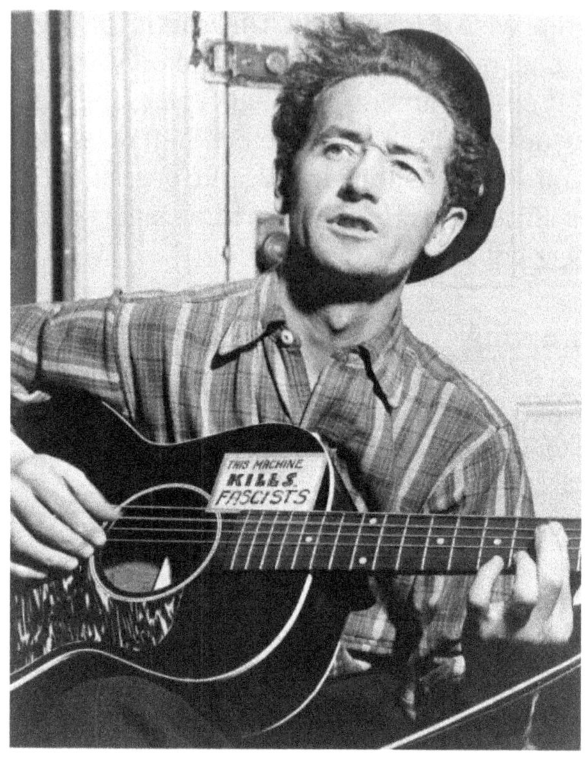

Woody Guthrie with guitar labeled
"This machine kills fascists" in 1943
(NY World-Telegram, Sun staff photographer: Al Aumuller /
Public domain / Wikimedia Commons)

Woody Guthrie

Another singer songwriter who would also avoid the 'narcotic effects' of music was Woody Guthrie (1912 – 1967). Brought up in Oklahoma, USA, Woodrow Wilson Guthrie was an American singer-songwriter, one of the most significant figures in American folk music. Guthrie wrote hundreds of political, folk, and children's songs, along with ballads and improvised works. One of his most famous songs "This Land Is Your Land" was inspired by his reaction to Irving Berlin's "God Bless America" on the radio.

Guthrie experienced hardship at first hand when he joined the thousands of migrants going to California to look for work during the Dust Bowl period. He became concerned by the conditions of life endured by working-class people and started writing songs about unemployment, migration, trade unions, labour struggles, and anti-fascist songs. All his life he believed in the power of music to change society and people's attitudes. He performed regularly and wrote thousands of songs, poems and prose reflecting the life of working-class people, neatly summing it up in the terse statement: "All you can write is what you see."[102]

Nueva Canción – 'oppositional in every respect'

By the 1960s, a counterculture movement was making inroads into popular culture with movements like Nueva Canción (New Song) in Argentina, Chile and Spain, the General Strike centered in Paris in May 1968 in France as well as the Civil Rights Movement in the USA. The Nueva Canción (NC) movement started in Chile and soon spread all over Latin America. It went through three main phases in Chile: "The first was one of protest, the second of direct political engagement and the third moved away from direct political engagement to focus on glorifying and documenting the life of working people."[103] On a formal level Nueva Canción used

> non-mainstream musical devices in their compositions such as traditional styles, and their rhythmic patterns, harmonic progressions and scales associated with folkloric music as well as Andean instruments in their arrangements. The songs were thus oppositional in every respect to the new 'invading' culture and embodied in sound and content something fresh but at the same time familiar which seemed to appeal to a mass of Chileans.[104]

---

[102] https://en.wikipedia.org/wiki/Woody_Guthrie

[103] http://www.nationalcollective.com/2013/12/10/the-power-of-music-in-political-struggle-part-3-education-and-imagining-the-new/

[104] http://www.nationalcollective.com/2013/12/10/the-power-of-music-in-political-struggle-part-3-education-and-imagining-the-new/

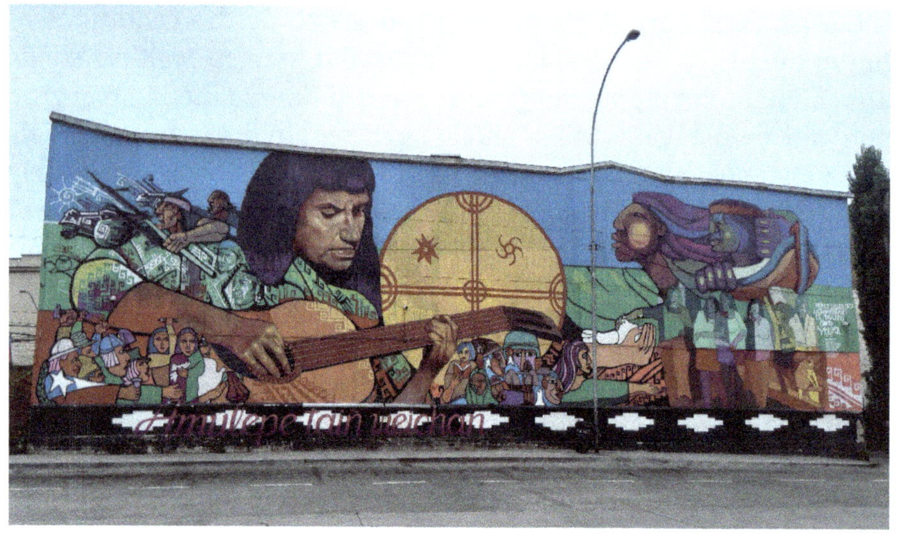

Violeta Parra depicted in mural at Valparaíso bus terminal
(Rec79 / CC BY-SA 4.0 / Wikimedia Commons)

Composers like Violeta Parra (1917–1967) (also songwriter, folklorist, ethnomusicologist and visual artist) and Argentine singer, songwriter, guitarist, and writer, Atahualpa Yupanqui (1908–1992) were two of the most important and influential figures in the Nueva Canción popular musical movement which "was anti-imperial in its stance" against commercialised American and European music while its content covered many issues associated with the peoples of the region such as "poverty, empowerment, imperialism, democracy, human rights, religion, and the Latin American identity".[105]

They led a movement which was anti-Romanticist in that they fought back against the narcotic effects of individualist, self-absorbed, introspective music and instead they encouraged a turning outward, an openness and interest in society and their position in that society, a positive attitude towards how society could be changed for the better.

---

[105] https://en.wikipedia.org/wiki/Nueva_canci%C3%B3n

The Romanticist escapist tradition in music
Jazz, Pop and Rock – 'part of the entertainment industry'

Earlier in the twentieth century jazz had been a popular form of music among the oppressed but it to fell victim to commercialisation. As Tim Blanning writes:

> From the time it emerged toward the end of the nineteenth century, jazz fit very well with the Romantic aesthetic, for it was nothing if not spontaneous, improvisatory and individual. Its African-American origins also made it the potential ally of liberation movements. During much of the twentieth century, however, for all of jazz's ability to express the suffering and aspirations of an oppressed community, the genre was very much part of the entertainment industry.[106]

Since the 1950s commercialised pop music had attained a huge market share in the recording industry, and in the early 1960s the Beatles continued a lively, dancing style developed by singers like Bill Haley and Elvis Presley. However, by the late 1960s, under the influence of the burgeoning drug culture, the tone changed and Romanticism gained the upper hand. In a style change in the late 1960s the Beatles opened up the way for some of the most introspective, narcotic music ever composed. Their music became "a music of introspective self-absorption, a medium fit for communicating autobiographical intimacies, political discontents, spiritual elevation, inviting an audience, not to dance, but to listen-quietly, attentively, thoughtfully'."[107]

While the Vietnam war was the basis of many radical outpourings during the late 1960s and had even influenced the pop music industry charts with politicised pop songs, by the 1970s the entertainment industry had recovered to produce some of the most 'tune in and drop out' music ever produced, by 'progressive' rock bands

---

[106] *The Triumph of Music: Composers, Musicians and Their Audiences, 1700 to the Present* by Tim Blanning (Penguin Modern Classics, 2008) p114

[107] *The Triumph of Music: Composers, Musicians and Their Audiences, 1700 to the Present* by Tim Blanning (Penguin Modern Classics, 2008) p121

such as Pink Floyd, Genesis, Led Zeppelin etc. During the 1970s, artists like David Bowie and Eric Clapton overreached, when Bowie gave a 'Nazi salute'[108] in London and Clapton stated that Britain was becoming a 'black colony'[109] at a concert in Birmingham, both in 1976. Indeed, in relation to Clapton, Blanning argues:

> Arguably the greatest living master of the electric guitar, Clapton personified the Romantic aesthetic: 'The classic Clapton pose-back to the crowd, head bowed over his instrument, alone with the agony of the blues-suggests a supplicant communing with something inward: a muse or a demon ... his entire career can be seen as a search for a form in which he could express the staple blues emotions - fear, loneliness, anger and humour- in a personally valid way'.[110]

Fear, loneliness and anger became mainstays of Romanticism in the pop music of the 1970s and 1980s music with Punk ('anger is an energy'), Morrissey ('the pope of mope') and U2 ('I Still Haven't Found What I'm Looking For'), not to mention the New Romantics and Heavy Metal. The nadir of Romanticist pop music, Gothic rock, became popular in the early 1980s with bands such as Joy Division, the Cure, Siouxsie and the Banshees, and Bauhaus. Like the late nineteenth-century art movement, Symbolism, Gothic music themes included "sadness, existentialism, nihilism, dark romanticism, tragedy, melancholy and morbidity" and was expressed through a "darker sound, with minor or bass chords, reverbs, dark arrangements or dramatic and melancholic melodies, having inspirations in gothic literature".[111]

In more recent years, U2's albums *Songs of Innocence* and *Songs of Experience* directly reference Romanticist William Blake's illustrated collection of poems of the same name.

---

[108] https://en.wikipedia.org/wiki/The_Thin_White_Duke

[109] https://ultimateclassicrock.com/eric-clapton-racist-remarks/

[110] *The Triumph of Music: Composers, Musicians and Their Audiences, 1700 to the Present* by Tim Blanning (Penguin Modern Classics, 2008) p118/9

[111] https://en.wikipedia.org/wiki/Gothic_rock

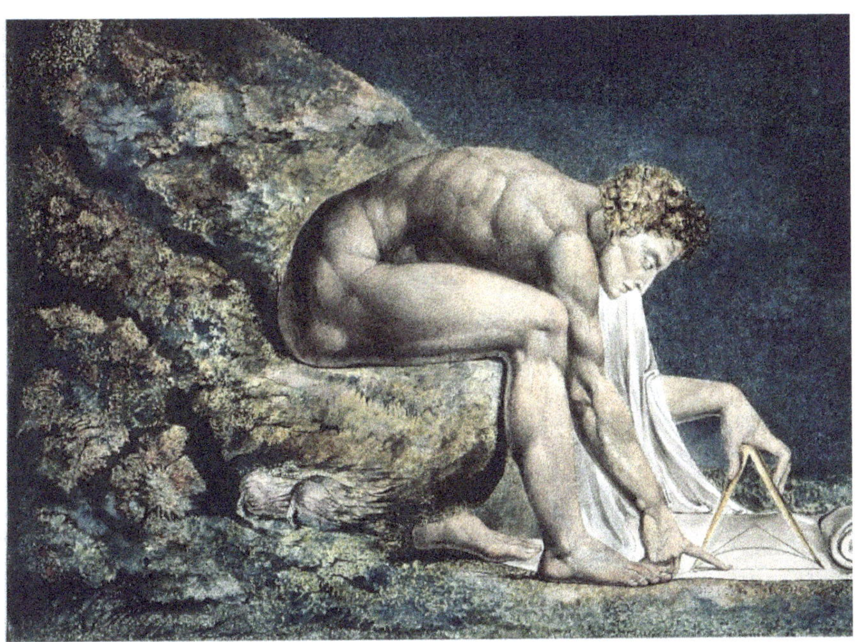

Blake's *Newton* (1795) demonstrates his opposition to the "single-vi-sion" of scientific materialism: Newton fixes his eye on a compass (recalling Proverbs 8:27, an important passage for Milton) to write upon a scroll that seems to project from his own head
(Public domain / Wikimedia Commons)

William Blake (1757–1827) was an English poet, painter, and printmaker who is considered a seminal figure in the history of the poetry and visual arts of the Romantic Age.

Blake held visionary religious beliefs and opposed the Newtonian view of the universe.[112] Living around the same time as Blake was the German writer Johann Wolfgang von Goethe (1749–1832), famous for the novel *The Sorrows of Young Werther* (1774) and is considered to have been one of the originators of the Romantic movement. However, later in life Goethe described Romanticism as a 'disease'.[113]

---

[112] *The Romantic Rebellion: Romantic Versus Classic Art*, Illustrated, by Sir Kenneth Clark (John Murray Pub., 1973) p167

[113] *The Roots of Romanticism* by Isaiah Berlin (Princeton Uni Press, 1999) p130

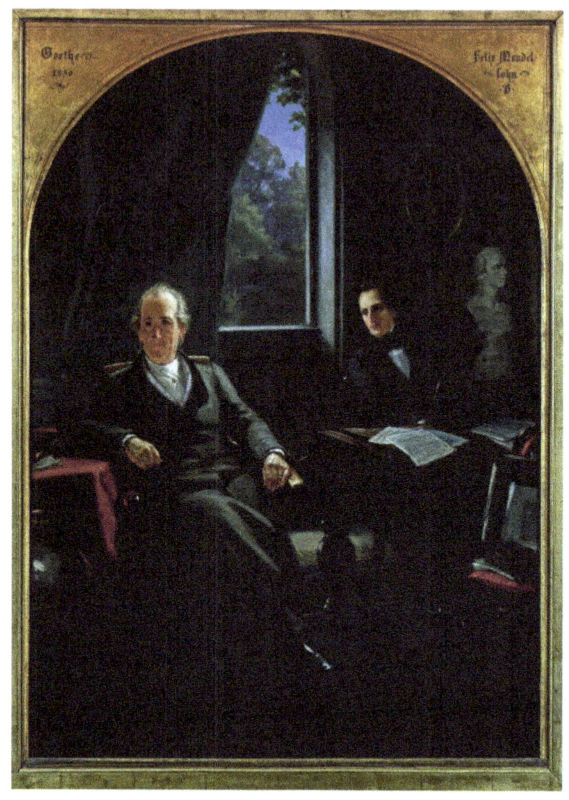

Mendelssohn plays to Goethe (1830), painting by Moritz Oppenheim
(1800–1882) in 1864
(Public domain / Wikimedia Commons)

The effect of the Romanticist 'disease' on music has been to turn it inward and convert its listeners into modern lotus eaters. In Homer's epic poem, the *Odyssey*, Book IX, Odysseus is blown off course but reaches a land inhabited by people who live on a food that comes from a kind of flower. He sends a few men to investigate but upon tasting the lotus they fall into a peaceful apathy and lose interest in going home until Odysseus drags them out and leaves at once. Similarly, much modern music has a narcotic effect on mass audiences who are overwhelmed by emotion while at the same time attain personal catharsis.[114]

The many geopolitical crises of the twenty-first century are in

---

[114] Homer, *Odyssey* (Penguin Classics, 1988) p141

need of mass political campaigns to bring about awareness and pressure against the drumbeats of a Third World War. Building collectivist movements with a radical collectivist culture and moving away from the individualism and irrationalism of Romanticist culture of the nineteenth and twentieth century is a necessary step towards real political change. Music, of all the arts, can be a powerful force in the creation of a collective consciousness. Composers of music and song highlighting the various issues affecting people today are necessary. Therefore, examining the issues around the form and content of music in society is an urgent requirement if music is to have an important cultural role in the future.

Chapter 5
Opera

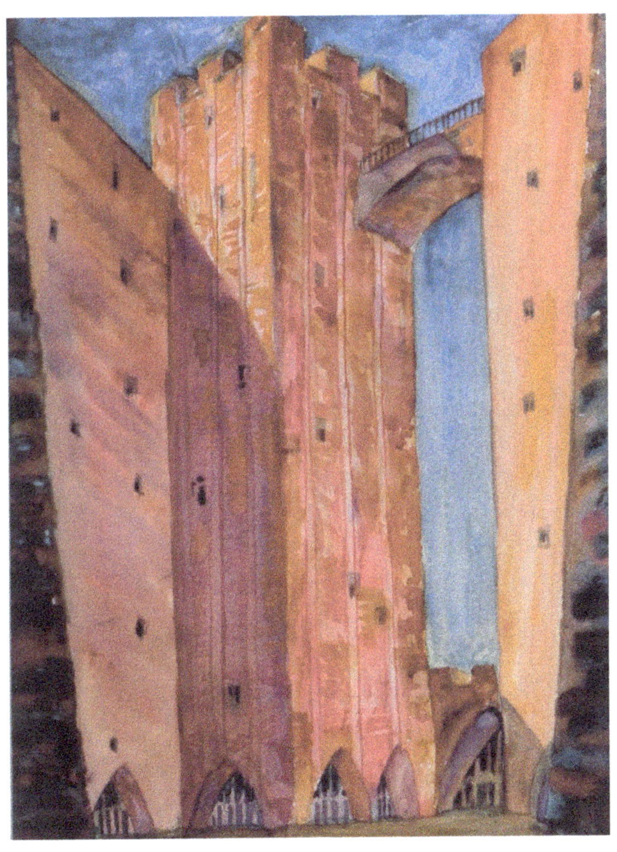

Ludwig van Beethoven's (1770–1827) *Fidelio* (1805), Act 1, prison yard (Halle, 1920) (Paul Thiersch / Public domain / Wikimedia Commons)

In life's springtime days, Happiness has escaped me. The truth, I dared speak it, and these chains are my reward.
Beethoven, *Fidelio*

Opera in Crisis: Can It be Made Relevant Again?

The world doesn't really need your version of your favourite book in college. Opera is a really demanding art form. If you're going to go to the trouble, you might as well make it about something important and essential rather than decorative and irrelevant.
Peter Sellars

It [opera] has reflected, in complex and mediated forms, the significant political personages and events that have shaped the modern Western world: kings and coups, classes and class conflict, rebels and revolutions.
John Bokina

Opera productions depend on much state support, which is in decline, as states themselves go further and further into debt. To try and overcome these problems there have been many attempts at changes in form and content and even transmission in recent years. But these changes do not solve cost or accessibility issues especially in an era where it is difficult to get people to go out to the much cheaper cinema house, let alone a phenomenally expensive opera production. Yet, nowadays one is more likely to experience opera as cinema than theatre. Can such an expensive medium become popular again? What makes an opera popular? Can opera be relevant to people's struggles today?

Here I will look at the origins and history of opera from the late 1590s until today. Like other forms of culture, opera was initially influenced by Enlightenment ideas in its Baroque (1590-1750) and

Classical periods (1750-1820), while the Romanticist (1800-1914) reaction predominated in the early nineteenth century up to the early twentieth century. Enlightenment and Romanticist influences could still be seen throughout the twentieth century with Verismo (c1890-1920) and Modernism respectively. The twenty-first century has brought interesting changes in form and content and a global appreciation of opera but it remains an essentially elite form of entertainment in terms of cost and audiences.

Early opera - 'did not normally furnish half the expense'

Jacopo Peri is credited with developing the first operas. His earliest surviving opera Dafne exists mainly as a libretto and fragments of music. The earliest surviving full opera is Peri's *Euridice* which was performed in 1600. Peri worked with Jacopo Corsi, also a composer of the time, both of whom were influenced by classical Greek and Roman works. They worked with the poet Ottavio Rinuccini, a member of the Florentine Camerata, who wrote the texts. The Florentine Camerata were a group of humanists, poets, musicians and intellectuals who met regularly in the 1570s in late Renaissance Florence who sought to produce new works more in keeping with the spirit of humanism in the form and style of the ancient Greeks.

Renaissance humanism was a revival in the study of classical antiquity, at first in Italy and then spreading across Western Europe from the 14th to the 16th centuries. The humanists emphasized the value and agency of human beings, individually and collectively and believed in the idea of human freedom and progress. Their aim was to educate people and create a participatory citizenry through the study of the *studia humanitatis*, today known as the humanities: grammar, rhetoric, history, poetry, and moral philosophy. The Renaissance contributed heavily to the spread of Enlightenment ideas which was a much broader movement.

The Florentine Camerata were influenced by the historian and humanist Girolamo Mei who believed that ancient Greek drama was mainly sung rather than spoken as the Greek Aristoxenus had written that speech should set the pattern for song.

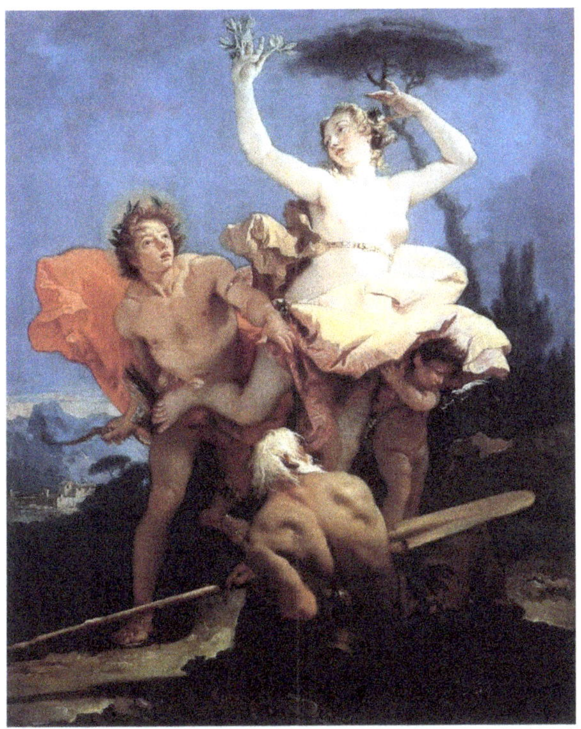

Daphne Chased by Apollo (1744)
by Giovanni Battista Tiepolo (1696–1770)
(Public domain / Wikimedia Commons)

The Camerata were critical of contemporary polyphony which was felt to be overused and obscured the words and their meanings. Therefore:

Intrigued by ancient descriptions of the emotional and moral effect of ancient Greek tragedy and comedy, which they presumed to be sung as a single line to a simple instrumental accompaniment, the Camerata proposed creating a new kind of music. Instead of trying to make the clearest polyphony they could, the Camerata voiced an opinion recorded by a contemporary Florentine, 'means must be found in the attempt to bring music closer to that of classical times.'[115]

---

[115] https://en.wikipedia.org/wiki/Florentine_Camerata

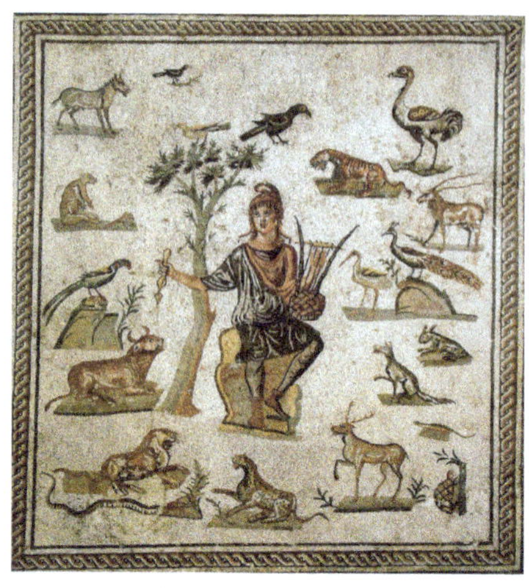

Orpheus surrounded by animals. Ancient Roman floor mosaic, from Palermo, now in the Museo archeologico regionale di Palermo
(Foto di Giovanni Dall'Orto / Wikimedia Commons)

These musical experiments were called monody and Peri's operas had the entire drama sung in monodic style with gambas, lutes, and harpsichord or organ for continuo as the main instruments. Thus, we see a radical development in musical form along with content coming from Greek mythology. This new 'music drama' was called 'opera' (work), as Paul Strathern writes:

the musicians of Florence were responsible for the birth of opera, which arose from two distinct sources. On the one hand, there was medieval liturgical drama: holy plays enacted publicly at various times in the Church calendar. Quite separate from these were the classical Greek dramas, with their choric interludes, which were revived and staged by the Florentine humanists. When these two forms were combined, the result was opera: non-religious work incorporating music and drama. The term takes its name from the Italian expression *opera in musica* (work in music); and the settings of these early operas were usually either legendary or mythical, requiring a new freer musical form.[116]

---

[116] Paul Strathern, *The Medici: Godfathers of the Renaissance*, (Pimlico: London, 2005), p.360

Over time other composers took up these new ideas and eventually synthesised monody and polyphony.

Peri's opera *Euridice* (first performed in Florence on 6 October, 1600) tells the story of Orpheus (Orfeo), a great musician, who journeyed to the underworld to plead with the gods to revive his wife Euridice after she had been fatally injured. Orpheus uses his legendary voice to convince Pluto the god of the underworld to return Euridice to life. He is successful and they return from the underworld and rejoice.

The use of this particular story from Greek mythology in 1600 showed the growing divide between the humanist intellectuals and the church. This was at an extremely difficult time when "the persecution of witches was the official policy of both the Catholic and Protestant Churches." According to Helen Ellerbe in *The Dark Side of Christian History*:

> Around 1600 a man wrote: Germany is almost entirely occupied with building fires for the witches ... Switzerland has been compelled to wipe out many of her villages on their account. Travelers in Lorraine may see thousands and thousands of the stakes to which witches are bound.[117]

The fear of the devil and hell had reached terrible proportions and any reasonable call for mercy or reconsideration, like the theme of *Euridice*, most likely would have been dangerous at that time, except in allegorical forms.

Not long after, the Italian composer Claudio Monteverdi (with a libretto by Alessandro Striggio) brought out an opera based on the same story in 1607 entitled *L'Orfeo*, an opera which is still regularly performed.

Monteverdi constructed the opera score out of a daring use of many different existing forms - the aria, the strophic song, recitative, choruses, dances, dramatic musical interludes. While there was an actual written score, instrumentalists were allowed freedom to elaborate musically and singers to embellish their arias. While the work was admired up to the 1650s it was soon forgotten until the

---

[117] Helen Ellerbe, *The Dark Side of Christian History* (Morningstar and Lark, 1995), p.136/7

nineteenth century due to changing styles and tastes. When first performed it was in front of a courtly audience of nobility and intellectual aristocrats. However, with the spread of interest in opera throughout Europe, public opera houses were built to hold larger and larger audiences by the end of the seventeenth century. Yet the expense of producing opera was becoming apparent as a French commentator noted in 1683:

> the nobility of Venice patronized the great opera theatres more for their *divertissement particular* than for any financial profit that might accrue, since income from opera 'did not normally furnish half of the expense'.[118]

Thus, we can see that opera was born in a time of church hierarchy and power, determined to wipe out dissent, resulting in widespread fear and danger while Renaissance humanists were focusing on ancient Greek ideas of democratic society, and values like mercy.

Classical - 'divesting the music entirely of abuses'

In France, the Enlightenment is traditionally dated from 1715 to 1789, i.e., from the beginning of the reign of Louis XV until the French Revolution. Enlightenment ideas focused on reason as the main source of knowledge and propagated ideals of liberty, progress, toleration, constitutional government, and separation of church and state in opposition to absolute monarchy and the dogmas of the Catholic church.The intellectuals of the Enlightenment believed that:

> humanity progressed through the rational acquisition and organization of knowledge, and that real knowledge resulted from observation and logic rather than tradition, speculation, or divine inspiration.[119]

---

[118] Daniel Snowman, *The Gilded Stage: A Social History of Opera* (Atlantic Books: London, 2010), p.36

[119] http://donelan.faculty.writing.ucsb.edu/Mozart.html

Enlightenment ideas also had a profound effect on different forms of culture, particularly in the creation of opera.

It was the German classical composer, Christoph Willibald Gluck who reformed opera in the 1700s at a time when the freedom allowed to musicians and singers to extrapolate was seen to have gotten out of hand. His first reform opera, *Orfeo ed Euridice*, was premiered in Venice in 1762 and then in Paris, in a revised French-version, in 1774. In his own words, Gluck sets out his reasons:

> When I undertook to set this poem, it was my design to divest the music entirely of all those abuses with which the vanity of singers, or the too great complacency of composers, has so long disfigured the Italian opera, and rendered the most beautiful and magnificent of all public exhibitions, the most tiresome and ridiculous. It was my intention to confine music to its true dramatic province, of assisting poetical expression, and of augmenting the interest of the fable; without interrupting the action, or chilling it with useless and superfluous ornaments; for the office of music, when joined to poetry, seemed to me, to resemble that of colouring in a correct and well-disposed design, where the lights and shades only seem to animate the figures, without altering the out-line.[120]

Gluck, like other classical period composers sought to simplify music emphasizing "light elegance in place of the Baroque's dignified seriousness and impressive grandeur. [...] Composers from this period sought dramatic effects, striking melodies, and clearer textures. One of the big textural changes was a shift away from the complex, dense polyphonic style of the Baroque, in which multiple interweaving melodic lines were played simultaneously, and towards homophony, a lighter texture which uses a clear single melody line accompanied by chords."[121]

---

[120] https://www.cengage.com/music/book_content/049557273X_wrightSimms/assets/ ITOW/7273X_41_ITOW%20Gluck.pdf
[121] https://en.wikipedia.org/wiki/Classical_period_(music)

Gluck playing his clavicord (1775),
portrait by Joseph Duplessis (1725–1802)
(Public domain / Wikimedia Commons)

Gluck, Franz Joseph Haydn and Wolfgang Amadeus Mozart were all major composers of the classical style. These composers were on the cusp of a major change in society with burgeoning capitalism changing the balance of power in the feudal aristocratic societies of Europe.

In the past the role of music was to entertain the wealthy and powerful in their mansions and castles while praising the glory of God in the churches. Composers, if they were lucky, had the job of *Kapellmeister*, or church composer who worked as artisans producing mainly hymns and oratorios or in-house for a noble patron.

Mozart sought to move away from this life to compose for a more bourgeois audience and become an independent contributor to intellectual life. This was part of the developing attitude of the intellectuals of Enlightenment Europe who believed in the improvement of humanity and civil society through increased secular knowledge.

Mozart's *Don Giovanni* was written in 1787, two years before the French Revolution, when there was an antipathy towards the aristocracy and a growing perception of them as a parasitic class. *Don Giovanni*, as James Donelan notes, gives audiences an exaggerated version of 'an aristocrat who does nothing but consume, and does so almost joylessly'. Furthermore:

> As the curtain opens, we see Figaro and Susanna; Figaro is counting off the measurements necessary for fitting a bed in his new room, and Susanna is admiring how she looks in the new hat she made for herself. You can already notice several things that indicate that something different from standard opera buffa is going on: this scene of domestic tranquility emphasizes Figaro's and Susanna's capabilities as the makers and doers of this world. You can assume he will build his own bed; Susanna has made her own hat, and this opera, based, as you know, on a subversive play, appeared at precisely the time in history when a new bourgeois class of traders, bankers, craftsmen, and merchants were gaining power and significance in European society, and the necessity of having a noble class was being questioned very seriously for the first time. The workers of the world and the bourgeois created wealth, and got things done; the sovereign provided them with a stable government, but what did the aristocracy do any more except hoard valuable resources and put on airs?[122]

The world of the aristocracy was in decline and a new world led by the bourgeoisie was in the ascent with its emphasis on emotion and individualism. The Romanticist reaction to the Industrial Revolution and the scientific rationalization of nature produced a new culture that opposed the aristocratic social and political norms of the Age of Enlightenment that could be seen in Classical opera.

---

[122] http://donelan.faculty.writing.ucsb.edu/Mozart.html

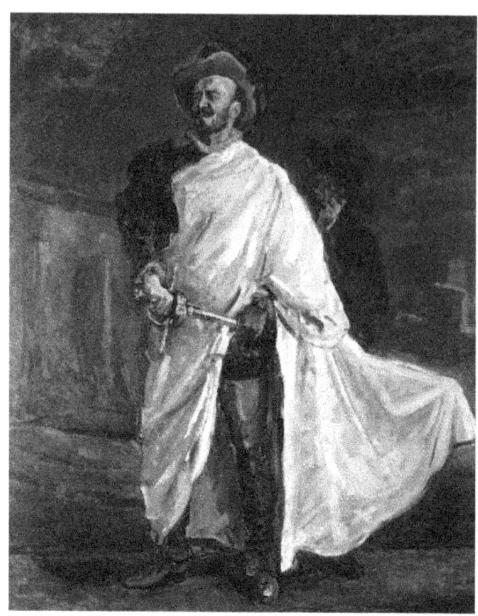

Portrait of Francisco D'Andrade in the title role of
Don Giovanni by Max Slevogt, 1912 (1868–1932)
(Public domain / Wikimedia Commons)

Romanticism, reaction with 'mysticism and turbid emotionalism'

This change in attitude from Classical to Romanticist was noted by Arnold Hauser in *The Social History of Art*. He writes:

> since the advent of romanticism all cheerfulness seems to have a superficial, frivolous character. The combination of carefree light-heartedness with the most profound seriousness, of playful exuberance with the highest, purest ethos transfiguring the whole of life, which was still present in Mozart, breaks up; from now on everything serious and sublime takes on a gloomy and careworn look. It is sufficient to compare the serene, clear and calm humanity of Mozart, its freedom from all mysticism and turbid emotionalism, with the violence of romantic music, to realize what had been lost with the eighteenth century.[123]

---

[123] Arnold Hauser, *The Social History of Art*, Vol. 3 (Vintage Books: New York, 1958), p.225

The Romanticists' attitude to modernity was one of outright rejection. They were radical and individualistic enough to lead bourgeois revolutions but soon saw the abyss and the potential for their own loss of power and dissolution as a class (if the burgeoning socialist movements were successful).

In Germany, Carl Maria von Weber's *Der Freischütz* (1821) started the style which became known as *Romantische Oper* along with other composers like Albert Lortzing (e.g. *Undine*, described as a *romantische Zauberoper* 'romantic magic opera'), Heinrich Marschner (e.g. *Der Vampyr* and *Hans Heiling*) and Louis Spohr (e.g. *Faust*). These composers based their operas on typical Romantic themes such as nature, the supernatural, the Middle Ages and popular culture, specifically folklore, culminating in Wagner's 'romantic operas', *Der fliegende Holländer* (*The Flying Dutchman*, 1843), followed by *Tannhäuser* (1845) and *Lohengrin* (1850).

Wagner's operas grew in scale with more nationalist overtones but focused on myths, legends and nature, such as *Der Ring des Nibelungen* (the *Ring* or "Ring cycle"), a set of four operas based loosely on figures and elements from Germanic mythology. As his fame and influence spread throughout Europe other composers took on board some elements of his style and rejected others.

As Romanticism spread and nationalists moved away from universalist Enlightenment ideas (such as equality of all before the law), opera came to emphasise a particular ethnic group, a particular national language, or the patriotism and culture of the 'folk' as the true basis of each nation state (at a time when working-class internationalism was beginning to take hold). Folk songs and folk dances as well as nationalist subjects formed the new content of the new operas. In Italy, Giuseppe Verdi's opera *Nabucco* contains the lyrics, "Oh mia Patria sì bella e perduta (Oh my Fatherland so beautiful and lost!)! In Russia Mikhail Ivanovich Glinka's *A Life for the Tsar* (1836) tells the story of the Russian peasant and patriotic hero Ivan Susanin who sacrifices his life for the Tsar by leading astray a group of marauding Poles who were hunting him. In Brazil, Carlos Gomes' (1836–1896) opera *Il Guarany* (1870) used references from the country's folk music and traditional themes while the Czech composer Antonín Leopold Dvořák used the Czech language for his librettos to convey the Czech national spirit.

The return of Enlightenment resistance to Romanticist diversion

Verismo - 'focusing on the hard-knock lives'

In Italy, the growth of Realism in art and literature was making itself felt among opera composers such as Pietro Mascagni (*Cavalleria Rusticana*, 1890), Ruggero Leoncavallo (*Pagliacci*, 1892), Umberto Giordano (*Mala vita*, 1892), Francesco Cilea (*L'arlesiana*, 1897) and Giacomo Puccini (*La bohème*, 1896) and they developed their own style called *verismo* (Italian for "realism", from *vero*, meaning "true").

Realism opposed Romanticist idealisation or dramatisation and focused more on working class people instead. The popularity of Wagner's work with its social and political mythologising had had its effects. As Adam Parker notes:

> The Italians took notice and, coping with their own political, economic and social upheavals, began to embrace a more realistic operatic style that strived to show aspects of everyday life and convey basic truths about human struggles. The music, too, changed. Standard arias — pauses in the action that showcased the talents of singers — gave way to a more unified structure and constant musical flow. Italian composers cast aside romantic fairy tales and stopped short of embracing Wagner's mythical realms, preferring to focus on the hard-knock lives of characters who often were simple village-dwellers, impoverished, lovelorn and prone to make mistakes.[124]

The Italian Verismo composers were highly influenced by the realistic literary works of Émile Zola, Honoré de Balzac and Henrik Ibsen and sought to bring opera down to earth by examining the lives of ordinary people, the lives of the poor, with themes such as infidelity, revenge, and violence.

---

[124] https://www.postandcourier.com/news/romanticism-gives-way-to-verismo-style/article_3632b474-9737-557a-a9e9-f13d9828d946.html

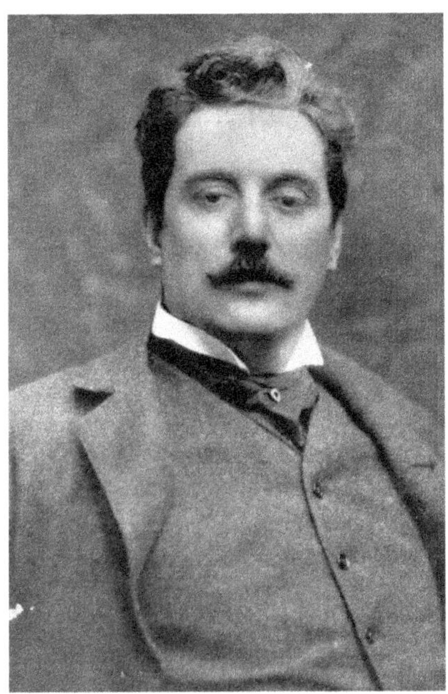

Giacomo Puccini, (1858–1924) one of the composers most closely associated with verismo
(Public domain / Wikimedia Commons)

The Verismo singing style brought in big changes from the elegant *bel canto* style of the 19th century. Verismo singers adopted a more declamatory singing style with a vociferous, passionate element to increase the emotional content of the opera.

Enlightenment and Romanticist ideas polarize

The Twentieth Century - 'losing much of its narrative power'

The twentieth century led to many changes as Modernism and Postmodernism, the children and grandchildren of Romanticism, settled in to Western culture while Realism and Social Realism, descendants of the universalist ideas of the Enlightenment, became state styles in the East. The Modernist composers rejected traditions such as classical ideas of form in art (harmony, symmetry, and order). As in literature and art, Modernist emphasis on new forms had their effect on opera as atonal, and then twelve-tone techniques were developed by Arnold Schoenberg and Alban Berg, while later in the century Philip Glass and John Adams became known for a pared-down style of composing called Minimalism.

Atonality, which describes music that lacks a key, became used from the early twentieth-century onwards and began a breakdown of the forms of classical European music which had existed from the seventeenth to the nineteenth centuries.

The knock-on effects were profound, as Andrew Clements writes:

With the collapse of tonality, music had lost much of its narrative power, they reasoned, and so storytelling need no longer be a prerequisite of opera either. The music would still contain, support and reinforce the onstage drama, but that drama didn't need to be linear: scenes could proceed simultaneously (as in Bernd Alois Zimmermann's *Die Soldaten*, 1965), present different versions of the same story (Harrison Birtwistle's *The Mask of Orpheus*), tell no story at all (Philip Glass's *Einstein on the Beach*) or dispense with a text altogether (Wolfgang Rihm's *Séraphin*, 1995).[125]

Meanwhile, in the East, the Russian Revolution saw the development of a different approach to opera, one focused more on rebellious peasants or the working class with Classical influences.

Historically, in Russia there had been many successful composers. Mikhail Glinka's (1804–1857) *A Life for the Tsar* was followed by Alexander Dargomyzhsky (1813–1869) and his opera *Rusalka* (1856) and revolutionary *The Stone Guest* (1872), Modest Mussorgsky's (1839–1881) *Boris Godunov*, Pyotr Tchaikovsky's (1840–1893) *Eugene Onegin* (*Yevgeny Onegin*), (1877–1878) and *The Queen of Spades* (*Pikovaya dama*) (1890) and the prolific Nikolai Rimsky-Korsakov (1844–1908) who completed fifteen operas.

---

[125] https://www.theguardian.com/music/2011/aug/20/opera-in-the-modern-age

The Soviet state encouraged opera and many new operas were produced by a new generation of composers. While the early operas were influenced by Modernism, things started to change as the 1934 Soviet Writers Congress instigated a policy of Socialist Realism and by 1946 the Zhdanov Doctrine was proposed which opposed "cosmopolitanism" (which meant native Russian accomplishments were to be emphasised more than foreign models but with an emphasis on the working-class) and the "anti-formalism campaign" (which saw 'formalism' as 'art for art's sake' as it did not serve a larger social purpose).

Most famously Dmitri Shostakovich's (1906–1975) *Lady Macbeth of the Mtsensk District* (performed in 1934) was criticised by *Pravda* in an article entitled Chaos Instead of Music in 1936. The story centres around a lonely woman in 19th-century Russia who falls in love with one of her husband's workers and is driven to murder. While there doesn't seem to have been any problem with the content, however, one can see the reaction to Western Modernism playing out in the description of the opera from the perspective of Classical opera:

From the first minute, the listener is shocked by deliberate dissonance, by a confused stream of sound. Snatches of melody, the beginnings of a musical phrase, are drowned, emerge again, and disappear in a grinding and squealing roar. To follow this "music" is most difficult; to remember it, impossible. Thus it goes, practically throughout the entire opera. The singing on the stage is replaced by shrieks. If the composer chances to come upon the path of a clear and simple melody, he throws himself back into a wilderness of musical chaos – in places becoming cacophony. The expression which the listener expects is supplanted by wild rhythm. Passion is here supposed to be expressed by noise. All this is not due to lack of talent, or lack of ability to depict strong and simple emotions in music. Here is music turned deliberately inside out in order that nothing will be reminiscent of classical opera, or have anything in common with symphonic music or with simple and popular musical language accessible to all.[126]

When an editor of *Pravda* was asked why Shostakovich was targeted, he replied:

We had to begin with somebody. Shostakovich was the most famous, and a blow against him would create immediate repercussions and would make his imitators in music and elsewhere sit up and take notice. Furthermore, Shostakovich is a real artist, there is a touch of genius in him. A man like that is worth fighting for, is worth saving ... We had faith in his essential wholesomeness. We knew that he could stand the shock ... Shostakovich knows and everyone else knows that there is no malice in our attack. He knows and everyone else knows that there is no desire to destroy him.[127]

Indeed, Shostakovich was awarded the USSR State Prize in 1941 (Piano Quintet), 1942 (Symphony No. 7), 1950 (Song of the Forests – The Fall of Berlin for chorus) and 1952 (Ten Poems for Chorus opus 88).

The first time the USSR State Prize was awarded for opera was to Uzeyir Hajibeyov for the opera *Keroghlu*[128] in 1941. It was the first opera in the Muslim East. *Koroghlu* was based on a regional legend about a young man who organized a rebellion against the khan (king), who had blinded his father out of spite. Hajibayov uses the rhythms of Azerbaijan's Yalli dance in the choir's singing to reflect the strength of the people and their yearning for freedom. The large choir conveys the unity of the people and glorifies their rebellion.[129]

Koroglu is a "classical opera complete with arias, choruses and ballet, but like so much of Hajibayov's work it also includes traditional rhythms and melodies. [...] Hajibayov included folk instruments such as the tar, zurna (pipe) and nagara (drum) in

---

[126] http://soviethistory.msu.edu/1936-2/upheaval-in-the-opera/upheaval-in-the-opera-text/chaos-instead-of-music/

[127] Alex Ross, *The Rest is Noise: Listening to the Twentieth Century* (Harper Perennial: London, 2009), p.249

[128] https://www.youtube.com/watch?v=fyFU6lmb_QU&list=PLFF5BD205A10CDFC4&index=9&t=3287s

[129] http://www.visions.az/en/news/108/06770a54/

the orchestra to heighten the sense of place. [...] The opera quickly gained popular acclaim and was performed widely."[130]

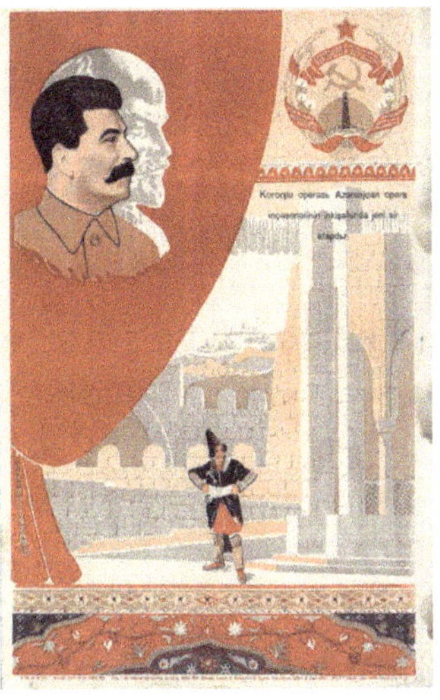

Poster of *Koroghlu*, Azerbaijan (1939)
(Lebeshev Boris Ilyich (1905-?) / Public domain / Wikimedia Commons)

Thus, we can see the huge gap that opened up between Romanticist modernist opera in the West, its influence in the East, and the influence of Classical opera style that was promoted in the Soviet Union.

Twenty-First Century - 'no use pretending something's not broken'

A couple of years ago Classical-Music.com asked leading opera singers to list their top operas. Five were composed in this century: Jake Heggie, *Dead Man Walking* (2000), Mark-Anthony Turnage, *The Silver Tassie* (2002), George Benjamin, *Written on Skin* (2012), Thomas Adès, *The Exterminating Angel* (2016). Despite the variety of themes and historical periods - showing that opera composition

---

[130] http://www.visions.az/en/news/108/06770a54/

and production is alive and well - in the words of Graham Vick (the-stage.co.uk): "we need to bend – there's no use pretending something's not broken."[131]

Recent writers on opera are well aware of the difficulties involved and have come at the problem from differing perspectives. For Vick, issues of form were uppermost in his thoughts. In an article entitled 'Opera needs radical overhaul to survive', he writes:

> We must stop believing that, if we work really hard, we might be almost as good as the legitimate theatre. Our agonising nostalgia for class (*Downton Abbey* only the most recent example) perpetuates philistine values. Crippled with self-doubt and privilege, the art form can hardly be heard in the wider society. A charge often levelled against it is that it is 'owned by the few'. It is this sense of possession and superiority that is its greatest enemy.[132]

He suggests different ways that opera companies can overcome these problems such as having touring versions and lowering seat prices by lowering performance costs.

For writers like Richard Morrison, chief music critic of *The Times*, content is a determining factor for future survival. In a recent article ('Is it appropriate for opera composers to write about modern-day atrocities?') he discusses Anthony Bolton's *The Life and Death of Alexander Litivinenko* (spy killed by polonium), John Adams's *Death of Klinghoffer* (hijacking of a cruise ship), and Tansy Davies's *Between Worlds* (about five people trapped in the World Trade Centre on 9/11). He questions the subject matter of recent operas which seems to be almost a strategy of using shock tactics to get punters back into the opera house:

> Can anything and everything be turned into art? Is the entire human condition fair game for a writer, painter or composer? Or are some real-life subjects so horrific or still so fresh

---

[131] Graham Vick, 'Opera needs radical overhaul to survive'. https://www.thestage.co.uk/opinion/graham-vick-opera-needs-radical-overhaul-to-survive

[132] Graham Vick, 'Opera needs radical overhaul to survive'. https://www.thestage.co.uk/opinion/graham-vick-opera-needs-radical-overhaul-to-survive

that they should be off limits, at least until those caught up in them are no longer around to be offended?[133]

Both of these are valid and important perspectives on the ongoing problems of the opera business. However, like cinema, the more expensive a cultural medium is, the more its ideology is tightly controlled by those who hold the purse strings. The mass media corporations control how everything is seen and understood, saturating the media with ideologies that favour the world outlook of the neoliberal elites.

For culture in general to inspire future interest and support it must move away from the narratives and objectives of the elites. Working class struggles have shaped the world and any improvements in living conditions have been won after years of often violent conflict and sacrifice. These stories, histories and even allegories of these stories have formed the basis of progressive culture in the past.

Ordinary people do not own their own mass communications media or opera houses but know art made in solidarity with their plight (whether it be local or abroad) when they see it. Therefore, anything and everything can be turned into art, that is, if it is made in such a way that empathy, solidarity and progress is the result of the work and not just a distant spectacle as a vehicle for Romanticist shock-horror or laughs. For opera to have distinctive, compelling, and meaningful engagements with people in the future it must first invest in its most important component: its audiences.

---

133 https://www.pressreader.com/uk/bbc-music-magazine/20190612/283794265287123

Chapter 6

Dance

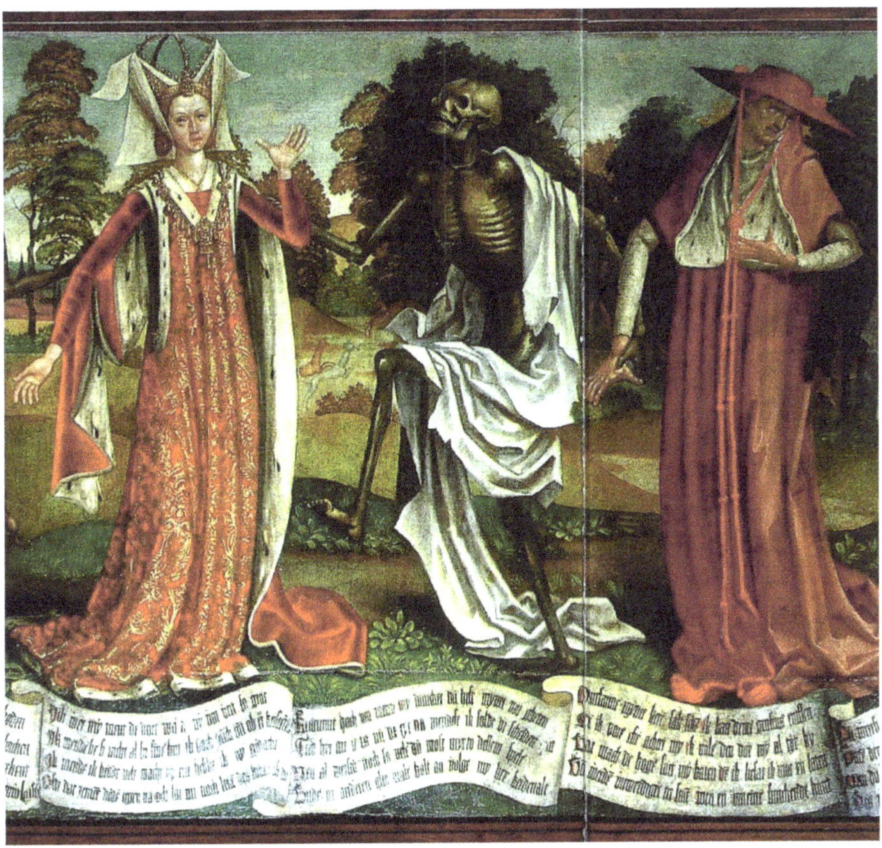

Surmatants (Totentanz) (Danse Macabre) by Bernt Notke
(c.1440–1509) from St. Nicholas' Church, Tallinn, end of 15th century
(today in the Art Museum of Estonia)
(Bernt Notke / Public domain / Wikimedia Commons)

The drum is always there. In life and death. In between is dance. Always the drum is everywhere.
Peniel Guerrier

Diversity in Dance Today

I don't think this world was made for a small minority to dance on the faces of everyone else.
H.G. Wells *In the Days of the Comet*

When the music changes, so does the dance.
African proverb

The dance group Diversity's 'I Can't Breathe' routine evoked around 24,500 complaints from members of the public when it aired on ITV on 5 September, 2020. The performance was inspired by the killing of George Floyd in the USA on May 25, 2020. Its choreography references progress from stock market bubbles, the growth of digital shopping, the effect of mobile phones on family life, the coronavirus pandemic and subsequent lockdowns, to the killing of George Floyd, and then ending with street protests and the riot police. The show was a spectacular mix of spoken word, song, visual and stage effects, as well as Diversity's trademark blend of complex routines, breakdancing, backflips and theatricality.

While the troupe garnered much international praise for the 4 1/2-minute anti-racist performance, the many complaints focused on its political content. According to Ashley Banjo, troupe member and choreographer, "We got bombarded with messages and articles … horrible stuff about all of us, our families … it's sad."[134] This level of negative public reaction to a dance routine on TV in the UK was unprecedented.

---

[134] https://metro.co.uk/2020/09/12/what-was-the-diversity-blm-dance-performance-that-sparked-over-15000-ofcom-complaints-13258721/

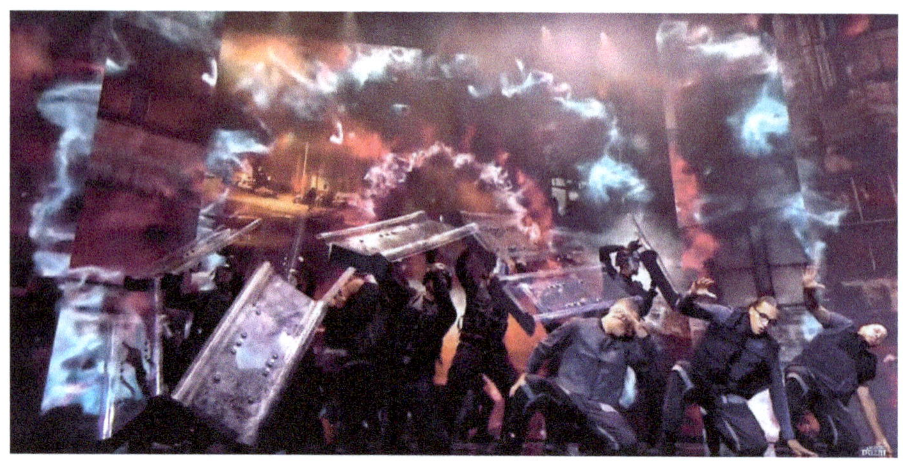

Diversity's 'I Can't Breathe' routine
(https://www.youtube.com/watch?v=kzFNKFitHjw - screenshot)

Dance has been an important part of TV entertainment, especially in the UK and the USA, since the 1960s with shows such as American Bandstand and Soul Train, dance groups on Top of the Pops and in more recent decades, Dancing on Ice, Dancing with the Stars, So You Think You Can Dance and Strictly Come Dancing.

However, maybe the innocuousness of such TV dance history has lulled people into seeing dance as pure entertainment, safe from the radical social commentary that other artforms put on display now and then in theatres, galleries and cinemas, thus producing the large amount of complaints.

The history of dance shows that it has always been with us, and, like with other art forms, dance has a mixed history of social and radical roles. It has also, like other art forms, been highly influenced by Enlightenment and Romanticist ideas in more recent centuries, changing how we see and understand the role of dance in society today.

Here we will look at how dance has changed since the Enlightenment and why it has had an increasing popularity in the last century. We will also look at the potential for a radical dance culture to become a vehicle for increasing social and political awareness on a global scale.

Early and medieval dance history

Dance has been a part of human culture from prehistoric times to Egyptian tomb paintings depicting dancing figures from c. 3300 BCE. Folk dance, in particular, has been an important part of festivals, seasonal celebrations and community celebrations such as weddings and births.[135]

In Europe during the Middle Ages there are references to circular dances called *carole* from the twelfth and thirteenth centuries. People also danced around trees holding hands in a leader and refrain style. These dances and songs became the carols we know today.[136]

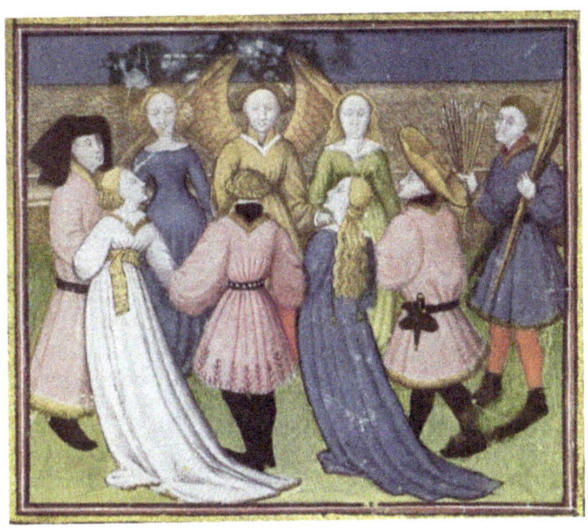

From a manuscript of *Le Roman de la Rose*
(*The Romance of the Rose*) (c. 1430), a medieval poem in Old French, styled as an allegorical dream vision
(Master of the Vienna Roman de la Rose / Public domain / Wikimedia Commons)

However, the literary history of dance, especially in terms of detailed descriptions goes back to Italy in the middle of the fifteenth century after the start of the Renaissance. During this time there also

[135] https://en.wikipedia.org/wiki/History_of_dance
[136] https://en.wikipedia.org/wiki/Medieval_dance

developed a divergence between court dances and country dances, between performance and participation. Court dancers trained for dances for entertainment, while anyone could learn country dances. At court formal display dancing would be followed by informal country dances for all to participate in.[137]

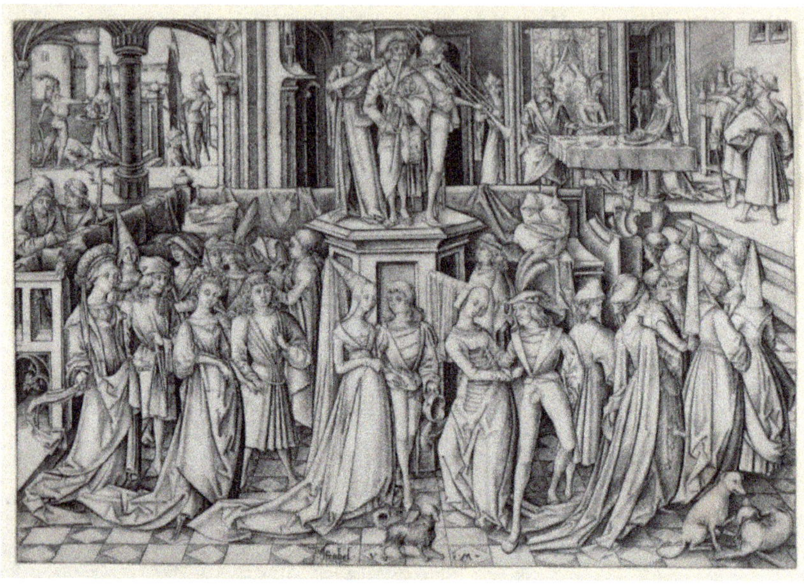

Dance at Herod's Court, ca. 1490, Israhel van Meckenem (c.1445–1503), engraving. Couples circling in a *basse danse*
(Public domain / Wikimedia Commons)

Ballet also began at this time developing out of court pageantry in Italy at aristocratic weddings. Its choreography was based on court dance steps and performers dressed in the formal gowns of the time rather than the later tutus and ballet slippers.

Ballet was then brought to France by Catherine de' Medici in the sixteenth century where it developed into a performance-focused art form during the reign of Louis XIV, where his "interest in ballet dancing was political motivated. He established strict social etiquettes through dancing and turned it into one of the most crucial elements in court social life, effectively holding authority over the

---

[137] https://en.wikipedia.org/wiki/Renaissance_dance

nobles and reigning over the state."[138] Louis XIV did this by encouraging:

> leading nobles to live at Versailles. This, along with the prohibition of private armies, prevented them from passing time on their own estates and in their regional power bases, from which they historically waged local wars and plotted resistance to royal authority. Louis thus compelled and seduced the old military aristocracy (the 'nobility of the sword') into becoming his ceremonial courtiers, further weakening their power.[139]

Louis XIV loved and promoted ballet, participating in court ballets during the early half of his reign, dancing 80 roles in 40 major ballets. In March 1661, Louis established the Académie Royale de Danse, founded by *Letters Patent* (a type of legal instrument in the form of a published written order), the first dance institution established in the Western world.[140] In 1669, he founded the Académie d'Opéra (later renamed Académie Royale de Musique, or the Opéra), within which arose the Paris Opera Ballet.[141] By the end of the seventeenth century ballet had become professionalised and its challenging acrobatic movements could "only be performed by highly skilled street entertainers."[142]

The Enlightenment and ballet in the 18th century

It was ballet that also became a focal point for criticism by the Enlightenment *philosophes* during the 18th century. The *philosophes* (French for 'philosophers') "were public intellectuals who applied reason to the study of many areas of learning, including philosophy, history, science, politics, economics, and social issues."[143]

---

[138] https://en.wikipedia.org/wiki/History_of_ballet
[139] https://en.wikipedia.org/wiki/Louis_XIV
[140] https://en.wikipedia.org/wiki/Acad%C3%A9mie_Royale_de_Danse
[141] https://en.wikipedia.org/wiki/Paris_Opera
[142] https://en.wikipedia.org/wiki/Classical_ballet
[143] https://en.wikipedia.org/wiki/Philosophes

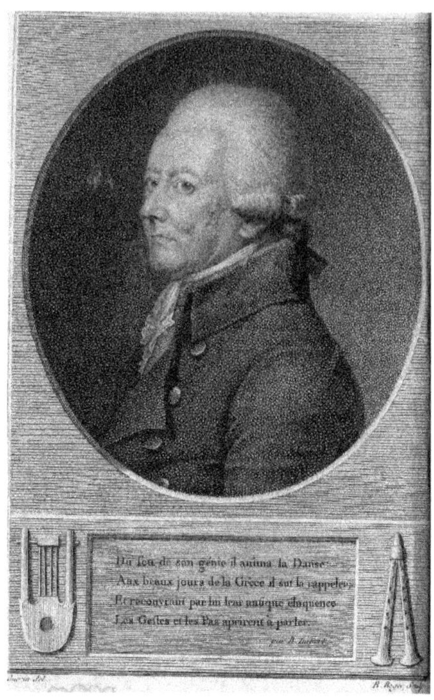

Noverre: frontispiece of *Lettres sur les arts* imitateurs, Paris, Collin,
The Hague, Immerzeel, 1807
Jean-Georges Noverre (1727–1810) was a French dancer and ballet-master, and is generally considered the creator of ballet d'action, a precursor of the narrative ballets of the 19th century. His birthday is now observed as International Dance Day.
(Barthélémy Joseph Fulcran Roger / Public domain / Wikimedia Commons)

The philosophes "argued [in general] that ancient supersti-tions and outmoded customs should be eliminated, and that reason should play a major role in reforming society." They desired to see "the development of art forms that gave meaningful expression to human thoughts, ideas, and feelings, and they disregarded merely decorative or ornamental forms of art."[144]

Denis Diderot, for example, (one of the editors of the quintes-sential enlightenment project: the *Encylopédie*) wrote in his essay 'Entretiens sur 'Le Fils Naturel'':

---

[144] https://www.encyclopedia.com/humanities/culture-magazines/enlightenment-and-ballet

I would like someone to tell me what all these dances performed today represent — the *minuet*, the *passe-pied*, the *rigaudon*, the *allemande*, the *sarabande* — where one follows a traced path. This dancer performs with an infinite grace; I see in each movement his facility, his grace, and his nobility, but what does he imitate? This is not the art of song, but the art of jumping. A dance is a poem. This poem must have its own way of representing itself. It is an imitation presented in movements, that depends upon the cooperation of the poet, the painter, the composer, and the art of pantomime. The dance has its own subject which can be divided into acts and scenes. Each scene has a recitative [type of singing that is closer to speech than song] improvised or obligatory, and its *ariette* [a short aria].[145]

To achieve this the philosophes argued for more naturalism in style and less of the "contrived sophistication and majesty" of earlier Baroque aesthetics. This criticism eventually led to new forms of ballet "that attempted to convey meaning, drama, and the human emotions" in particular the *ballet d'action*: "a dance containing an entire integrated story line".[146]

Ballet in the 19th century: Romanticism

Enlightenment ideas which led to the 'Age of Reason' and classical ideas of order, harmony and balance gave way to Romanticist emphasis on emotion, individualism and anti-rationalist medievalism. The 'vogue for exotic, escapist fantasy which dominated Romanticism in all the other arts' soon affected ballet in two major aspects: a new preoccupation with the supernatural, and the exotic. The plots in Romantic ballet:

were dominated by spirit women—sylphs [imaginary spirits of the air], *wilis* [a type of supernatural being in Slavic

[145] https://www.encyclopedia.com/humanities/culture-magazines/enlightenment-and-ballet
[146] https://www.encyclopedia.com/humanities/culture-magazines/enlightenment-and-ballet

folklore], and ghosts—who enslaved the hearts and senses of mortal men and made it impossible for them to live happily in the real world. Women dancers were dressed in diaphanous white frocks with little wings at their waist, and were bathed in the mysterious poetic light created by newly developed gas lighting in theatres. They danced in a style more fluid and ethereal than 18th-century dancers and were especially prized for their ballon [the ability to appear effortlessly suspended while performing movements during a jump] as they tried to create the illusion of flight.[147]

The second important Romanticist influence in ballet was:

a fascination with the exotic, which was figured through gypsy or oriental heroines and the use of folk or national dances from 'foreign' cultures (such as Spain, the Middle East, and Scotland). Such dances were considered highly expressive both of character and of exotic local colour, though in some countries, such as Italy, indigenous dances were featured in ballets whose plots reflected that region's surge of nationalist feeling.[148]

An early example of the Romantic ballet is *La Sylphide* which was first performed at the Paris Opera in 1823 starring Marie Taglioni:

La Sylphide is a story ballet about a supernatural female creature, half-woman, half-bird, who is doomed to an eternity of dancing. The Sylphide falls in love with a peasant man, James, who is soon to be married. However, James falls in love with the sylphide and leaves his wedding to spend his life with her. The ballet takes a turn when James consults a witch on how to keep the Sylphide from flying off. The witch tells him to tie a scarf around the Sylphide's waist, and James obeys. The scarf ends up killing the Sylphide, and James is ultimately killed by the witch in an attempt to avenge her

---

[147] https://www.oxfordreference.com/view/10.1093/oi/authority.20110803100427645
[148] https://www.oxfordreference.com/view/10.1093/oi/authority.20110803100427645

death. The Sylphide is symbolic of an unattainable dream, and James is the naive hero who pursues her. This ballet was the first romantic ballet and typifies the romantic themes of fantasy, supernaturalism and man vs. nature.[149]

However, it was also the 19th century which saw the creation of what is considered by many to be the finest achievement of the Classical style, *Sleeping Beauty*. As Victoria Rose Niblett writes:

Sleeping Beauty is opulent, returning to the intermingling of traditional French court dances in the choreography and the refinement of the Apollonian [relating to the rational, ordered, and self-disciplined aspects of human nature as opposed to Dionysian characteristics of excess, irrationality, lack of discipline, and unbridled passion] expression. This was a shift away from the emotional exploration of the Romantic period and back to reason and rational philosophy. [...] In the Romantic period, dance was designed by the external power of the music, but in the Classical period choreographers had a more influential role with the construction of the symphony. This involvement allowed choreography to follow an academic, pattern-oriented structure that insured the association between dance and music. [...] While Romantic ballet focused on fragile and emotional femininity, Classical ballet focused more on the type of femininity that could be expressed in the refinement, strength, and charm of the female character.[150]

While this era saw the rise of ballet as a truly international art form, Romanticism in ballet declined rapidly "as ballets were so weighted towards the feminine and the febrile", while "male dancers were frequently relegated to the role of porteur [supporting the ballerina]".[151]

---

[149] https://sites.google.com/site/ugadancehistory/make-donations

[150] https://victorianiblett.weebly.com/dance-scholarship/romantic-v-classical-ballet#

[151] https://www.oxfordreference.com/view/10.1093/oi/authority.20110803100427645

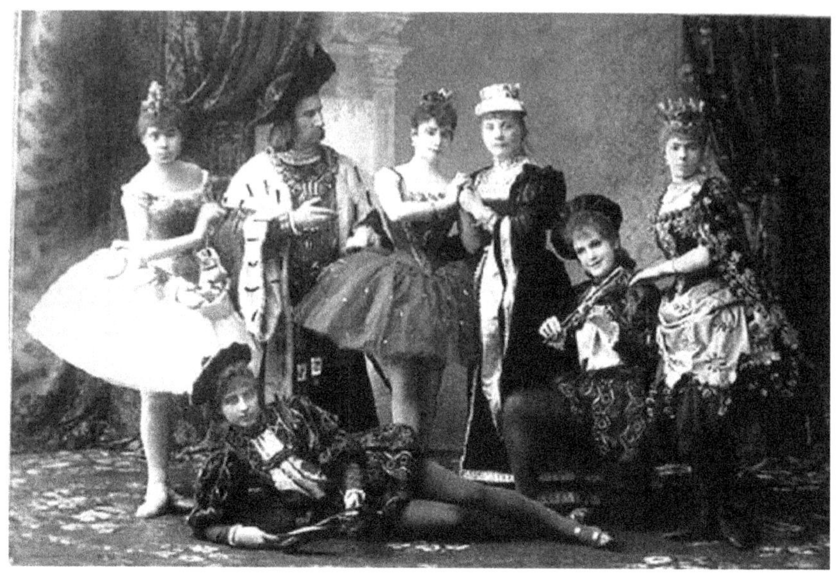

A publicity photo for the premiere of Tchaikovsky's ballet
The Sleeping Beauty (1890)
Original cast members costumed for Act I. At center is Carlotta
Brianza as Aurora. Mariinsky Theatre, St. Petersburg, 1890
(Public domain / Wikimedia Commons)

Folk dance and Herder

The rise of nationalist feeling in the 19th century was also associated with the new emphasis on local culture and traditions. Folk dances attained a new significance as the spread of nationalist and socialist ideas gave a new emphasis and importance to the culture of the peasants and the working classes. In Ireland, for example, *céilí* dances were collected country-wide and popularised by Conradh na Gaeilge (Gaelic League) in its goal to promote Irish cultural independence and de-anglicisation.[152]

It was the eighteenth-century Enlightenment philosopher Johann Gottfried von Herder (1744–1803) who recognised the importance of traditional culture. Herder established fundamental ideas concerning the intimate dependence of thought on language

---

[152] https://en.wikipedia.org/wiki/Ceili_dance

which "appears in its greatest purity and power in the uncivilized periods of every nation." Hence Herder's interest in collecting ancient German folk songs and his focus upon language and cultural traditions as the ties that create a 'nation' "were extended to include folklore, dance, music and art."[153]

Herder developed his folk theory to the point of believing that "there is only one class in the state, the Volk, (not the rabble), and the king belongs to this class as well as the peasant".[154] His idea that the Volk was not the rabble was a new idea at this time, and thus Herder laid the basis for the idea of "the people" as the basis for later democratic ideologies.

Therefore, as Vicki Spencer writes:

Herder's intention, then, was not to urge moderm intellectuals and artists to reject the philosophical and intellectual features of their own culture in favor of the simple naivety of earlier folk literature. Instead, he argued that their relationship to their own culture needed to change, in order to capture the complexities and spontaneity in the way of life, language, and character of their own unique culture.[155]

Moreover, Herder believed it was important to look back through history for the nation to 'grow organically' into the future. According to David Denby:

Herder believes in a human drive towards perfection and self-improvement, but this is a process which operates always in given contexts and within given constraints, which must be understood and respected historically. It is when societies are denied the opportunity to grow organically that they fail to progress. Tradition and progress are not opposites: progress must emerge out of a social and historical tradition if it is to take root, and, conversely, 'a living tradi-

---

[153] https://en.wikipedia.org/wiki/Johann_Gottfried_Herder
[154] https://en.wikipedia.org/wiki/Johann_Gottfried_Herder
[155] Vicki Spencer, 'In Defense of Herder on Cultural Diversity and Interaction', *The Review of Politics*, Winter, 2007, Vol. 69, No. 1 (Winter, 2007), pp. 79-105 Published by: Cambridge University Press for the University of Notre Dame du lac on behalf of *Review of Politics*

tion was inconceivable without the progressive emergence of new goals'.[156]

Later, Herder's ideas on folk culture became strongly associated with Romanticism and national chauvinism. However, Herder "understood and feared the extremes to which his folk-theory could tend" and he "refused to adhere to a rigid racial theory, writing that 'notwithstanding the varieties of the human form, there is but one and the same species of man throughout the whole earth'."[157]

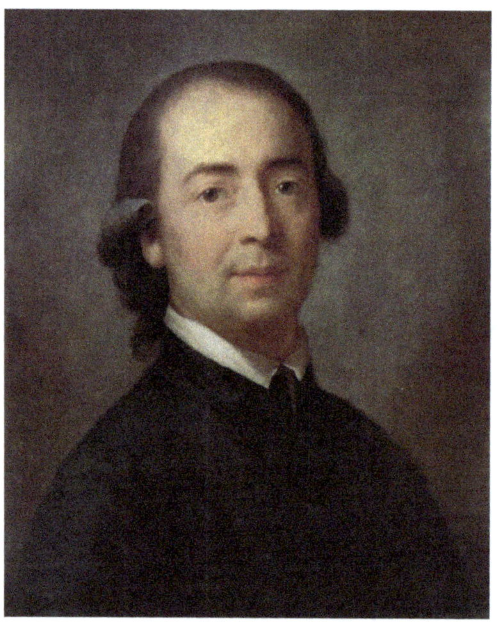

Herder (1785) by Anton Graff (1736–1813)
(Public domain / Wikimedia Common)

Thus, Herder saw the importance of understanding one's own culture as a foundation stone for future national projects to be built upon, and not about seeing the past as a Golden Age to be nostalgic about as in Romanticist theory.

---

[156] David Denby, 'Herder: culture, anthropology and the Enlightenment', History of the Human Sciences Vol. 18 No. 1. © 2005 Sage Publications (London, Thousand Oaks, CA and New Delhi) pp. 55–76

[157] https://en.wikipedia.org/wiki/Johann_Gottfried_Herder

Dance in the twentieth century

Enlightenment influences

By the beginning of the twentieth century folk dance was firmly established and formed an important part of national culture. Many countries around the world had state folk dance ensembles by the middle of the century. In particular this could be seen in the Soviet Union after the Russian revolution of 1917 where the state supported and promoted folk dance as part of the culture of the people. The Red Army Choir, an official army choir of the Russian armed forces, was set up in the 1920s, and by the 1930s was touring with an ensemble of dancers.[158]

Ballet also continued life after the revolution but with new revolutionary content. As Georg Predota writes:

> Ballet companies had to cope with a mass exodus of leading figures of the stage, but also defend against grassroots Communist voices that decried ballet as an artificial, frivolous art form, a decadent playground for grand dukes hopelessly out of touch with reality. Yet gradually, government policy opened the former bastions of imperial high culture to the masses, making ballet performances available to a wider audience by distributing free or subsidized tickets.[159]

For example, the Russian ballet, *The Red Poppy*, with a score written by Reinhold Glière, was created in 1927 and was a huge success. It had a modern revolutionary theme, as Predota notes:

> Set in a port in Kuomintang China in the 1920's, The Red Poppy eventually became the first truly Soviet ballet. The story tells of the love between a Soviet sailor and a Chinese girl, who is eventually killed by the sailor's capitalist rival. The tyrannical British imperialist commander of the port sanc-

---

[158] https://interlude.hk/red-poppy-reinhold-gliere-yekaterina-geltzer/
[159] https://interlude.hk/red-poppy-reinhold-gliere-yekaterina-geltzer/

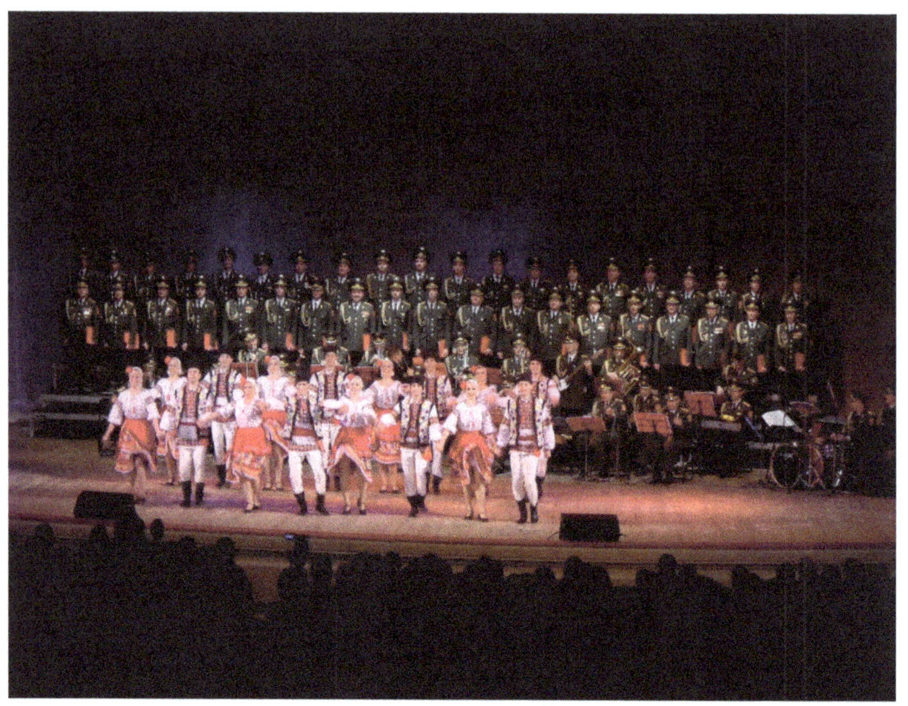

The Alexandrov Choir with Dance Ensemble, Warsaw 2009
(Also known as the Red Army Choir and the Song and Dance Ensemble of the Russian Army)
(Loraine / CC BY-SA 4.0 / Wikimedia Commons)

tions her murder, as Tao-Hoa tries to escape her homeland on board a Soviet ship. As she falls dying, she gives her compatriots a red poppy as an emblem in their fight for freedom.[160]

Romanticist influences

In Europe, the ballet company Ballet Russes, was formed in 1909 and toured Europe as well as North and South America. Although set up by the Russian impresario Serge Diaghilev (and even used Russian dancers), the company never performed in Russia.

---

[160] https://interlude.hk/red-poppy-reinhold-gliere-yekaterina-geltzer/

It became part of the Modernist movement with music commissioned from Rimsky-Korsakov and Stravinsky and the designs of Picasso, Rouault, Matisse, and Derain.[161]

Modernism - an extension of Romanticist thinking - emphasised individualism, art for art's sake, suspicion of reason, and subjectivism. In the arts, Modernism tended to emphasise constantly changing form over sociopolitical content and this became particularly notable in the twentieth century.

Dance in general also developed in many different directions in the twentieth century but the Modernist movement set the stage for dance trends and styles in the United States and Europe which tended to emphasise individualism and diversion, and then later developed into freestyle. This could be seen in western concert or theatrical dance where modern dance continued as an art form:

Modern dance is a broad genre of western concert or theatrical dance, primarily arising out of Germany and the United States in the late 19th and early 20th centuries. Modern dance is often considered to have emerged as a rejection of or rebellion against, classical ballet. Socioeconomic and cultural factors also contributed to its development. In the late 19th century, dance artists such as Isadora Duncan, Maud Allan and Loie Fuller were pioneering new forms and practices in what is now called aesthetic or free dance for performance. These dancers disregarded ballet's strict movement vocabulary, the particular, limited set of movements that were considered proper to ballet and stopped wearing corsets and pointe shoes in the search for greater freedom of movement.[162]

Later in the twentieth century, as in the other arts, dance was affected by Postmodernism from the 1960s to the 1980s. While Postmodernism rejected the grand narratives (e.g. Christian ideology, Freudian psychology, political democracy etc.) and the ideology of Modernism, it was similar to Modernism in that it also rejected

---

[161] https://www.britannica.com/topic/Ballets-Russes-ballet-company
[162] https://en.wikipedia.org/wiki/Modern_dance

Enlightenment ideas and was thus yet another descendant of Romanticism.

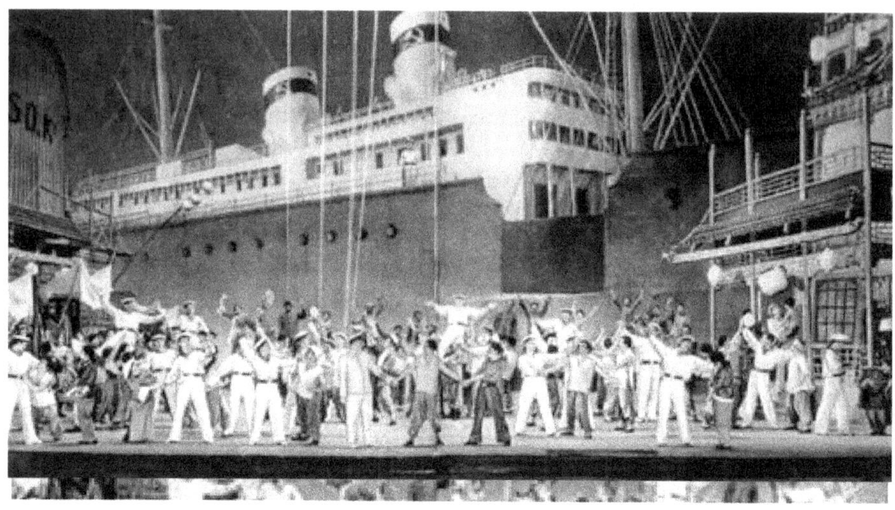

A scene from the 1927 production of *The Red Poppy*
(Public domain / Wikimedia Commons)

With Postmodernism, the politicisation of dance or the use of dance as a form of collective resistance to capitalism and imperialism, became a more remote prospect as "the postmodern dance movement rapidly developed to embrace the ideas of postmodernism, which rely on chance, self-referentiality, irony, and fragmentation." For example, Postmodern dance incorporated "improvisation, spontaneous determination, and chance", cast non-trained dancers, and changed the relationship of dance to the tempo of accompanying music. Later it became more conceptual and abstract while distancing "itself from expressive elements such as music, lighting, costumes, and props."[163]

As Postmodern dance distanced itself from the masses, popular dances in the form of commercialised novelty and fad dances went to the other extreme, regularly spreading among the people like wildfires that soon burnt themselves out. They took different forms: solo dances, partner dances, group dances and freestyle dances.

---

[163] https://en.wikipedia.org/wiki/Modern_dance

From 1909 to the mid-1940s there was: The Grizzly Bear, Charleston, Duckwalk, Carioca, Suzie Q, The Lambeth Walk, Thunder Clap, Conga, and the Hokey cokey. During the 1950s there was Bomba, The Chicken, Bunny Hop, The Hop, The Meatstick, Madison, The Stroll, and Hully Gully. The 1960s had Shimmy, Twist, The Chicken Walk, The Gravy ("On My Mashed Potato"), The Loco-Motion, Martian Hop, Mashed Potato, The Monster Mash, The Swim, Watusi, Chicken Dance, Hitch hike, Monkey, The Frug, Jerk, The Freddie, Limbo, Batusi, and The Shake.

In the 1970s it was Sprinkler, Penguin, Hustle, Time Warp, Bump, Tragedy, Grinding, Car Wash, Electric Slide, Robot, The Running Man, Y.M.C.A., and Little Apple. The 1980s saw Moonwalk, Cotton-Eyed Joe, Harlem Shake, Agadoo (aka Agadou), Superman (aka Gioca Jouer), The Safety, Lambada, Thriller, The Hunch, Wig Wam Bam, Cabbage Patch, Da Butt. In the 1990s there was The Carlton, Locomía, Boot Scootin' Boogie, Do the Bartman, Hammer, The Humpty, Vogue, The Urkel, Achy Breaky Heart (Line dance), Macarena, Saturday Night, Tic, Tic Tac, Thizzle, La Bomba (not to be confused with Bomba), The Roger Rabbit, and Tootsee Roll.[164]

As can be seen from the quantity cited and the regularity of change there is no end to Modernism's ability to move with the markets or keep up with the constantly changing mass consumer pop music scene. A few styles of dance had periods of mass popularity and are still going today as social dances encouraged by regular classes in, for example, jive, salsa, and ballroom dancing.

Cinema also aided the popularity of dance in the twentieth-century as can be seen in films featuring ballet in the 1940s (*The Red Shoes*), tap dancing in the 1950s (*Singin' in the Rain*), modern dance in the 1960s (*West Side Story*), disco in the 1970s (*Saturday Night Fever*), club/performance partner dancing in the 1980s (*Dirty Dancing*), tango in the 2000s (*Chicago*) and modern dance theatre in the 2010s (*Pina*). The global popularity of Hollywood musicals and Bollywood song-and-dance sequences have made dance an important element to be considered in any new film musical.[165]

---

[164] https://en.wikipedia.org/wiki/Novelty_and_fad_dances
[165] https://en.wikipedia.org/wiki/Dance_in_film

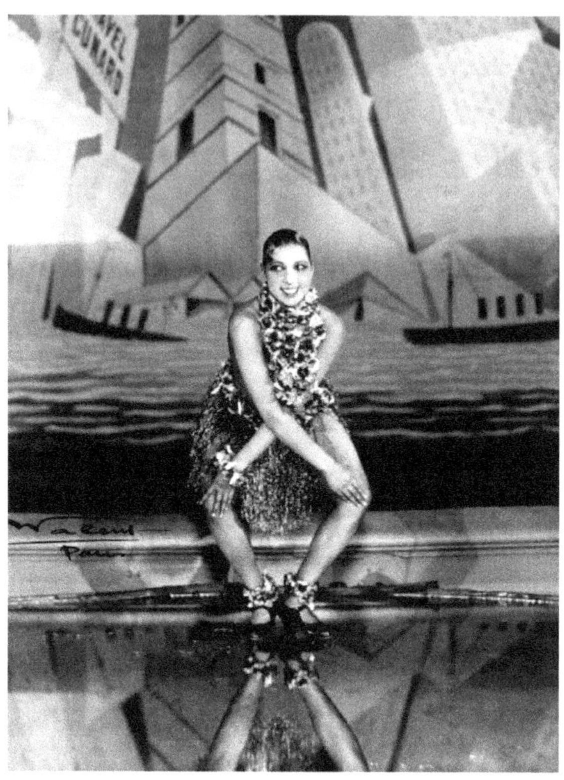

Josephine Baker dancing the Charleston at the Folies Bergère, Paris, in 1926
(Walery, Polish-British, 1863-1929 / Public domain / Wikimedia Commons)

In terms of live performance (and folk dance), the Irish stage show, Riverdance, featuring Irish step-dancing, opened in Dublin in 1995. It went on to perform in over 450 venues worldwide and has "been seen by over 25 million people, making it one of the most successful dance productions in the world." The show also incorporated international dance elements of flamenco and tap dancing.[166]

Thus, the twentieth-century has seen an explosion in interest in dance in general, and in the quantity of styles and techniques. It also has seen the overt politicisation of dance in nationalist and socialist struggles, and as an art form as affected by Romanticist and Enlightenment ideas as every other major art form.

---

[166] https://en.wikipedia.org/wiki/Riverdance

The twenty-first century and new debates

Dance has become even more prevalent in the twenty-first century with the internet and global satellite media, for example, through apps like TikTok and dance shows on TV. Riverdance is still touring and ballet is as popular as ever. Novelty and fad dances still come and go. Social dancing and traditional dance are still in demand due to classes, competitions and people's natural love of dance as a form of socialising.

However, it could be asked if popular dance has simply become a form of social catharsis, and performance dance as escapism and diversion? Is there a role for dance in progressive culture? The negative reaction to Diversity's 'I Can't Breathe' radical narrative may have been simply an overreaction in a society unused to seeing dance used in a critical setting, yet the connection between dance and story has become relevant again as Modernist and Postmodernist aesthetic strategies have waned in popularity.

Twenty-first-century ballet has seen discussion revolving around narrative or story ballet (has plot and characters), as Alastair Macaulay writes: "Nowhere more than in narrative has ballet become the land of low expectations. Audiences regularly sit through a poverty of dance-narrative expression that they would never tolerate in a movie, a novel, an opera, a play or even a musical."[167]

Hanna Rubin discusses issues relating to choreography:

Choreographing story ballets that will appeal to contemporary audiences presents unique challenges even for experienced dancemakers. A too-literal approach or too-traditional staging can seem quaint or flat. And what makes a suitable narrative for those coming of age in a digital era, where there are no strictures on what can be searched, seen and shared? How can a story ballet hold audiences' attention? If mere distraction becomes the goal, how can a ballet achieve the resonance that will give it continued life?[168]

[167] 'For Ballet, Plots Thicken, or Just Stick?' https://www.nytimes.com/2010/08/08/arts/dance/08storyballet.html

[168] 'Story Ballets for the 21st Century: What Are the Secret Ingredients of Today's Successful Narrative Works?' https://www.pointemagazine.com/contemporary-story-ballets-2412872540.html

However, choreographer Helen Pickett notes that "[n]ew stories are being created from other people's histories". She points out that traditional ballerina roles haven't always been empowering ones. "Putting the female on the pedestal was a way to say she is untouchable, but not in an elevated way — in a way that she is perhaps suffering [...] There was a lot of that in the Romantic era: Giselle goes nuts for her love."[169]

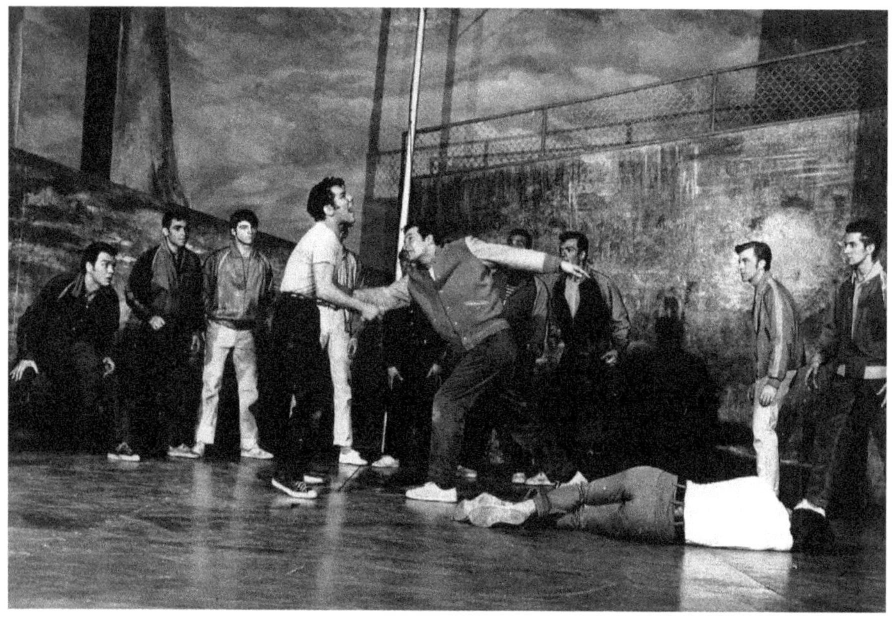

Tony stabs Bernardo in the 1957 Broadway production
(Photo by Fred Fehl / Public domain / Wikimedia Commons)

The ballet *Spartacus*, the Bolshoi Ballet's biggest hit of the last half-century, has seen a comeback in recent years in both live and film versions. *Spartacus* is a ballet by Aram Khachaturian (1903–1978) following the exploits of Spartacus, the leader of the slave uprising against the Romans known as the Third Servile War. The 1968 production, choreographed by Yury Grigorovich, made the bal-

---

[169] 'Where Are Today's Dynamite Ballerina Roles?' Joseph Carman https://www.dancemagazine.com/ballet-choreography-today-2569989256.html

let famous and became one of Khachaturian's best-known works.[170] David Mead, in his review of a cinematic version, writes about the importance of the ballet 'as a beacon of hope':

> From the premiere in 1968, Spartacus has been judged through the lens of the Cold War. [...] Now, just short of half a century later, this ballet, continuously in the repertoire of the Bolshoi, can be seen for the profound and great work that it is. In 1968, it was a very daring production for the Bolshoi and, rather than be viewed against the backdrop of US/Soviet relations, should be regarded as it was: contemporaneous with the Vietnam war, Paris student revolts, waves of strikes in the UK and youth tuning in and dropping out in the US. [...] Spartacus, in all his myth and mystery, has served as a beacon of hope for the oppressed throughout the centuries. In 2016 the world is still plagued with inequality, slavery, oppression and poverty not to mention wars and political crises. It is this that makes this ballet as heart-rending as ever, its technical demands always subsumed into the dramatic necessities.[171]

In her own work, Pickett has featured strong female characters, and has worked on an adaptation of Arthur Miller's *The Crucible* for the Scottish Ballet. This is certainly an interesting direction as *The Crucible* was a "dramatized and partially fictionalized story of the Salem witch trials that took place in the Massachusetts Bay Colony during 1692–93. Miller wrote the play as an allegory for McCarthyism, when the United States government persecuted people accused of being communists."[172]

In a review of a three-week run of Bolshoi's *Spartacus* at the Royal Opera House in London in 2019, Roslyn Sulcas discusses the technical aspects of the production as the "ballet moves with impetuous sweep through impassioned virtuosic solos and lyrical pas de deux, full of spectacular overhead lifts and slung-across-the back swirls" and notes that "the ballet, for all its focus on soloist virtuosity,

---

[170] https://en.wikipedia.org/wiki/Spartacus_(ballet)

[171] https://www.seeingdance.com/the-bolshoi-ballet-in-cinema-spartacus/

[172] https://en.wikipedia.org/wiki/The_Crucible

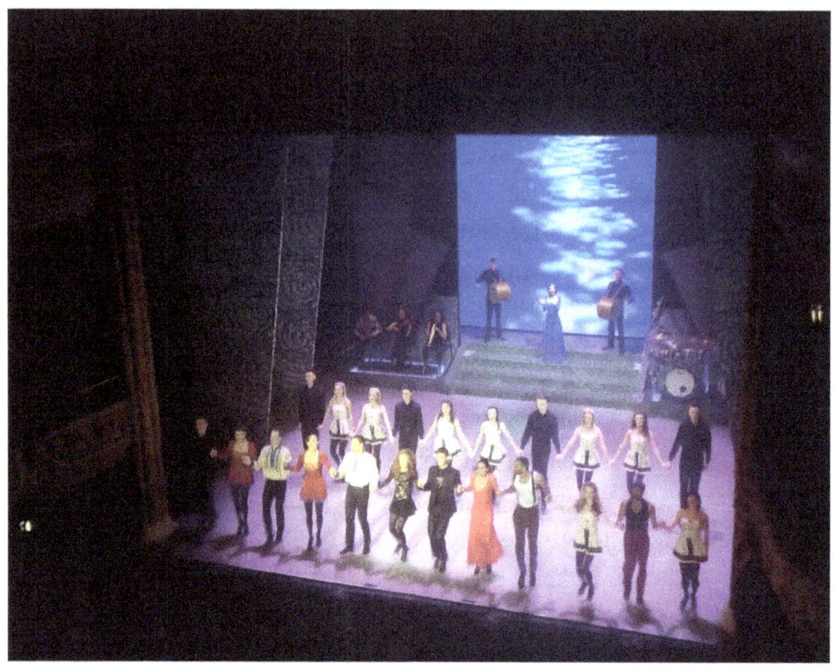

Riverdance cast at the Gaiety Theatre, Dublin, 2019
(Sheila1988 / CC BY-SA 4.0 / Wikimedia Commons)

is also an ensemble tour de force, a marvellous display of might from the Bolshoi corps. *Spartacus* is still a ballet for the masses, on stage and off."[173]

Finding the right balance between form and progressive content in ballet may be one of the biggest challenges of the 21st century for many reasons: conservative owners/backers/critics, the negative effects of Modernism and Postmodernism on form and ideology, and the lingering effects of Romanticist over-emphasis on emotion and the individual rather than on context and sociopolitical struggles.

Similarly, with other forms of dance. The synthesis of the new with the old can make for exciting and engaging art (like 'I Can't Breathe') when it is based on the stories of people's actual lived lives.

While Diversity have the luxury of prime-time television and a

---

[173] https://www.theguardian.com/stage/2019/aug/04/bolshoi-ballet-spartacus-review-royal-opera-house

mass audience to present their views and choreographies, other choreographers work on their stories in more difficult situations, as Veronica Jiao writes:

> There are countless choreographers who have dedicated their entire body of work to the story-telling of blackness in America (Kyle Abraham, Camille Brown, Okwui Okpokwasili and the collaborators/choreographers of Urban Bush Women, to name a few). There are the nameless choreographers working four part-time jobs in order to share their stories and experiences in a downtown factory-turned-studio-turned-theatre.[174]

Dance has truly taken its place as a significant global cultural movement. While there are still social divisions in dance today as in the past, the difference is that the performance dances of the elites today have the potential to be radical and progressive, just as the group dances of the masses today can be self-absorbed and escapist.

The future of participative dance will also depend on the level of engagement of people in sociopolitical struggle. In the past, in Ireland, for example, people flocked to traditional dance as it tied in with their nationalist and socialist beliefs. It was a way of connecting their past to a perceived or hoped for future. Similarly, in sport the Irish people flocked to Gaelic games while the previous mass support for cricket dropped dramatically as cricket was now perceived to be a 'British' sport. People seek what gives their life meaning as they become more politicised, and this leads to pride in their own radical culture and radical history as a form of resistance. Participative dance will no doubt change again on this more conscious basis because it is an important part of people's social and cultural lives.

Dance has had a long journey through human history. It has always been associated with peoples' celebrations and festivities as a collective expression of human emotions. However, over time particular dances became more and more associated with different

---

174 'Op-Ed: The Problem With So You Think You Can Dance's Fast-Food Activism,' Veronica Jiao
   https://www.dancemagazine.com/so-you-think-you-can-dance-2480300942.html

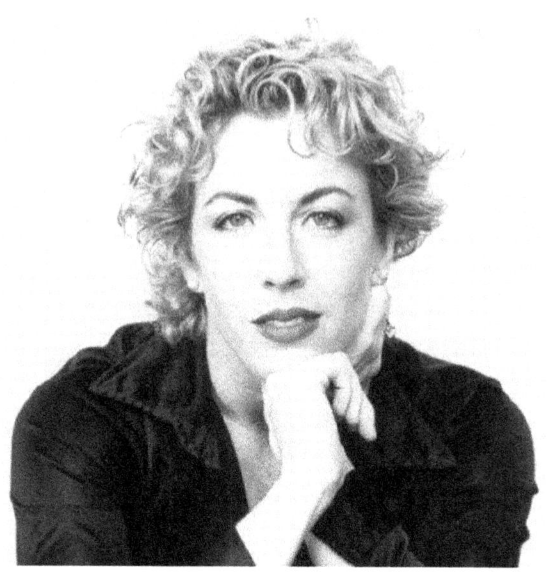

Choreographer Helen Pickett
Scottish Ballet's The Crucible was shown at Theatre Royal, Glasgow in 2019. Based on the play by Arthur Miller, Helen Pickett notes: "The real trick of telling the story of *The Crucible* through dance is not to overexplain everything." (The Scotsman)
(https://www.scotsman.com/arts-and-culture/edinburgh-festivals/theatre-and-stage/edinburgh-international-festival-preview-scottish-ballets-crucible-1412172)
(Image: KCBalletMedia / CC BY 2.0 / Wikimedia Commons)

classes and groups as societies grew ever more complex.

During the time of the Enlightenment, dance became a focus of research and criticism. Performance dance became imbued with Classical ideals and participative dance was seen in a new way as an important part of the heritage of all the people, and not backward or even inferior as in the past.

Later, such dances took on even more powerful roles with revolutionary content and state folk ensembles. However, Romanticist ideas turned dance in on itself, shearing it of sociopolitical ideals and progressive content. That is, until Diversity hit the stage with a performance which may yet prove to be the beginning of a new chapter in the history of dance.

Chapter 7

Poetry

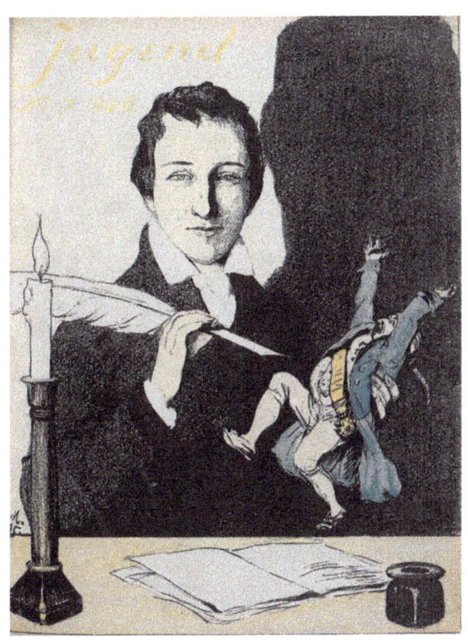

Heinrich Heine (1797–1856) *Jugend* magazine (1906) "Where they burn books, in the end they will also burn human beings" (Dort, wo man Bücher verbrennt, verbrennt man am Ende auch Menschen) *Almansor* (written 1821–1822)

(Sergey Solomko (1867-1928) / Public domain / Wikimedia Commons)

With your bitter, twisted lies,
You may trod me in the very dirt
But still, like dust, I'll rise.
Maya Angelou

The Dialectics of Rhyme

"Doomed be the king, the rich man's king,
Who would not be moved by our suffering,
Who tore the last coin out of our hands,
And let us be shot by his blood-thirsty bands...
We weave; we weave.
"Doomed be the fatherland, false name,
Where nothing thrives but disgrace and shame,
Where flowers are crushed before they unfold,
Where the worm is quickened by rot and mold...
We weave; we weave.
"The loom is creaking, the shuttle flies;
Nor night nor day do we close our eyes.
Old Germany, your shroud's on our loom,
And in it we weave the threefold doom; ...
We weave; we weave!"
Heinrich Heine

Poetry is often associated with genteel people and laid-back life-styles, yet over the decades since the Enlightenment many poets have been actively involved in the most radical of political and art movements. Setting up a solid foundation for such attitudes was the poet extraordinaire, Alexander Pope. In this chapter I shall look at the connection between poetry and socio-political struggles over the centuries. From Pope to the Chartists, and from the Irish revolutionary poets to the postcolonial writers of Africa, poetry has played an important part in social change.

The New Augustans v Medievalism – 'shall not Britain now reward his toils?'

Imagine being one of the generation of poets to follow Shakespeare. In the eighteenth-century, the Enlightenment poet's attitude towards Shakespeare was that Shakespeare was good but not perfect. They looked back to Roman times, to that of Augustus (63 BCE–CE 14) for a more political and satirical model for their poetry. Alexander Pope (1688–1744) was highly influenced by the poet Horace (65 BCE–8 BCE) whose work was created during a momentous time when Rome changed from a republic to an empire. Pope's poem *Epistle to Augustus* (addressed to George II of Great Britain) initiated The New Augustans, as they were known, and they created new and bold political work in all genres as well as sharp and critical satires of contemporary events and people. The Augustan era in English poetry is well known:

> for its fondness for wit, urbanity, and classical (mostly Roman) forms and values. Named for the Augustan period or "Golden Age" in Roman poetry, the English Augustans both translated and modeled their own verse after poets such as Virgil, Horace, and Propertius. [...] Practitioners of Augustan models included Pope, John Dryden, John Gay, Jonathan Swift, and Samuel Johnson. These poets are famous for their long verse narratives or mock epics, which are often satirical and imitate classical models.[175]

Pope's best known works *The Rape of the Lock*, *The Dunciad*, and *An Essay on Criticism* made him famous in his own time for their biting criticism and wit. Equally satirical but with more emphasis on prose than poetry was his contemporary, Jonathan Swift (1667–1745), the Anglo-Irish satirist, essayist, pamphleteer, poet and cleric whose *A Tale of a Tub* (1704), *An Argument Against Abolishing Christianity* (1712), *Gulliver's Travels* (1726), and *A Modest Proposal* (1729) led to the creation of the term 'Swiftian' for such sharp satire.

The Augustan era was also known by other Enlightenment

---

[175] https://poets.org/text/brief-guide-augustans

names such as the age of neoclassicism and the Age of Reason. It was a time of increased availability of books and a dramatic decrease in their cost. This in turn meant that education was less confined to the upper classes and that writers could hope to make more money through the sale of their works and therefore be less dependent on patrons.

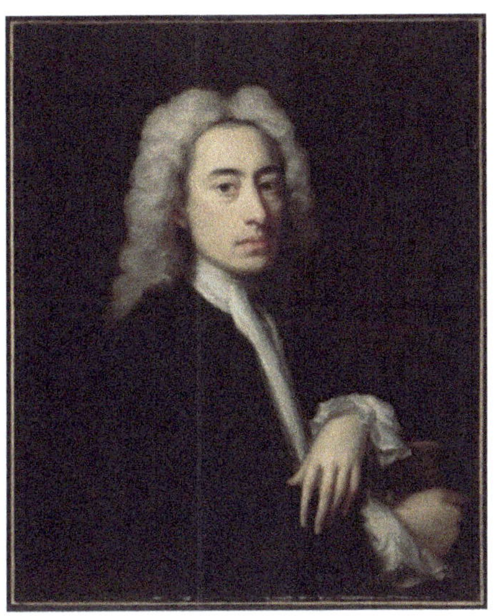

Alexander Pope (c.?1736), painting attributed to English painter Jonathan Richardson (1667–1745), Museum of Fine Arts, Boston
(Public domain / Wikimedia Commons)

The greatest patron of the arts throughout the Middle Ages was the Church. Patronage was also used by nobles, rulers, and very wealthy people to endorse their political ambitions, social positions, and prestige. Leonardo da Vinci (1452–1519) and Michelangelo (1475–1564), William Shakespeare (1564–1616), and Ben Jonson (c.1572–c.1637) all looked for and received the support of noble or ecclesiastical patrons.

The sales from Pope's works allowed him to live a life less determined by other people's wealth, and this independence is reflected in his lines from Epistle to Dr. Arbuthnot:

> Oh let me live my own! and die so too!
> ('To live and die is all I have to do:')
> Maintain a poet's dignity and ease,
> And see what friends, and read what books, I please.[176]

While Pope read a lot of philosophy, his concerns were mainly poetic. As David Cody writes:

Like many of his contemporaries, Pope believed in the existence of a God who had created, and who presided over, a physical Universe which functioned like a vast clockwork mechanism. Important scientific discoveries by men like Sir Isaac Newton, who explained, in his Principia, the nature of the laws of gravitation which helped to govern that universe, were seen as corroborating that view. 'Nature, and Nature's Laws lay hid in Night,' Pope wrote, in a famous couplet intended as Newton's epitaph, but 'God said, Let Newton be! and All was Light.' This view of the universe as an ordered, structured place was an aspect of the Neoclassical emphasis on order and structure which also manifested itself in the arts, including poetry.[177]

Pope was famous for his biting criticism which spoofed the mores of society or mocked his literary rivals. His critical political savvy was also on show in lines like:

> 'Tis George and Liberty that crowns the cup,
> And zeal for that great House which eats him up.
> The woods recede around the naked seat,
> The sylvans groan—no matter—for the fleet;
> Next goes his wool—to clothe our valiant bands;
> Last, for his country's love, he sells his lands.
> To town he comes, completes the nation's hope,
> And heads the bold train-bands, and burns a pope.
> And shall not Britain now reward his toils,
> Britain, that pays her patriots with her spoils?

---

[176] https://www.poetryfoundation.org/poems/44895/epistle-to-dr-arbuthnot
[177] http://www.victorianweb.org/previctorian/pope/phil.html

> In vain at court the bankrupt pleads his cause;
> His thankless country leaves him to her laws.[178]

Pope's poetry reflected the Enlightenment popularisation of science through scientific and literary journals, the development of the book industry, and the promulgation of encyclopedias and dictionaries. The new ideas spread like wildfire through learned academies, universities, salons and coffeehouses. While the Enlightenment period lasted from the beginning of the reign of Louis XV (1715) until the turn of the nineteenth century, it was soon followed by the Romantic period from about 1800 to 1860.[179]

Chartism v Romanticism – 'How comes it that ye toil and sweat?'

The Romanticists preferred intuition and emotion to the rationalism of the Enlightenment and placed a high value on the achievements of "heroic" individualists and artists. They turned inwards, seeing art as an individual experience and emphasising such emotions as apprehension, horror and terror, and awe. Romanticism looked backwards to folk art, ancient customs and medievalism. As the bourgeoisie achieved their main aims of wresting control of land and power from the aristocracy, the responsibility for continuing the struggle for the principles of *'liberté, égalité, fraternité'* fell upon the organisations of the working classes.

In England, Chartism was a major working-class movement called after the People's Charter of 1838 and was a movement for political reform in Britain until 1857. The movement's strategies were constitutional and they used petitions and mass meetings to put pressure on politicians to concede manhood suffrage. The Charter demanded: a vote for every man twenty-one years of age, secret ballots, payment of Members (so working people could attend without loss of income), equal constituencies, and annual Parliamentary elections. The Chartist movement was a reaction to the passing of the Reform Act 1832, which failed to extend the vote beyond those owning property. The political leaders of the working class felt that

---

[178] https://oll.libertyfund.org/title/boynton-the-complete-poetical-works-of-alexander-pope
[179] https://en.wikipedia.org/wiki/Age_of_Enlightenment

the middle class had betrayed them.

In conjunction with Chartist demonstrations and strikes, the Chartist press as the voice of radicalism existed in the form of *The Poor Man's Guardian* (bearing the heading: "Published contrary to 'law' to try the power of 'might' against 'right'.") in the 1830s and was succeeded by the *Northern Star and Leeds General Advertiser* between 1837 and 1852. The press covered news, editorials, and reports on international developments while becoming the best-selling provincial newspaper in Britain with a circulation of 50,000 copies. It also became an organ for the publication of working-class poets and poems.[180]

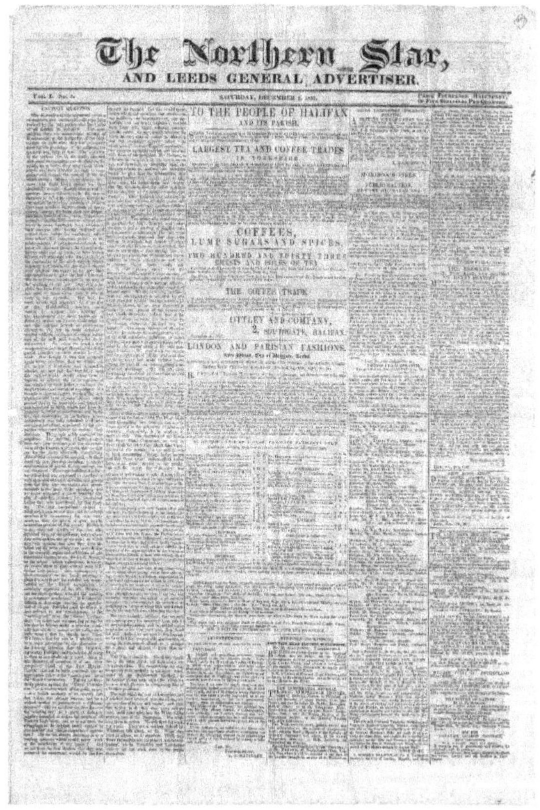

Front page of *The Northern Star* and *Leeds General Advertiser*, 1837
(The Northern Star, Nineteenth-Century Serials Edition / Public domain / Wikimedia Commons)

---

[180] https://en.wikipedia.org/wiki/Chartism

With such a wide circulation, it was no wonder that so many sent their poems in for consideration. According to Mike Sanders:

The Northern Star's poetry column was not an attempt to impose 'culture' from above, rather it was a response to a popular demand that poetry could and should speak to working-class desires and needs. From the start, literally hundreds of Chartists sent in their poems and quite a few appear to have pestered the editor with enquiries as to when their work would appear.[181]

It is believed that up to 1,000 poems by up to 400 Chartist and working-class poets were published in the Northern Star between 1838 and 1852. Michael Sanders notes that:

Most have names, but a high percentage are published either under initials, under a pseudonym or anonymously, presumably by writers who would fear reprisals, such as dismissal or blacklisting, if they were known to be writing for the Northern Star. By and large, we know nothing of these people. They are permanently lost to history. But these poems show us that poetry was once central to the way working-class communities expressed themselves both politically and otherwise.[182]

Ordinary people used poetry as a way of demonstrating their humanity in the face of grinding poverty and dehumanising industrial capitalism. By composing poetry, they showed they could produce 'beauty' as well as surplus value.[183]

An example of an anonymous poet's endeavour is AW's poem To The Sons Of Toil published in 1841:

---

[181] 'Making Better Rhymes: Chartist Poetry and Working Class Struggle' Mike Sanders https://www.culturematters.org.uk/index.php/arts/poetry/item/2209-making-better-rhymes-chartist-poetry-and-working-class-struggle

[182] 'Lost voices of Victorian working class uncovered in political protest poems' https://www.theguardian.com/uk/2007/mar/15/books.booksnews1

[183] https://www.culturematters.org.uk/index.php/arts/poetry/item/2209-making-better-rhymes-chartist-poetry-and-working-class-struggle

> How comes it that ye toil and sweat
> And bear the oppressor's rod
> For cruel man who dare to change
> The equal laws of God?
> How come that man with tyrant heart
> Is caused to rule another,
> To rob, oppress and, leech-like, suck
> The life's blood of a brother?[184]

We still don't know anything about AW but he or she is an example of many men and women who turned to poetry to express their desires for social justice. However, several important poets did arise out of the Chartist movement such as Ernest Charles Jones (1819–1869), novelist and Chartist. In 1845, Jones 'joined the Chartist agitation, quickly becoming its most prominent figure, and vigorously carrying on the party's campaign on the platform and in the press. His speeches, in which he openly advocated physical force, led to his prosecution, and he was sentenced in 1848 to two years' imprisonment for seditious speeches. While in prison he wrote, it is said in his own blood on leaves torn from a prayer-book, The Revolt of Hindostan, an epic poem.'[185]

Thomas Cooper (1805–1892) was a leading Chartist and known for his prison rhyme the Purgatory of Suicides (1845). Gerald Massey (1828–1907) was only twenty-two when he published his first volume of poems, *Voices of Freedom and Lyrics of Love* (1850). George Binns (1815–1847) was a New Zealand Chartist leader and poet.

Ebenezer Elliott (1781–1849) was known as the Corn Law rhymer for his leading the fight to repeal the Corn Laws which were causing hardship and starvation among the poor. Though a factory owner himself, his single-minded devotion to the welfare of the labouring classes won him a sympathetic reputation long after his poetry ceased to be read. John Bedford Leno (1826–1894) was a Chartist, radical, poet, and printer who acted as a "bridge" between Chartism and early Labour movements, he was called the "Burns of

---

[184] 'Lost voices of Victorian working class uncovered in political protest poems' https://www.theguardian.com/uk/2007/mar/15/books.booksnews1

[185] https://en.wikipedia.org/wiki/Ernest_Charles_Jones

Labour" and "the poet of the poor" for his political songs and poems, which were sold widely in penny publications, and recited and sung by workers in Britain, Europe and America.

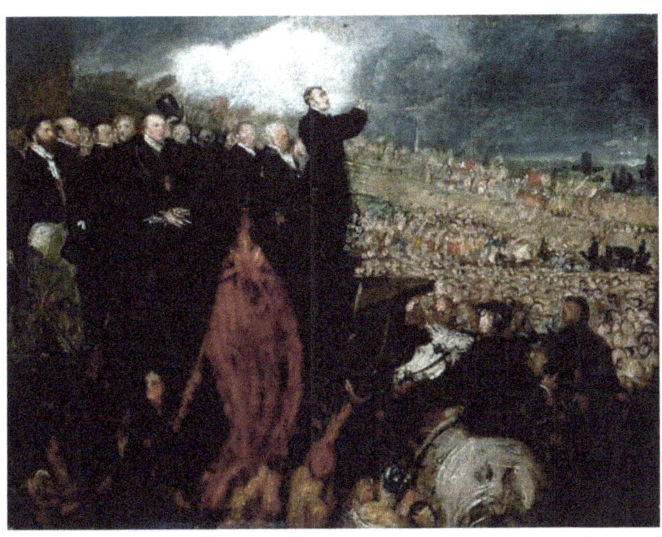

Meeting of the Birmingham Political Union (1832-1833), oil on canvas,
by Benjamin Haydon (1786-1846)
(Public domain / Wikimedia Commons)

The Poets' Revolution v Modernism – 'Viewing human conflict from a social perspective'

The connection between the radical poets and the working class continued into the twentieth century even when Romanticist modernism took hold. Modernism rejected the ideology of realism, while promoting a break with the immediate past, technical innovation, and a philosophy of 'making it new'. As such:

Modernist poetry in English is generally considered to have emerged in the early years of the 20th century with the appearance of the Imagist poets. In common with many other modernists, these poets were writing in reaction to what they saw as the excesses of Victorian poetry, with its emphasis on traditional formalism and overly flowery poetic diction. [...] Additionally, Modernist poetry disavowed the traditional aesthetic claims of Romantic poetry's later phase and no longer sought "beauty" as the highest achievement of verse. With this abandonment of the sublime came a turn away from pastoral poetry and an attempt to focus poetry on urban, mechanical, and industrial settings.[186]

Despite the modern context and simpler language, Modernist poets moved further away from Realism as they developed literary techniques such as stream-of-consciousness, interior monologue, as well as the use of multiple points-of-view, undermining what is meant by realism.[187] Thereby moving further away from the kind of narrative and descriptions of external reality that seekers of political change and social justice use as an art form to create and propagate awareness of their social conditions.

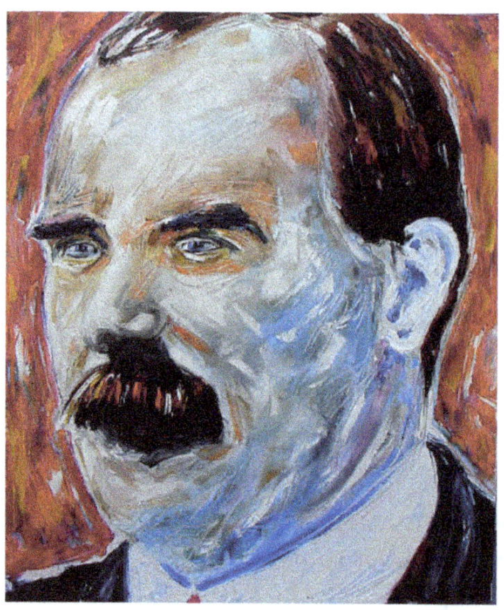

Painting of James Connolly by Caoimhghin Ó Croidheáin

The Chartist tradition of radical politics associated with radical content in poetry was continued in Ireland whose revolutionary

---

[186] https://www.cs.mcgill.ca/~rwest/wikispeedia/wpcd/wp/m/Modernist_poetry_in_English.htm
[187] https://en.wikipedia.org/wiki/Literary_modernism

radicals perceived in the First World War an opportunity encapsulated in the slogan, "England's difficulty is Ireland's opportunity". The culmination of nationalist and radical politics of the previous centuries was demonstrated in the Easter Rising of 1916. Indeed, it is often described as The Poets' Revolution as three of the men who signed the Proclamation in 1916, Patrick Pearse (1879–1916), Thomas MacDonagh (1878–1916), and Joseph Plunkett (1887–1916), were published poets, while many other participants were also writers of plays, songs and ballads. The leader of the Irish Citizens Army, James Connolly wrote:

> Our masters all a godly crew,
> Whose hearts throb for the poor,
> Their sympathies assure us, too,
> If our demands were fewer.
> Most generous souls! But please observe,
> What they enjoy from birth
> Is all we ever had the nerve
> To ask, that is, the earth.[188]

The leaders of the Irish revolution were generally a young, artistic group of revolutionaries and their executions by the British colonists sent shock waves throughout Ireland leading to the War of Independence (1919-1921) and the Civil War (1922–1923).

Later in the 1920s and 1930s a more politically conscious working-class poetry developed. In the United States the combination of influences from the Soviet Union and the Great Depression led to the growth of many new leftist political and social discourses. Milton Cohen summarised the aesthetic, stylistic, and political concerns being debated at the time. He noted that poets were expected to:

(1) View human conflict from a social perspective (as opposed to personal, psychological, or universal) and see society in terms of economic classes.

(2) Portray these classes in conflict (as Marx described

---

[188] https://www.marxists.org/archive/connolly/1907/xx/wewnerth.htm

them): workers versus bosses, sharecroppers versus land-owners, tenants versus landlords, have-nots versus haves. (3) Develop a 'working-class consciousness,' that is, identify with the oppressed class in these conflicts, rather than maintaining objective detachment.

(4) Present a hopeful outcome to encourage working-class readers. Other outcomes are defeatist, pessimistic, or 'confused.'

(5) Write simply and straightforwardly, without the aesthetic complexities of formalism.

(6) Above all, politicize the reader. Revolutionary literature is a weapon in the class struggle and should consciously incite its readers if not to direct action then to a new attitude toward life, 'to recognize his role in the class struggle.'[189]

These 'proscriptions' ran straight in the face of every tenet of Modernist poetry which emphasised the personal imagination, culture, emotions, and memories of the poet. Major poets of the radical movement in the United States include Langston Hughes (1902–1967), Kenneth Fearing (1902–1961), Edwin Rolfe (1925-1954), Horace Gregory (1898–1982), and Mike Gold (1894–1967).[190]

Post-colonial poetry v postmodernism –
'The bitter taste of liberty'

As the United States suffered under the heightened political repression of McCarthyism in the 1950s the mantle of radical culture moved to the countries who wrestled themselves out of British colonial stranglehold in the form of postcolonial literature. The English language was imposed in many colonised countries, yet came to be the language of radical anti-colonial poets during liberation struggles and afterwards in the independence era. African poets, for

---

[189] https://en.wikipedia.org/wiki/American_proletarian_poetry_movement See also: Milton Cohen, *Beleaguered Poets and Leftist Critics, University of Alabama Press,* (Tuscaloosa, 2010), p.24

[190] https://en.wikipedia.org/wiki/American_proletarian_poetry_movement

example, were able to use poetry to communicate to the world not only their "despairs and hopes, the enthusiasm and empathy, the thrill of joy and the stab of pain … but also a nation's history as it moved from 'freedom to slavery, from slavery to revolution, from revolution to independence and from independence to tasks of reconstruction which further involve situations of failure and disillusion'."[191]

David Diop's poem Africa weighs up past and present political complexities:

Africa, my Africa
Africa of proud warriors in ancestral savannahs …
Is this you, this back that is bent
This back that breaks under the weight of humiliation
This back trembling with red scars
And saying yes to the whip under the midday sun …
That is Africa your Africa
That grows again patiently obstinately
And its fruit gradually acquires
The bitter taste of liberty.[192]

The development of the postcolonial in the South paralleled the development of the postmodern in the West. The philosophical bases of postmodernism did not sit easily with the practical contingencies of newly achieved nationhood.

Postmodernism rejected the grand narratives and ideologies of modernism, and like modernism (and Romanticism), called into question Enlightenment rationality itself. The tendencies of postmodernism towards self-referentiality, epistemological and moral relativism, pluralism, and irreverence would make it an uncomfortable bedfellow with the socialist and revolutionary nationalist exigencies of the newly decolonised. As the Kenyan writer Ngugi wa Thiong'o notes:

---

[191] 'African English Poetry: Some Themes and Features' Dr. (Mrs) Jaya Lakshmi Rao V. http://www.postcolonialweb.org/africa/jvrao5.html

[192] 'African English Poetry: Some Themes and Features' Dr. (Mrs) Jaya Lakshmi Rao V. http://www.postcolonialweb.org/africa/jvrao5.html

Literature does not grow or develop in a vacuum; it is given impetus, shape, direction and even area of concern by the social, political and economic forces in a particular society. The relationship between creative literature and other forces cannot be ignored especially in Africa, where modern literature has grown against the gory background of European imperialism and its changing manifestations: slavery, colonialism and neo-colonialism. Our culture over the last hundred years has developed against the same stunting, dwarfing background.[193]

In a way the radical political changes wrought by anti-colonial struggles kept the culture tied down and anchored to the values and aspirations of the masses. Postcolonial ideology was relevant to society in a way that postmodernism was not. It could be argued that postmodernism actively sought to remove itself from political relevance by decrying grand narratives and elevating relativism.

Radical poetry today? – 'only injustice and no resistance?'

Until relatively recently it seemed that the sentiments of Bertolt Brecht's (1898-1956) poem *To Posterity* had become almost universally true in the twenty-first century:

For we went, changing our country more often than our shoes.
In the class war, despairing
When there was only injustice and no resistance.[194]

However, there has been a sea change in attitude with people demonstrating on the streets in many cities globally in recent years. The eruption of protests and violence in Chile, for example, started with students demonstrating against the proposal to raise the subway fares. This was unexpected as Sofía del Valle noted:

---

[193] https://en.wikipedia.org/wiki/Poetry_in_Africa
[194] https://allpoetry.com/To-Posterity

Economists have long called Chile's economy 'the miracle' of Latin America, where GDP per capita has noticeably grown from $2,500 in 1990 to $15,346 in 2017. However, these numbers hide a fundamental problem: they do not account for inequality. Chile's late poet Nicanor Parra said it best: 'There are two pieces of bread. You eat two. I eat none. Average consumption: one bread per person.'[195]

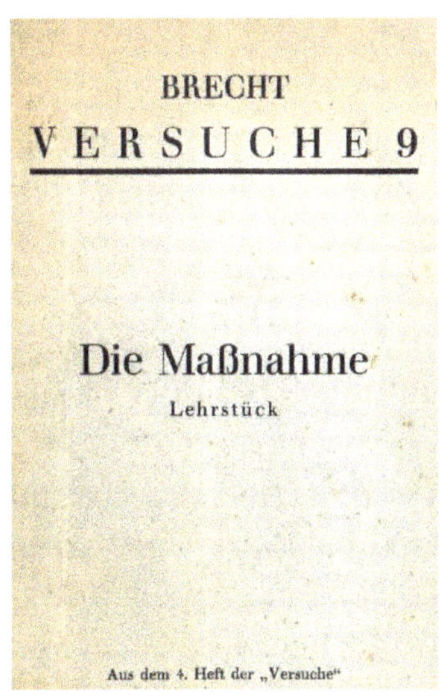

The Decision (Die Maßnahme), frequently translated as The Measures Taken, is a Lehrstück and agitprop cantata by Bertolt Brecht, consisting of eight sections in prose and unrhymed, free verse, with six major songs.
(Gustav Kiepenheuer Verlag 1930, (Description: CHRISTIAN HESSE AUKTIONEN), (Public domain / Wikimedia Commons)

She also states that the people themselves are starting to participate in political activity with the "proliferation of *"cabildos ciudadanos,"* or self-organized participatory meetings of citizens that have gathered to discuss problems and solutions for the country we dream to be."[196]

---

[195] 'The protests in Chile's streets are about inequality' Sofía del Valle https://politicsofpoverty. oxfamamerica.org/protests-chile-inequality-social-justice/

[196] 'The protests in Chile's streets are about inequality' Sofía del Valle https://politicsofpoverty. oxfamamerica.org/protests-chile-inequality-social-justice/

This has led to the connection between the masses and poetry, similar to Chartist times, being restored to Chile. According to Vera Polycarpou, the people on the streets are "singing the songs of Victor Jara, listening to symphonic music in the squares, making street theatre and reciting the poems of Pablo Neruda, declaring that it will not tolerate military rule, repression and injustice again."[197]

The Chilean Pablo Neruda (1904–1973) was a Nobel Prize winning poet-diplomat who wrote in a variety of styles, including surrealist poems, historical epics, overtly political manifestos, a prose autobiography, and passionate love poems, from a very young age. Neruda was living in Madrid at the outbreak of the Spanish Civil War (1936 to 1939) and with some friends had formed the Alliance of Anti-Fascist Intellectuals bringing popular theater to the people, plays from Cervantes to Lorca. The assassination of the Spanish poet Federico García Lorca (1898–1936), a friend of his, a month into the war profoundly affected Neruda. According to Mark Eisner:

Beyond the horror of a friend's assassination, Lorca's death represented something more: Lorca was the embodiment of poetry; it was as if the Fascists had assassinated poetry itself. Neruda had reached a moment from which there was no turning back. His poetry had to shift outwardly; it had to act. No more melancholic verse, love poems dotted with red poppies, or metaphysical writing, all of which ignored the realities of rising Fascism. Bold, repeated words and clear, vivid images now served his purpose: to convey his pounding heart and to communicate the realities he was experiencing in a way that could be understood immediately by a wide audience.[198]

This shift away from Romanticism can be seen clearly in Neruda's poem *I Explain Some Things*:

---

[197] 'AKEL, Chile: - Many years may have passed but the great avenues have reopened' Vera Polycarpou http://www.solidnet.org/article/AKEL-Chile-Many-years-may-have-passed-but-the-great-avenues-have-reopened/

[198] 'What We Can Learn from Neruda's Poetry of Resistance' Mark Eisner https://www.theparisreview.org/blog/2018/03/26/pablo-nerudas-poetry-of-resistance/

You will ask why his poetry
doesn't speak to us of dreams, of the leaves,
of the great volcanoes of his native land?
Come and see the blood in the streets,
come and see
the blood in the streets,
come and see the blood
in the streets![199]

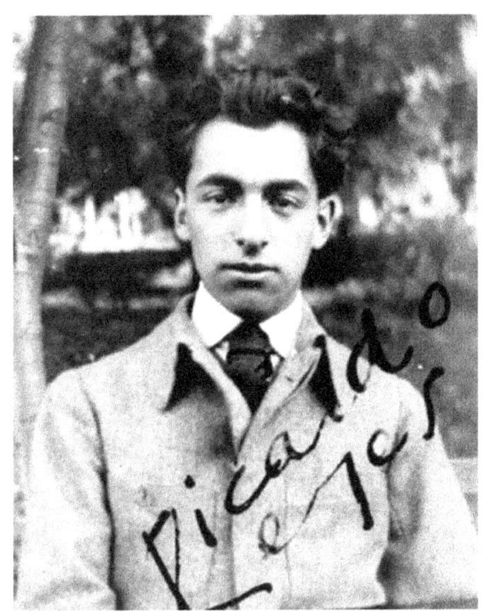

Pablo Neruda (1904–1973)
(Unknown author / Public domain / Wikimedia Commons)

The demonstrations in Chile have also seen the return of the *cacerolazo* or 'casserole' a form of popular protest used globally consisting of people making noise by banging pots, pans, and other utensils at demonstrations. The Chilean rapper Ana Tijoux has sung about this form of protest, called Cacerolazo[200] where she raps about *cacerolazos* as a form of massive protest in defiance of police and military violence describing them as "[w]ooden spoons against your shooting":

[199] 'What We Can Learn from Neruda's Poetry of Resistance' Mark Eisner https://www.theparisreview.org/blog/2018/03/26/pablo-nerudas-poetry-of-resistance/

[200] https://www.youtube.com/watch?v=lItbHicquo4

> Vivita, guachita, Chile despierta
> Cuchara de palo frente a tus balazos
> Y al toque de queda, ¡cacerolazo!
> No somos alienígenas ni extraterrestres
> No cachai na', es el pueblo rebelde
> Sacamos las ollas y nos mataron
> A los asesinos ¡cacerolazo!
> (Vivita, guachita, Chile wake up
> Wooden spoon in front of your bullets
> And at the curfew, cacerolazo!
> We are not aliens or extraterrestrials
> Don't shit, it's the rebel people
> We took out the pots and they killed us
> To the killers cacerolazo!)[201]

Tijoux's parents went into exile during Augusto Pinochet's dictatorship in Chile, an experience which affected her artistic career as a hip-hop protester and activist, and her interest in political and social issues. A song she wrote 2011, Shock, became popular again in Chile recently. When asked to comment about this, she replied: "That song was inspired by the protests going on there. For the song to come back around means the demands of the people continue and that the government is not listening to them. It's the same demands."[202]

Since the time of Alexander Pope, poetry has played an important part in the struggle for change and social justice and the potential for poetry to consolidate people's feelings, aspirations and desires has remained strong. The Chartists may not have had the access to the internet or video production of Ana Tijoux but their newspapers achieved large distributions and sales, spreading a similar culture of revolt and opposition. The decision by poets, themselves, to participate and apply their art to the issues at hand has reinforced and inspired people the world over.

---

[201] 'Chilean Folk Music Comes Back To Life During Crisis' Camila Rayen Huecho Pozo https://chile-today.cl/chilean-folk-music-comes-back-to-life-during-crisis/

[202] https://www.mtv.com/news/3144846/ana-tijoux-cacerolazos-chile-protest-anthem/

Chapter 8

Literature

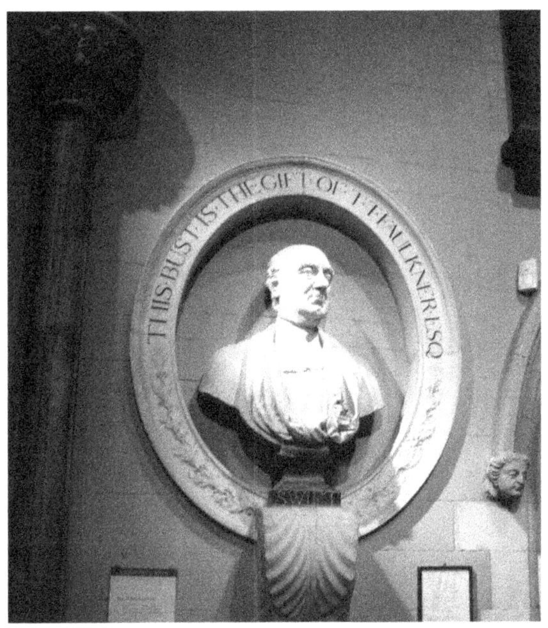

Bust of Jonathan Swift (1667–1745) near his burial spot in
St. Patrick's Cathedral, Dublin
(Wknight94 / CC BY-SA 3.0 / Wikimedia Commons)

Swift has sailed into his rest;
Savage indignation there
Cannot lacerate his breast.
Imitate him if you dare,
World-besotted traveller; he
Served human liberty.
W. B. Yeats translation of Jonathan Swift's Latin epitaph

Literature Serving Human Liberty

Resistance literature calls attention to itself, and to literature in general, as a political and politicized activity. The literature of resistance sees itself furthermore as immediately and directly involved in a struggle against ascendant or dominant forms of ideological and cultural production.
Barbara Harlow

Haven't we heard critics who demand of African writers that they stop writing about colonialism, race, colour, exploitation, and simply write about human beings? Such an attitude to society is often the basis of some European writers' mania for man without history - solitary and free - with unexplainable despair and anguish and death as the ultimate truth about the human condition.
Ngugi wa Thiong'o

As in other areas of the arts, cultural and political differences among writers meant that Romanticist and Enlightenment ideas on literature from the eighteenth to the twenty-first century has been a highly debated and polemical arena, showing how, from the earliest days, literature has been a battleground for the future of culture itself. Enlightenment influences on literature led to the concept of progressive culture which took many forms through to today. From realism, social realism, the proletarian novel and socialist realism, concepts of progressive culture have constantly changed in opposition to Romanticist ideas of 'art for art's sake'. Here we will look at these changes over time and examine some suggested definitions of progressive literature for the future.

Enlightenment and Romanticist literature

The Enlightenment was an intellectual movement during the eighteenth century in which philosophers and scientists spread their ideas through literary salons, coffeehouses and printed books, pamphlets and journals. It was a time of dramatically increasing literacy and a growing reading audience encouraged by cheaper printed material. Reading habits changed from public reading of a few books, to extensive private reading as books got cheaper. The Enlightenment was a time for satirists and humorists attacking the conservative monarchical institutions of the eighteenth century. Writers such as Jonathan Swift (1667–1745) and Alexander Pope (1688–1744) in Ireland and and Voltaire (1694–1778) in France blended criticism, satire and fiction into a new type of literature.

During the Age of Enlightenment there arose the literary genre of European literary sentimentalism. The sentimental novel was influenced by sentimentalism in philosophy, by writers such as Anthony Ashley Cooper, 3rd Earl of Shaftesbury[203] and Jean-Jacques Rousseau's doctrine of the natural goodness of man, focusing on developing a more humanist and sympathetic attitude towards the poor, criminals, and slaves.[204] The most well-known sentimental novels in English are Samuel Richardson's *Pamela, or Virtue Rewarded* (1740), Oliver Goldsmith's *Vicar of Wakefield* (1766), Laurence Sterne's *Tristram Shandy* (1759–67), *Sentimental Journey* (1768), Henry Brooke's *The Fool of Quality* (1765–70), Henry Mackenzie's *The Man of Feeling* (1771) and Maria Edgeworth's *Castle Rackrent* (1800).

While Enlightenment influences tended to be based on reason and science looking outwards, the Romanticist reaction stressed "sensibility", or feeling and tended towards human psychology and looking inwards. Romanticist literature put more emphasis on themes of isolation, loneliness, tragic events and the power of nature. A heroic view of history and myth became the basis of much Romanticist literature. The Scottish poet James Macpherson's (1736–1796) Ossian cycle of poems (published in 1762) were a

---

[203] https://en.wikipedia.org/wiki/Sentimentalism_(literature)

[204] https://en.wikipedia.org/wiki/Sentimental_novel

huge influence on Goethe (1749–1832) and Walter Scott (1771–1832). *Ivanhoe*, published in 1819, was Walter Scott's most popular historic novel and reflected the Romanticist interest in medievalism.

In Germany, it was Johann Wolfgang von Goethe's novel *The Sorrows of Young Werther* (1774) that had the most influence on burgeoning German Romanticism. However, the introverted, fatalistic aspect of Young Werther was eventually rejected by Goethe himself who described the Romanticist movement as "everything that is sick."

Literary Realism

After literary sentimentalism went on the wane, Enlightenment ideas took off in a different direction from Romanticism as the scientific method had its influence on literature in the form of the depiction of "objective reality". Known as Literary Realism, and beginning in the mid-nineteenth century, writers such as Stendhal (1783–1842) in France and Alexander Pushkin (1799–1837) in Russia led the realist movement with a view to representing "subject matter truthfully, without artificiality and avoiding artistic conventions, as well as implausible, exotic and supernatural elements."[205]

In this sense Realism opposed Romanticist idealisation or dramatisation and focused on lower class society's everyday activities and experiences in a more empirical way. This led to the development of the social novel which can be seen as a "work of fiction in which a prevailing social problem, such as gender, race, or class prejudice, is dramatized through its effect on the characters of a novel" and covering topics such as "poverty, conditions in factories and mines, the plight of child labor, violence against women, rising criminality, and epidemics because of over-crowding, and poor sanitation in cities."[206]

Early examples of the social novel were Charles Kingsley's (1819–1875) *Alton Locke* (1849) and Elizabeth Gaskell's (1810–1865) first industrial novel *Mary Barton* (1848). However, it was

---

[205] https://en.wikipedia.org/wiki/Literary_realism
[206] https://en.wikipedia.org/wiki/Social_novel

Charles Dickens (1812–1870) whose depictions of poverty and crime that shocked readers the most and even led Karl Marx (1818–1883) to write that Dickens had "issued to the world more political and social truths than have been uttered by all the professional politicians, publicists and moralists put together".[207] Dickens' novels, *Oliver Twist* (1839) and *Hard Times* (1854), explored many important social questions relating to the negative aspects of the industrial revolution.

Around the same time in France, Victor Hugo (1802–1885) published his historical novel *Les Misérables* (1862). The novel follows the lives of several characters and in particular the struggles of an ex-convict Jean Valjean. Hugo uses the form to elaborate his ideas on many topics from the history of France to politics, justice, religion and even the architecture and urban design of Paris. He outlines his purpose in a famous Preface to *Les Misérables* in which he writes:

> So long as there shall exist, by reason of law and custom, a social condemnation, which, in the face of civilization, artificially creates hells on earth, and complicates a destiny that is divine with human fatality; so long as the three problems of the age — the degradation of man by poverty, the ruin of women by starvation, and the dwarfing of childhood by physical and spiritual night — are not solved; so long as, in certain regions, social asphyxia shall be possible; in other words, and from a yet more extended point of view, so long as ignorance and misery remain on earth, books like this cannot be useless.[208]

Despite the controversy surrounding his play *Hernani*, Hugo was a statesman and human rights campaigner, and recognized as the most influential Realist writer of the 19th century. As he grew older "he became a passionate supporter of republicanism, and his work touches upon most of the political and social issues and artistic trends of his time."[209]

---

[207] https://en.wikipedia.org/wiki/Social_novel

[208] https://en.wikipedia.org/wiki/Les_Mis%C3%A9rables

[209] https://www.cs.mcgill.ca/~rwest/wikispeedia/wpcd/wp/v/Victor_Hugo.htm

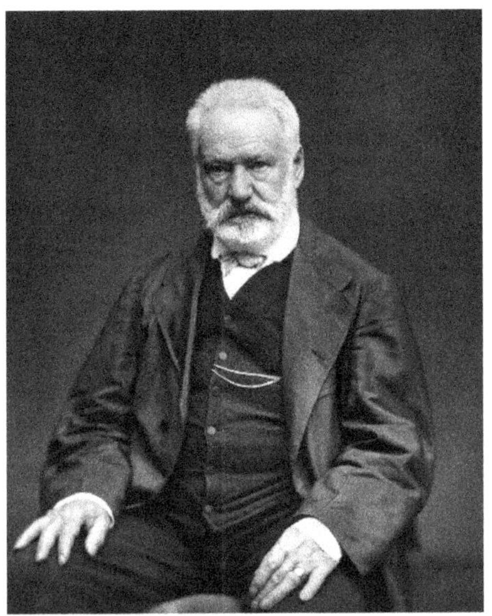

Victor Hugo (1876) by Étienne Carjat (1828–1906)
(Bibliothèque nationale de France / Public domain / Wikimedia Commons)

The American journalist and novelist Upton Sinclair (1878–1968) put his political and social ideas into practice when he spent seven weeks gathering information while working incognito in the meatpacking plants of the Chicago stockyards in 1904. This resulted in the 1906 novel, *The Jungle*, which exposed the harsh conditions, health violations, and unsanitary practices in the American meat packing industry of the time. The novel was hugely controversial at the time with publishers initially refusing to publish it but eventually the conditions described in the book led to public pressure to pass the Meat Inspection Act and the Pure Food and Drug Act.[210]

The proletarian novel

As the nineteenth century progressed enlightenment ideas were taken up by socialist movements and produced a new class-conscious proletarian literature created by working class writers.

---

[210] https://en.wikipedia.org/wiki/The_Jungle

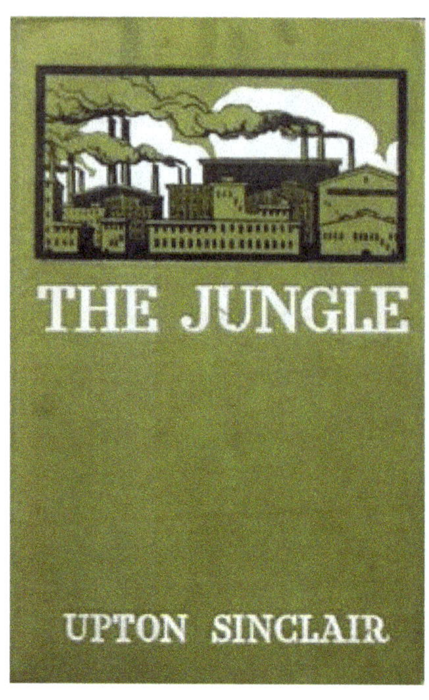

The Jungle is a 1906 novel by the American journalist and novelist
Upton Sinclair (1878–1968)
(Public domain / Wikimedia Commons)

The proletarian novel is a political form of the social novel which comments on political events and was used to promote social reform or political revolution among the working classes. The proletarian novel achieved significance in different countries in the early twentieth century.

In the United States, examples of American proletarian writing include Mike Gold, *Jews Without Money* (1930) (set in a slum populated mainly by Jewish immigrants from Eastern Europe), B. Traven, *The Death Ship* (1926) (scathing criticism of bureaucratic authority, nationalism, and abusive labor practices), Edward Dahlberg, *Those Who Perish* (1934) (first American anti-Nazi novel) and Jack Conroy, *The Disinherited* (1933) (the 1920s and 30s worker experience through the eyes of Larry Donovan).

In the Soviet Union, there were authors like Feodor Gladkov, *Cement* (1925) (worker comes home from the revolution and gets involved in the reorganization of the local cement factory), Nikolai Ostrovsky, *How the Steel Was Tempered* (1936) (follows the life of Pavel Korchagin, his fighting in, and aftermath of, the Russian Civil War), and Leonid Leonov, *The Russian Forest* (1953) (acclaimed by the authorities as a model Soviet book on World War II).

An early example of a working-class novelist from Britain was Robert Tressell, who wrote *The Ragged-Trousered Philanthropists* (1914) (a house painter's efforts to find work in the fictional English town of Mugsborough to stave off the workhouse for himself, his wife and his son). Some other examples from the time include Walter Greenwood, *Love on the Dole* (1933) (set in Hanky Park, the industrial slum in Salford where Greenwood was born and brought up), James Hanley, *The Last Voyage* (1931), (stoker John Reilly, who is still working only because he lied about his age, now faces his last voyage) and James C. Welsh, *The Underworld* (1920) a miner and trade unionist, who worked in mines from the age of 12, an experience which informed his first novels.[211]

Proletarian literature came to prominence during a time of rising fascism during the 1930s when Nazi book burnings were being carried out in Germany and Austria. The general political polarisation of the time is evidenced by the writers' meetings that took place when the First American Writers Congress (1935) in the USA, the International Writers' Congress for the Defence of Culture (1935) in France, and the First Congress of Soviet Writers (1934) in the Soviet Union were all held.

Progressive literature emphasised social development and was part of the general progressive movement of those who wanted science and technology to lead the way for a better society for all. It was opposed to the content and values of what the Indian writer K. Damodaran (1912–1976) called 'regressive literature', such as:

Despair, mysticism, the thought that man is helpless and incapable of building one's own future, complete degradation, sexual vagaries, respect for war and massacres, condescension to cultural values, faith in the evil of man and the disbelief in the generosity of mankind, hatred towards ideals,

---

[211] https://en.wikipedia.org/wiki/Proletarian_literature

all of these are the main trends of regressive literature. Such regressive trends are advertised behind a veil of arguments which state that art does not have any other responsibility beyond that of being art in itself.[212]

Such a description of regressive literature covers some aspects of Romanticist influences too, for example, art as diversion and art for art's sake.

What is progressive literature today?

Damodaran set out his beliefs on progressive literature as a literature in which the writer should adopt a scientific approach towards viewing things, try to eradicate superstitions and blind practices, and not isolate himself or herself from society. He also believed in literatures that preserved regional languages.[213]

One writer who puts such ideas into action in both fiction and prose is Ngugi wa Thiong'o, (not to mention Swiftian satire). While there are many African writers writing social literature about the lives of African people today, Ngugi has been important for his emphasis on the formal qualities of language as well the radical content of his novels. His use of his local Gikuyu language as the original language of his novels is an important anti-colonial aspect of his purpose for writing.

Examples of his novels include: *A Grain of Wheat* (1967) (weaves together several stories set during the state of emergency in Kenya's struggle for independence), *Petals of Blood* (1977), (deals with the repercussions of the Mau Mau rebellion as well as with a new, rapidly westernizing Kenya), the first modern novel in Gikuyu, *Caitaani mũtharaba-Inĩ* (*Devil on the Cross*) (1980) (focuses on politically challenging the role of international money and culture in Kenya) and *Mũrogi wa Kagogo* (*Wizard of the Crow*) (2004) (set in the imaginary Free Republic of Aburĩria, autocratically governed by one

---

[212] 'What is Progressive Literature? Why?' K. Damodaran http://transworkshoptps.blogspot.com/2014/03/what-is-progressive-literature-why.html?m=1

[213] 'What is Progressive Literature? Why?' K. Damodaran http://transworkshoptps.blogspot.com/2014/03/what-is-progressive-literature-why.html?m=1

man, known only as the Ruler).[214]

As English moves from being the dominant hegemonic language of earlier colonised countries (e.g. Ireland and Kenya) to being super hegemonic globally due to influences (such as satellite broadcasting and the internet), the linguistic strategies of Ngugi may become more significant when formally 'major' languages themselves also start to come under threat.

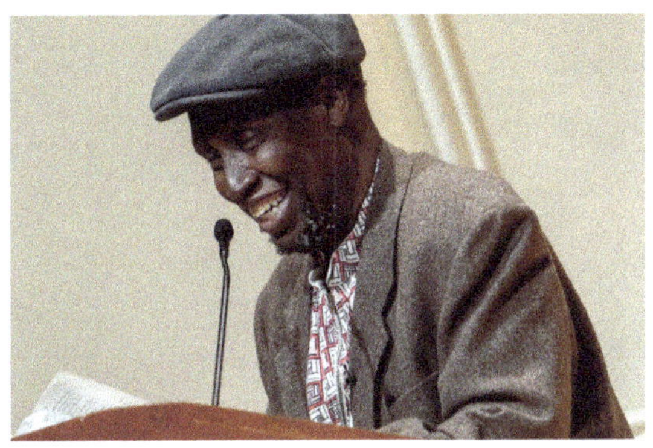

Ngũgĩ wa Thiong'o reading at the Library of Congress in 2019
(Library of Congress Life / CC0 / Wikimedia Commons)

While there have been obvious influences of Romanticism on writers like Dickens and Hugo, it could be argued that the realist impulse was a stronger drive and that both Dickens and Hugo knew and understood the poverty they described so well in their novels. This drive to incorporate and expose all forms of oppression in literary work could be described as one of the fundamentals that links the writers in the centuries old development of progressive literature. But, however progressive literature is defined into the future, one can be sure that its writers will not be appreciated for exposing the dark side of human oppression except by those whose voices too often remain unheard.

---

[214] https://en.wikipedia.org/wiki/Ng%C5%A9g%C4%A9_wa_Thiong%27o

Chapter 9

Theatre

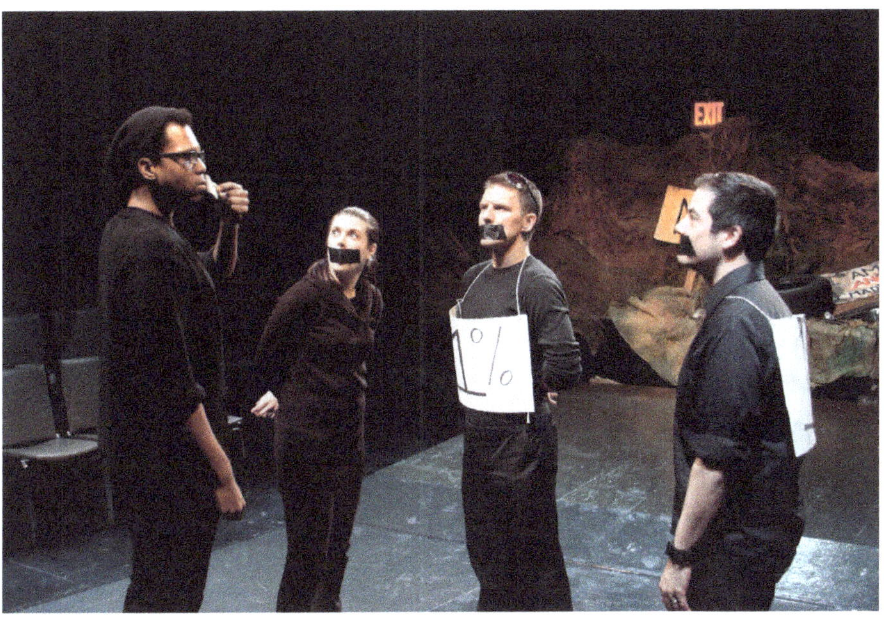

Created Equal is the second production this season for The Red Fern Theatre Company, whose mission is "to provoke social aware-ness and change through its theatrical productions and outreach."
(Photo: Steven Williams)

When the play ends, what begins?
Seeking conscientization:
awareness leading to action.
Sarah Thornton

Popular Theatre as Cultural Resistance

It is not enough to demand insight and informative images of reality from the theater. Our theater must stimulate a desire for understanding, a delight in changing reality.
Bertolt Brecht

Theatre is a form of knowledge; it should and can also be a means of transforming society. Theatre can help us build our future, rather than just waiting for it.
Augusto Boal

The importance of theatre in society today is demonstrated by the prevalence and variety of forms it takes both locally and globally. Indeed, over the centuries theatre has played an important sociological and ideological role. In an Enlightenment rational sense theatre has been used both by communities and elites to propagate and spread ideas for: the consolidation of society (Morality plays), social improvement (Neoclassical plays) as well as instigating and promoting revolutionary social ideas (Brechtian theatre). The Romanticist reaction in theatre meant that the formalized rules of Neoclassical theatre (e.g. the general and representative) were cast aside for celebrations of the individual and the drama of the subjective imagination as well as a revived backward-looking medievalism (e.g. the courtly romance and intrigues of the controversial play *Hernani* (1830) by Victor Hugo).

All around the world today theatre is funded by states through state theatres — playing national repertoires as well as showing international plays translated and/or modernised. However, as political and economic crises grow, so does the widening gap between two forms: community and state theatre. The global economic crisis has seen theatre once more developing into a useful community tool for highlighting important local issues (e.g. policing excesses) and global issues (e.g. climate change), and in many different ways (such as mass demonstrations and public squares). It will be argued that, in general, the state deals with any upsurge in popular resistance by attempting to appropriate radical working-class culture into preexisting structures to neutralise opposition. As with other art-forms, the influence of Enlightenment and Romanticist ideas can still be felt today. I will look at the development of general movements in theatre from the seventeenth century, beginning with Neoclassical theatre as an Enlightenment reaction to Restoration bawdiness, the influence of Romanticism, the rise of Realism, political theatre of the 1930s leading to the Documentary theatre of recent decades, and the contrasting ideology of state and community theatres of contemporary society.

Fifteenth to Eighteenth Centuries –

Neo-Classicism v Medievalism

Medieval theatre was mainly religious and moral in its themes, staging and traditions, emerging around 1400 and developing until 1550. Theatre was an ideal way to solve the difficulties of spreading the faith to a largely illiterate population. Certain biblical events were dramatised for feast days and performed by priests. In England there were many mystery plays such as the York Mystery Plays, the Chester Mystery Plays and the Wakefield Mystery Plays.[215] The word 'mystery' was used in the sense of 'miracle', and covered themes such as the Creation, Adam and Eve, and the Last Judgment.

Around the middle of the sixteenth century began English Renaissance theatre which was based on the rediscovery and imitation of classical works. Playhouses were established and became the sites for the production of plays by playwrights such as William Shakespeare (1564–1616), Christopher Marlowe (1564–1593) and

---

[215] https://en.wikipedia.org/wiki/Medieval_theatre

Ben Jonson (1572–1637). Genres of the period included the history play, tragedy and comedy, including satirical comedies. All a far cry from biblical stories and Christian morality: the classical influence bringing the subject matter down to earth.

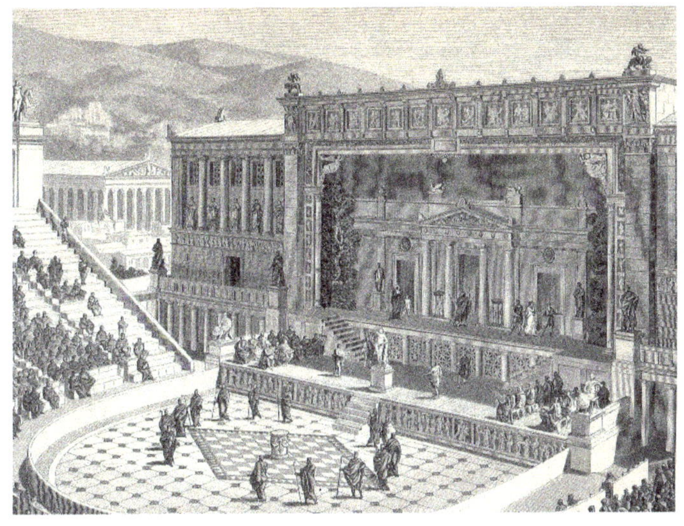

Artist rendering of the Theatre of Dionysus
(Joseph Kürschner (ed.) 1891 / Public domain / Wikimedia Commons)

This period lasted until the ban on theatrical plays enacted by the English Parliament in 1642. This ban, effected by the Puritans, lasted 18 years and ended in 1660 when the theatres were reopened. The strict moral codes of the Puritans were upended and comedies became the predominant mark of Restoration plays. These plays were a form of social commentary — recurring themes were cuckolding, shaming, seduction and the inversion of wealth, class and property. However, these themes also represented the upper class who tended to make up the typical audience (unlike the Morality plays) especially as most ordinary people could not afford the price of admission.

Restoration comedies were seen by many as bawdy, and Neoclassical theatre was a reaction to the decadence of these Charles II era productions. Neoclassical writers were influenced by Enlight-

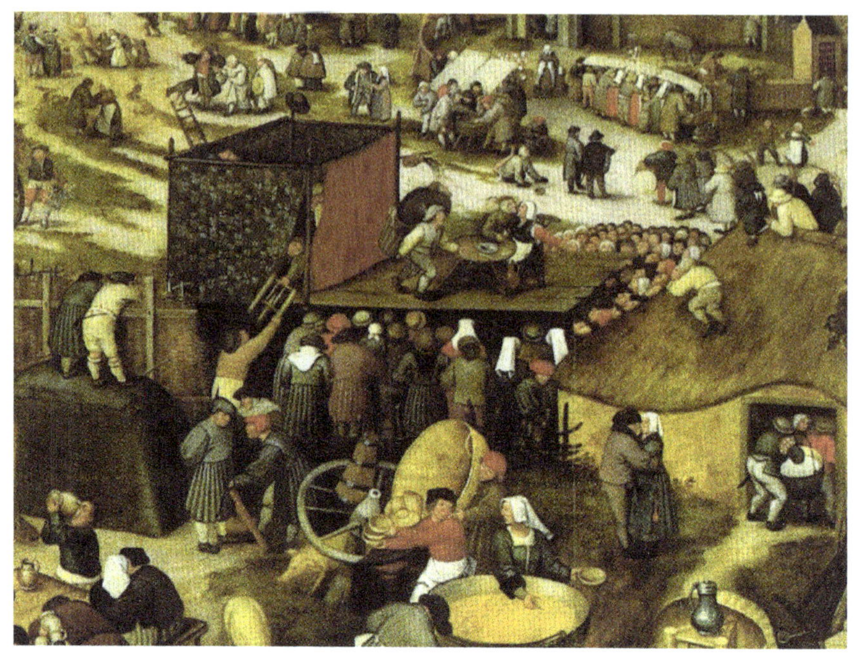

Village feast with theatre performance circa 1600
(Artist from the circle of Pieter Bruegel the youngr /
Public domain / Wikimedia Commons)

enment ideas and advocated a return to the values and conventions of classical Greek drama. The movement's aim was to restore the ideals of ancient Greek and Roman art, a time when many people began to think for themselves outside of the restrictions imposed by religion and traditional authority.

They believed that previous styles put far too much emphasis on emotions and the individual and looked to the classical style for inspiration on how to get people to see society in a more positive, collective manner by encouraging virtuous behavior. The Neoclassical attitude could be seen in the humanism of the plot lines which encouraged the audience to empathise with the characters rather than laugh at them. The rise of sentimental comedy reflected the Enlightenment idea that without emotion, imagination and sympathy, people would not be able to have the moral feelings that lead to our general ideas of justice and virtue.

The Neoclassicists developed a set of guidelines for the theatre, for example, they:

included five basic rules: purity of form, five acts, verisimilitude or realism, decorum and purpose. Play houses generally rejected scripts or productions that did not meet these requirements. Playwrights and actors in the Neoclassical period officially recognized just two types of plays: comedy and tragedy. They never mixed these together, and the restriction led to use of the now well-known pair of happy and sad masks that symbolize the theatrical arts. [...] Comedies, which were either satires or comedies of manners, tended to focus on the lower ranks of society, while tragedies portrayed the complex and fateful lives of the upper classes and royals.[216]

There was great social change and upheaval during the Neoclassical period as the middle class gained more power and prestige and the legitimacy of monarchies was questioned.

The search for natural law, beyond kings (who were above the law) and individual subjective experience, led to the desire to create the basis for a more stable and just society, so that, for example:

1. to Neoclassical minds, natural passions aren't necessarily good; natural passions must be subordinated to social needs and strictly controlled.

2. social needs are more important to Neoclassical society than individual needs. This conflicts with our modern preoccupation with the individual - in our time, the needs of the individual tend to be considered the most important, but this wasn't true in the Neoclassical period.

3. Neoclassical thinkers believed that man could find meaning in order itself - in the order of nature, social hierarchies, government, religion, even in the order within literary forms.[217]

---

[216] 'What Is Neoclassical Theatre?' L. Baran https://www.wisegeek.com/what-is-neoclassical-theatre.htm

[217] http://theatreforall.weebly.com/neo-classicism.html

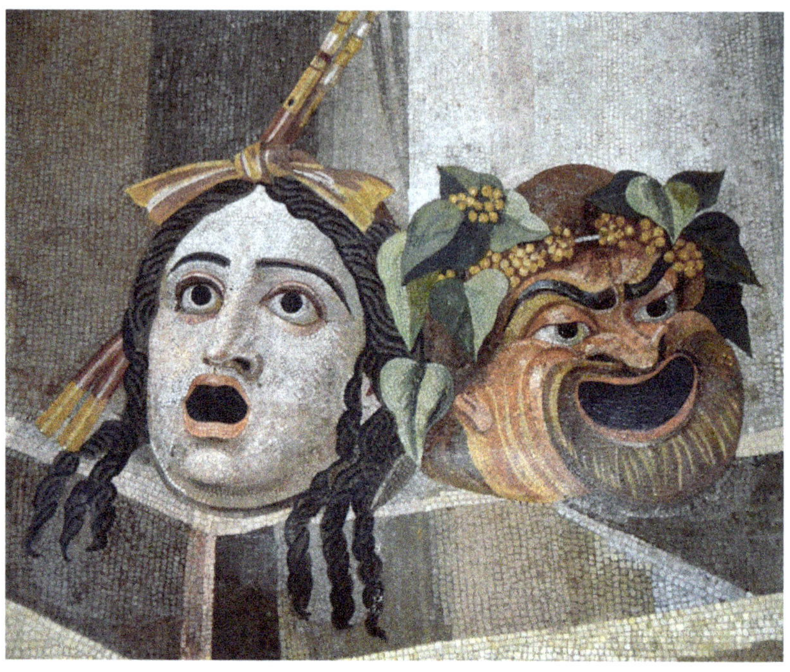

Theatrical masks of Tragedy and Comedy. Mosaic, Roman artwork, 2nd century CE. Capitoline Museums, Rome
(Capitoline Museums / Public domain / Wikimedia Commons)

In France the National Assembly instituted the freedom of theatres with the Chapelier Law in 1791 which resulted in a less autocratic censor and an increase in the number of theatres. New theatres with large capacities of up to two thousand people allowed for greater working-class access and political engagement with the debates of the time, and French theatre became famous for the quantity and quality of the plays produced.

The Nineteenth Century – Romantic reaction and the rise of Realism

The growth of Romanticism in Germany and France eventually affected writing for the theatre as Romanticist nationalism, with a growing interest in a return to medievalist faith in feeling and instinct, acted as a guide to moral behavior. These two opposing philosophies of Neoclassicism (Enlightenment ideas rooted in science and reason) and Romanticism (based on feeling and faith) eventually clashed in France where the Comédie Française maintained a strong Neoclassical hold over the repertory.

The tensions between the two opposing outlooks eventually resulted in conflict. On the night of the premiere of the drama *Hernani* by Victor Hugo (1802–1885) in 1830, riots erupted. They became known as the "Battle of Hernani", whereby:

> The large crowd that attended the premiere was full of conservatives and censors who booed the show for disobeying the classical norms and who wanted to stop the performance from going forward. But Hugo organized a Romantic Army of bohemian and radical writers to ensure that the opening would have to go ahead. The resulting riot represented the rejection in France of the classical traditions and the triumph of Romanticism.[218]

Hugo's Romantic army of writers and artists attacked Classicist positions and exclaimed: "Down with theories and systems! Let us tear away the old lath-and-plaster hiding the face of art! There are neither rules nor models; or, rather, no rules but the general laws of Nature!"[219]

This triumph of Romanticism meant a move away from structure and realism and the rise of a more personalised, individualistic philosophy looking inwards to the self, not to mention an irrational rejection of progress and a return to ideas of faith and hierarchy.

By the 1870s political events and social reforms led to the popularity of the Realist movement and a rejection of Romantic idealism. The Realist movement began in the mid-19th century as a reaction to the irrationalism of Romanticism. However, it was also a reaction to neoclassicism which had become elitist and aristocratic in its assumption of knowledge of Greek and Roman history and myth. The Realists returned to basic ideas of equality, influenced by the French

---

[218] https://en.wikipedia.org/wiki/Nineteenth-century_theatre
[219] https://www.mtholyoke.edu/courses/rschwart/hist255/bohem/thugo.html

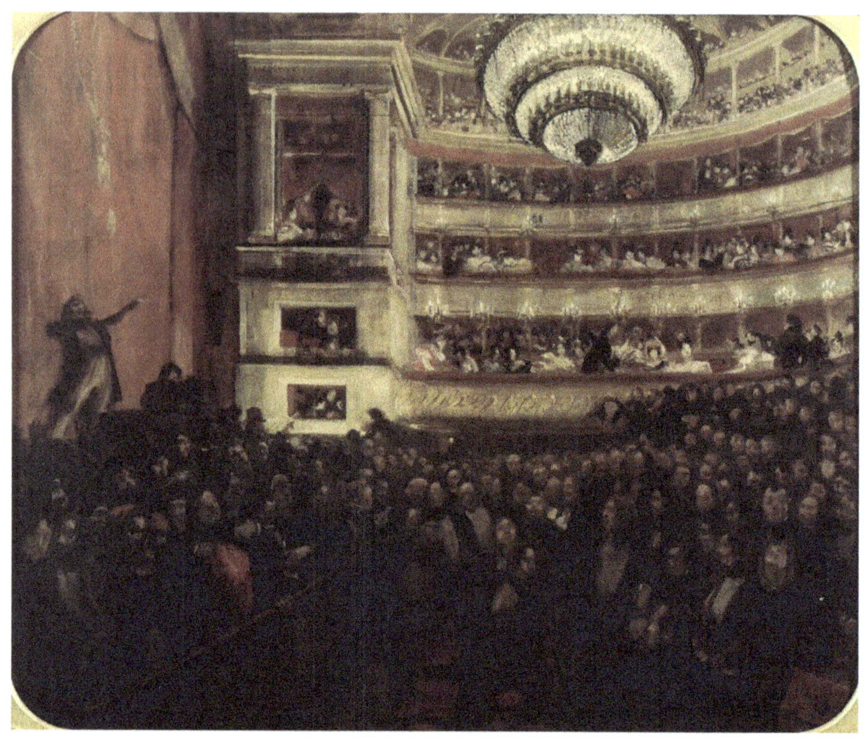

Premiere of the drama *Hernani* by Victor Hugo in 1830
(Paul-Albert Besnard / Public domain / Wikimedia Commons)

revolution and the Utopian Socialists. Realist ideas had a profound effect on both the theatre and its audiences:

> The achievement of realism in the theatre was to direct attention to the social and psychological problems of ordinary life. In its dramas, people emerge as victims of forces larger than themselves, as individuals confronted with a rapidly accelerating world.[220]

Henrik Ibsen (1828–1906), the Norwegian playwright, is known as the "Father of Realism" and he wanted a theatre that was closer in style to real life on the stage. Ibsen attacked middle-class society's values and his plays were based on unconventional subjects, e.g.,

---

[220] https://en.wikipedia.org/wiki/Realism_(arts)

euthanasia, the role of women, war and business, and syphilis in *A Doll's House*. Ibsen questions the roles of men (main provider of the family, public image) and women (limited education) in marriage and society, as well as showing poverty and failed relationships. Realism offered a new type of drama, one in which the public and society could relate to. Ibsen developed the form of the Well-Made play:

1. Soliloquies and asides were discarded
2. Exposition in the plays was motivated
3. Causally related scenes
4. Inner psychological motivation was emphasized
5. Recognition of environmental influences
6. Acknowledgement of socio-economic milieu[221]

He encouraged a style of dialogue which would be more realistic and easier to understand. However, what Realism did have in common with Neo-Classicism was the desire to make theatre more useful in the progressive development of society:

The mainstream theatre from 1859 to 1900 was still bound up in melodramas, spectacle plays (disasters, etc.), comic operas, and vaudevilles. [...] Technological advances were also encouraged by industry and trade, leading to an increased belief that science could solve human problems. But the working classes still had to fight for every increase in rights: unionization and strikes became the principal weapons workers would use after the 1860s—but success came only from costly work stoppages and violence. In other words, there seems to be rejection of Romantic idealism; pragmatism reigned instead. The common man seemed to feel that he needed to be recognized, and people asserted themselves through action.[222]

Other writers in the Realistic form include George Bernard Shaw (1856-1950) in England and Anton Chekhov (1860-1904) in Rus-

---

[221] https://novaonline.nvcc.edu/eli/spd130et/realism.htm
[222] https://novaonline.nvcc.edu/eli/spd130et/realism.htm

sia. Shaw made fun of society's norms for the purpose of educating and changing society. He used witty humor to present contemporary views and then showed their consequences by putting forward his own ideas. Chekhov's plays concentrated on psychological reality showing people trapped in social situations and having hope in hopeless situations.

The Twentieth Century and Modernism

The influence of Realism continued into the twentieth century where it morphed into different forms such as Naturalism and Socialist realism. Naturalism is the idea that all beings and events in the universe are natural (i.e. not supernatural) and can therefore be scientifically investigated. In the arts this led the idea of actions, inclinations, or thoughts based only on natural desires and instincts. Naturalism has also been used in theatre and cinema to present scenes or content verbatim i.e. with no editing.

Meanwhile the Romanticist basis of Modernism could be seen in the characteristic emphasis on an internal life of dreams and fantasies in Symbolist theatre[223] and in the subjective perceptions of reality in Expressionist theatre in Germany.

Realism, on the other hand, flourished in Russia where Konstantin Stanislavski (1863–1938) and Vladimir Nemirovich-Danchenko (1858–1943) founded the Moscow Art Theatre in 1897. Both were committed to the idea of a popular theatre. Stanislavski developed "psychological realism" which differed from his own Naturalistic early stagings:

> Naturalism, for him, implied the indiscriminate reproduction of the surface of life. Realism, on the other hand, while taking its material from the real world and from direct observation, selected only those elements which revealed the relationships and tendencies under the surface. The rest was discarded. [224]

---

[223] https://en.wikipedia.org/wiki/Symbolism_(arts)#Theatre
[224] https://en.wikipedia.org/wiki/Realism_(theatre)

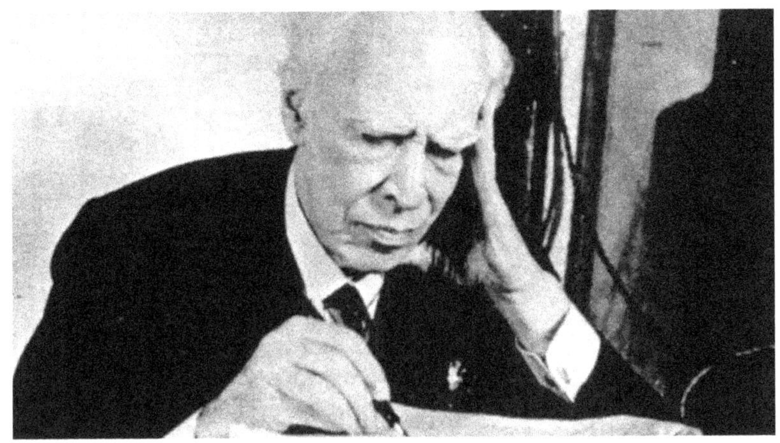

Stanislavski at work in the final year of his life
(Public domain / Wikimedia Commons)

The revolt against theatrical artifice with Realism and later Naturalism produced a new type of theatre which made Stanislavski famous and his theatre very successful.

Later in the 1930s Stanislavski's method would become an important element in the Socialist Realist ideology introduced by the USSR Union of Writers in the mid-1930s. The aim of Stanislavski's method was ultimately to absorb the audience completely in the fictional world of the play.[225]

The contemporary playwright, Bertolt Brecht (1898–1956) in Germany, reacted to this method which he believed was 'escapist' as he felt that any radical content would be blunted, that catharsis would leave the audience complacent. However, Stanislavski believed the audience would observe and learn from the action on stage (using the dialectics of thesis/antithesis/synthesis) in an updated politicised Neo-Classicism. If action proceeded from awareness, then the audience would not be complacent but would achieve catharsis through political action instead.

Brecht, in the Modernist fashion, developed what he called Epic theatre which sought to historicize and address social and political issues. He used innovative techniques, one of which he called the *Verfremdungseffekt* (translated as 'defamiliarization effect', 'dis-

---

[225] https://en.wikipedia.org/wiki/Konstantin_Stanislavski

tancing effect', or 'estrangement effect'). To do this,

> Brecht employed techniques such as the actor's direct address to the audience, harsh and bright stage lighting, the use of songs to interrupt the action, explanatory placards, the transposition of text to the third person or past tense in rehearsals, and speaking the stage directions out loud.[226]

The contrast between the Stanislavski's and Brecht's methods show very differing attitudes of the audience's capacity for understanding and assimilating the content of a play. Charlie Chaplin (1889–1977) used one of these 'distancing effects' when speaking directly to the audience at the end of his film *The Great Dictator*, which some believe led to a decrease in his popularity. The audience may feel that the actors are speaking down to them, or insisting on radical action without first knowing and understanding all aspects of the issue being presented. It has to be questioned whether it is necessary to 'knock people out of their complacency', and instead to give an audience credit for their ability to understand the message solely from the action on stage. The Modernist experimentation with forms also led to elite forms of culture such as James Joyce's (1882–1941) *Finnegans Wake* as the ultimate abstruse example.

As the century wore on other types of political theatre emerged such as the differing forms of Documentary theatre of the 1960s and 1970s. This style of theatre

> uses pre-existing documentary material (such as newspapers, government reports, interviews, journals, and correspondences) as source material for stories about real events and people, frequently without altering the text in performance. The genre typically includes or is referred to as verbatim theatre, investigative theatre, theatre of fact, theatre of witness, autobiographical theatre, and ethnodrama.[227]

While the presentation of pre-existing material may seem dry

---

[226] https://en.wikipedia.org/wiki/Bertolt_Brecht
[227] https://en.wikipedia.org/wiki/Documentary_theatre

and undramatic, it was the partisan interpretation and presentation of the material which gives it its artistic power. In other words, its Realist, rather than Naturalist, interpretation made all the difference to what may appear to be a Naturalist form (i.e. using material verbatim).

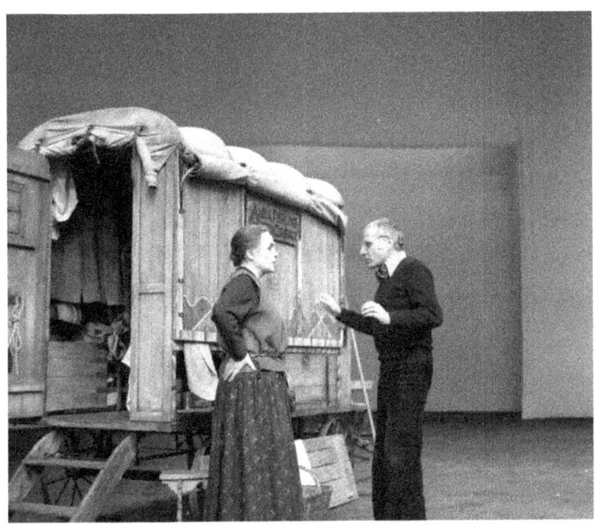

Manfred Wekwerth and Gisela May during rehearsals of *Mother Courage and Her Children* (1978), a play written in 1939 by the German dramatist and poet Bertolt Brecht (1898–1956)
(Bundesarchiv, Bild 183-T0927-019 / Katja Rehfeld /
CC-BY-SA 3.0, CC BY-SA 3.0 DE / Wikimedia Commons)

Another type of alternative theatre which emerged in the late twentieth century (though in some countries it has been around a lot longer) is Community theatre. It refers to a style of theatre which exists in the community itself and can be created entirely by the community, as a collaboration between the community and professionals or put on by professionals especially for that community. Ideologically it can have a very wide outreach and can be seen:

to contribute to the social capital of a community, insofar as it develops the skills, community spirit, and artistic sensibilities of those who participate, whether as producers or audience-members. It is used as a tool for social development, promoting ideas like gender equality, human rights, environment and democracy. Most of the community theatre practices have been developed based on the philosophy of education theorist Paulo Freire's approach of critical pedagogy in theatre and implementation techniques built by Augusto Boal, known as Theatre of the Oppressed.[228]

Paulo Freire's (1921–1997) method was to promote social change by getting the audience to participate in critical thinking through dialogue, identifying concerns, solutions and examining different perspectives. Augusto Boal's (1931–2009) plays would be performed "on streets, public places, in traditional meeting spaces, schools, prisons, or other institutions, inviting an alternative and often spontaneous audience to watch."[229]

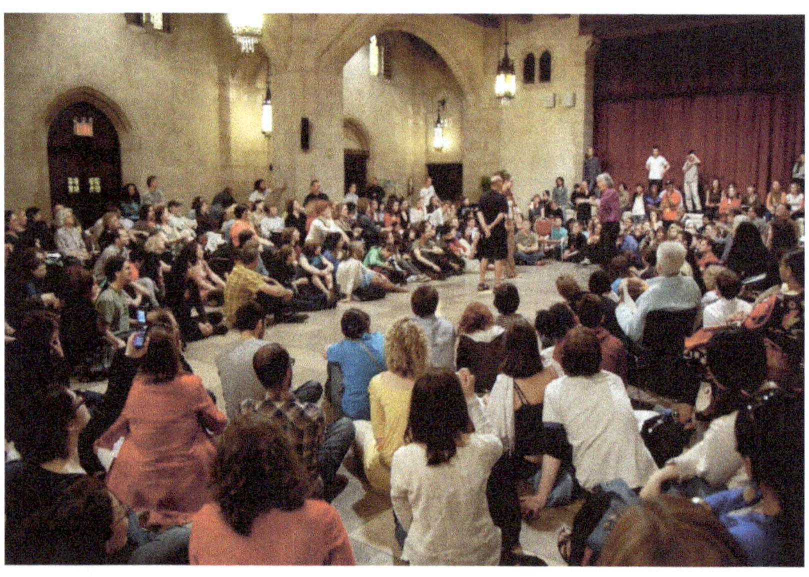

Augusto Boal presenting his workshop on the Theatre of the Oppressed. Riverside Church, May 13, 2008
(Thehero / CC BY-SA 3.0 / Wikimedia Commons)

Boal's approach also breaks down the 'invisible wall' between

---

[228] https://en.wikipedia.org/wiki/Community_theatre
[229] https://en.wikipedia.org/wiki/Community_theatre

actors and audience but the difference being that the audience determines the action on stage not the playwright. For example, Boal writes:

> The spectators feel that they can intervene in the action. The action ceases to be presented in a deterministic manner, as something inevitable, as Fate. Man is Man's fate. Thus Man-the-spectator is the creator of Man-the-character. Everything is subject to criticism, to rectification. All can be changed, and at a moment's notice: the actors must always be ready to accept, without protest, any proposed action; they must simply act it out, to give a live view of its consequences and drawbacks.[230]

Twenty-First Century – State Theatre v Community Theatre

In the twenty-first century State Theatre and Community Theatre exist side by side but as the global economic crisis deepens the traditional repertoire of the State theatre may seem to become outdated and distant from social issues.

Community theatre is a form which, like the ballad form in music, is capable of tackling and analysing contemporary issues in a very short period of time. However, the tendency of the state is to try to absorb all opposition into its own conservative narrative and 'de-fang' it. This tendency is discussed by the poet Fran Lock in detail:

> This matters, because the people traditionally holding the purse strings, controlling the presses; the people responsible for funding us and publishing us, are the same power elites who decide what constitutes a valid working-class voice, and an acceptable working-class identity. Arts Council England, for example, has nothing to gain from supporting people and projects who challenge or threaten their traditional

---

[230] *Theatre of the Oppressed*, Augusto Boal (Pluto Press: London, 1998), p.134.

business model, and most major publishers are wary of a working-class poetics that openly and explicitly acknowledges the politics of its own oppression. To have your work "out there" in any meaningful sense, to secure the invaluable financial assistance by which a creative project lives or dies, is to accept that your work, and that you, as a person, will be mediated, filtered and enmeshed, by and in the machinery of a grossly unequal hierarchy. By this method we are compromised. We tailor and shape our voices and ourselves to fit their image of us, and our working-classness is depoliticised and de-fanged through an act of caricature. By this mechanism is the triumph of working-class representation transformed into the tool by which working-class participation in the arts is edited, eroded and policed.[231]

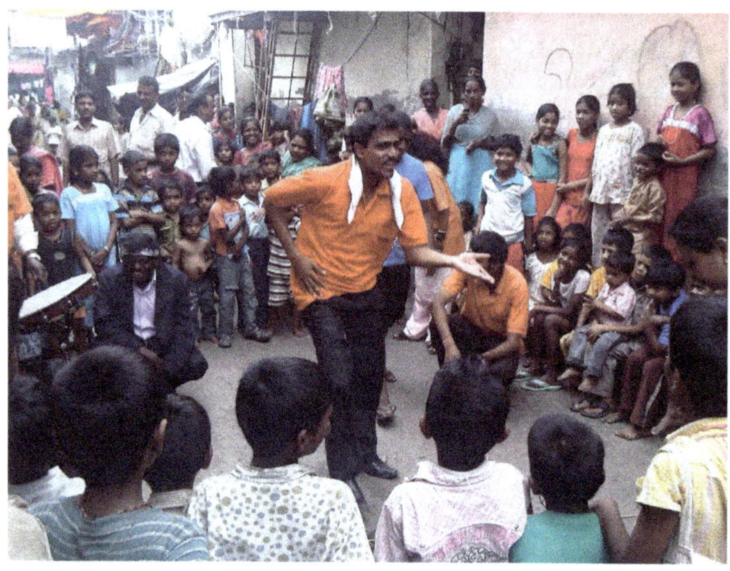

A street play (nukkad natak) in Dharavi slums in Mumbai
(GiveWell / CC BY 3.0 / Wikimedia Commons)

Another important aspect which she alludes to is the problem of monolithism ('shape[ing] our voices and ourselves to fit their image

---

[231] 'Don't mention the word class! The theft of working-class culture', Fran Lock https://www.culturematters.org.uk/index.php/arts/poetry/item/2901-don-t-mention-the-word-class-the-theft-of-working-class-culture

of us') which is the way dissent can be silenced by portraying minority groups as being made up of similar people all sharing similar views. As Kenan Malik writes:

> Multiculturalists tend to treat minority communities as if each was a distinct, singular, homogenous, authentic whole, each composed of people all speaking with a single voice, each defined primarily by a singular view of culture and faith. In so doing, they all too often ignore conflicts within those communities. All the dissent and diversity gets washed out. As a result, the most progressive voices often get silenced as not being truly of that community or truly authentic, while the most conservative voices get celebrated as community leaders, the authentic voices of minority groups.[232]

These are the kinds of difficulties community theatre faces, in particular, problems which are more accentuated where access is provided by a State theatre. However, in the streets, manipulation or outright censorship/rejection is much more difficult. And like the original Morality plays, the community theatre may have an ideological aspect which is equally difficult to moderate.

The Romantic/Modernist influence can still be seen in 'mainstream' (non-community theatre) in the emphasis on formal experimentation over sociopolitical content in projections of the future of theatre, for example, one critic M. A. Haridy writes:

> Firstly, in the experimental works in the new theatre groups and companies, which we call; the off existing established theatres [e.g. off-Broadway, off-West End]. Secondly, in the rise of the theatrical movements of the early and mid last century. Thirdly, in the works of some established theatres; and here we stress the word 'some'; that works is done mainly by some courageous directors.[233]

---

[232] 'What's the problem with multiculturalism?', Kenan Malik. See: https://kenanmalik.com/2014/10/16/whats-the-problem-with-multiculturalism/

[233] 'Theatre in 21st Century', M A Haridy. See: https://medium.com/@mikeaharidy/theatre-in-21st-century-760a865dd696

However, not all writers are blind to the growing sociopolitical and economic crises developing globally, as another writer writes regarding the future predictions of trends in theatres:

> it is true that technology has really affected theatres in terms of audience attendance and also changes in the overall appearance of the live performances in order to attract more audiences but will there be changes in the 21st-century trends in the cinema industry? Well, experts project the following changes in future: Need for community and people interactions will lead more people to the theatres. The increase in smaller theatres located in all parts of the country to attract more people to the theatres. Younger directors and actors will ensure more performances in the smaller theatres and the main focus will be on issues, news, and concerns of the immediate community.[234]

Thus, it can be seen there are mixed opinions on the future of 'official' theatre based in large and small theatres. It could be speculated that the 'small theatre' end and community-based theatre would be set for conflict as the professional and the amateur clash over what is to be portrayed and how, particularly if the issues raised and their resolution are perceived from widely differing ideological perspectives.

Throughout the last four centuries theatre has been pushed and pulled in many directions. It has been used by cliques for their own class entertainment. It has been forced many times in the direction of benefiting the greater good and dragged back again to serve elite agendas. However, the capability of theatre for examining social, political, and more recently, animal and climate issues in an immediate and negotiable way, will ensure that theatre as a mirror of society will be a difficult form for the state to control.

---

[234] http://www.nyctheatretickets.net/spiderman-turn-off-the-dark-foxwoods-theatre/

Chapter 10

Architecture

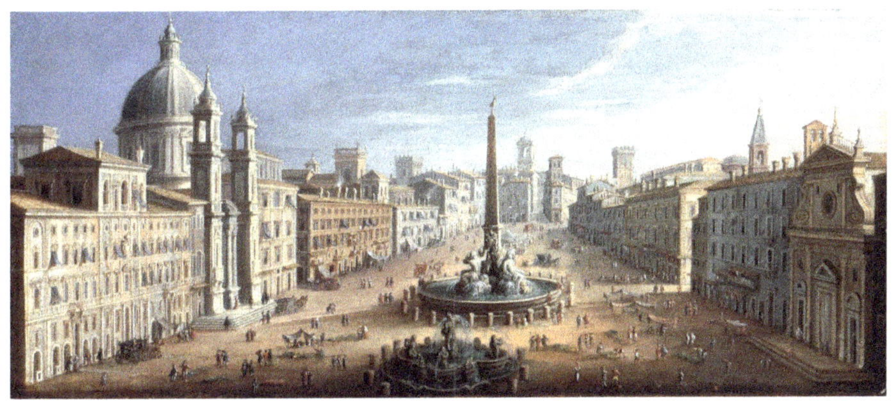

View of Piazza Navona (c. 1730) by Hendrik Frans van Lint (1684–1763)
(Public domain / Wikimedia Commons)

People ignore design that ignores people.
Frank Chimero

Neoliberalism, Climate Change and Architecture

> *We used to build temples, and museums are about as
> close as secular society dares to go in facing up to the
> idea that a good building can change your life
> (and a bad one ruin it).*
> Alain de Botton

> *Like medicine (architecture)
> must move from the curative to the preventive.*
> Cedric Price

What is the future for architecture in these times of climate change
and economic crises? Should sustainability and affordability be a
major factor in the design and development of future buildings?
What about aesthetics? There are many individual examples of
modern buildings today that have positive aesthetic qualities, but
can major future problems, like climate change, be resolved by individual efforts? Or will it take the role of the state with grand visions
for the future? While architecture may not seem to be an important
issue compared with unemployment or poverty, it is one of the most
important of the arts in terms of longevity, function and expense.
And its meaning can go beyond mere buildings to symbolism of the
state and national values.

The question of aesthetics is complex as modern architectural
design is "caught between the diminished architecture of the 99%
and the austere architecture of the 1%", while at the same time architecture is pulled between popular opinion of what is good design
and elite views that often contradict.

It is also well known that the production of cement is polluting. Therefore, many architectural projects now emphasize sustainability, like housing schemes to be built from cross-laminated timber and powered by renewable energy, bricks made of recycled construction waste, schemes that will be carbon neutral and function off-grid, plans for the world's first wooden football stadium, and other housing schemes that will be made from sustainably harvested local wood and save 100s of megatons of carbon in the process.[235]

However, no matter how sustainable these projects are, there is no escaping the aesthetic values of design which will ultimately sustain the building into eternity or see it eventually blown up to the smiles of hordes of ill-wishers.

So why is design so important for something which is ultimately functional? Is it because we have to look at these buildings for a very long time once they are constructed? How do we decide what is beautiful and why?

The whole history of architecture is riddled with controversies. Often what is considered beautiful now was criticized during its own time. Buildings have been knocked down and blown up in many different kinds of situations. Indeed, some have even been rebuilt exactly as before under controversial circumstances or postwar.

Today the debate still goes on about aesthetics and architecture with functional styles overtaking decorative styles only to be overtaken by decorative styles again. What determines these changes? Do political and economic systems play an important role in the kind of aesthetics which become preeminent? And if so, why? Did socio-political-economic systems such as hierarchical feudalism, industrialized capitalism, or state socialism play important roles? Does Neo-liberalism today? How relevant have the opinions of the users and builders of these edifices been?

Maybe more than all the other arts, architecture has been highly affected by the conflict between Enlightenment and Romanticist ideas ever since the Italian architect and designer Brunelleschi visited Rome to study the ancient ruins of classical Roman architecture in 1432. The Romanticist reaction to Neoclassical architecture

---

[235] https://www.dezeen.com/tag/sustainable-architecture/

materialized later in the form of Neo-Gothic architecture from the 1740s onwards. Since then architecture has been influenced by, *inter alia*, Modernism, Postmodernism and Neoliberalism. Now other pressures are coming to bear on architectural design such as sustainability in the face of climate chaos, and criticism such as that by the architect Juhani Pallasmaa who argues against 'cities of alienation' and for a 'human architecture'.

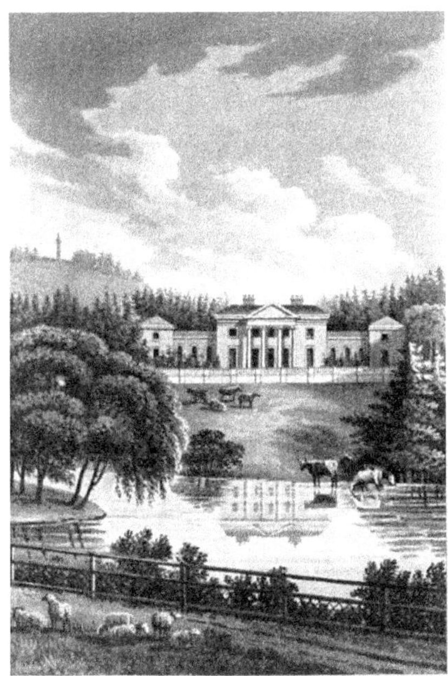
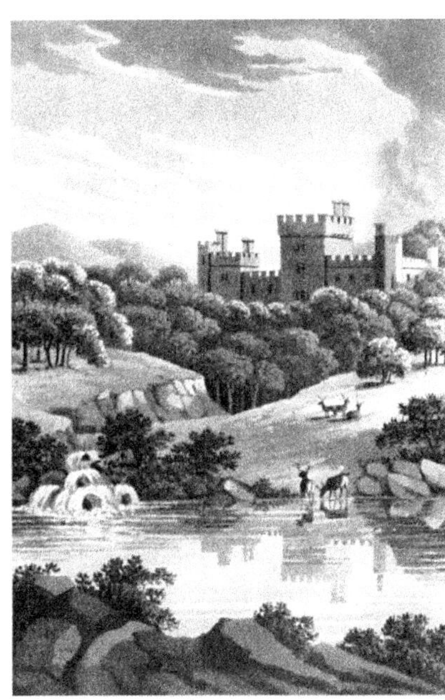

A Feb. 1st 1816 print (published J. Taylor, London) which exemplifies the contrast between neo-classical vs. romantic styles of landscape and architecture (or the "Grecian" and the "Gothic" as they're termed here). This engraved plate accompanied Humphry Repton's 1816 book *Fragments on the Theory and Practice of Landscape Gardening* (Public domain / Wikimedia Commons)

Renaissance architecture

The rise of the bourgeoisie in the form of the Medicis in Italy guided a major change in architecture from the Romanesque and Gothic styles of earlier times to the new Renaissance designs based on ancient Greek and Roman architecture. The earlier medieval styles had been largely used by feudal kings, and bishops of the powerful Catholic church for their castles and cathedrals. Gothic had grown organically out of Romanesque designs over time, for example, the small roof on medieval belfries became taller and thinner until it was eventually incorporated into the belfry as a Gothic spire.

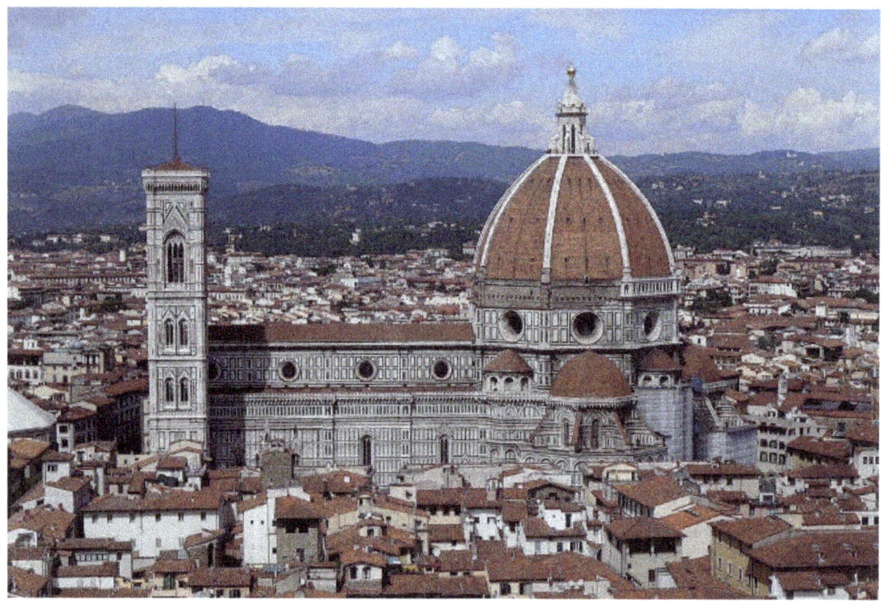

Filippo Brunelleschi (1377–1446), in the building of the dome of Florence Cathedral (Italy) in the early 15th century (1296-1436), not only transformed the building and the city, but also the role and status of the architect
(Bruce Stokes on Flickr / CC BY-SA 2.0 / Wikimedia Commons)

The revival of Classical learning in Rome went along with Enlightenment ideas, Renaissance humanism, and the development of science and engineering. It is interesting to note that Brunelleschi's first architectural commission was the Ospedale degli Innocenti (1419–c. 1445), or Foundling Hospital, designed as a home for orphans. His next project was the Basilica of San Lorenzo the location of the tombs of the Medici family who sponsored the church – rather than castles or cathedrals.

The study of the ancient ruins in Italy (Rome and Pompeii) and Greece (Athens) led to a clearer understanding of the difference between Greek and Roman architecture and subsequently to consciously Greek, Roman and Greco-Roman hybrids of Neoclassical design.[236]

This knowledge was expressed in the Renaissance style, a style which was consciously brought to fruition through learning and a desire to revive the ideas of the 'Golden Age'. The humanistic learning of the time set forth a positive conception of man (in opposition to the 'fallen man' of the established church) and was seen in Ovid's *Metamorphoses* (7 CE), where he describes the lost Golden Age as a time in which nature and reason were aligned and produced naturally good men:

> The Golden Age was first; when Man, yet new,
> No rule but uncorrupted Reason knew:
> And, with a native bent, did good pursue.
> Unforc'd by punishment, un-aw'd by fear.[237]

This view reflected the new learning that man could have an optimistic view of the future and control nature to create a better life for all. In Renaissance architecture, "symmetry, proportion, geometry and the regularity of parts", would reflect a more dignified mode of existence combined with concepts of equality, citizenship and republican organization of society. Renaissance architecture depicted "orderly arrangements of columns, pilasters [rectangular columns] and lintels [horizontal supports], as well as the use of semicircular arches, hemispherical domes, niches [shallow recesses] and aediculae [small shrines] replaced the more complex proportional systems and irregular profiles of medieval buildings."[238]

---

[236] http://www.essential-humanities.net/western-art/architecture/neoclassical-romantic/
[237] https://en.wikipedia.org/wiki/Golden_Age
[238] https://en.wikipedia.org/wiki/Renaissance_architecture

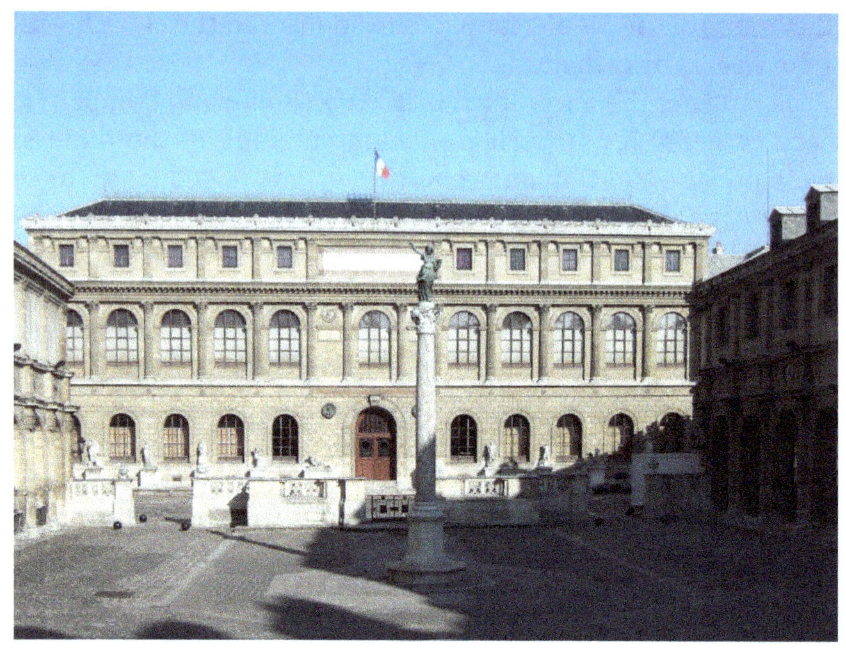

Palais des études of the École nationale supérieure des Beaux-Arts, Paris, 1830
(Selbymay / CC BY-SA 3.0 / Wikimedia Commons)

Neoclassical architecture

By the mid eighteenth-century Renaissance architecture developed into full blown Neoclassicism and became an international style as it was adopted by progressive circles in other countries particularly for the design of public buildings. The Neoclassical style incorporated many decorations such as mascarons [symbolic faces], cartouches [oval or oblong designs], festoons [wreaths or garlands], corbels [a type of bracket], various leaves and branches, rustications [contrasting textures], trophies, horns of abundance, lion heads, female faces or designs from other applied arts. The enduring popularity of Neoclassical architecture and the type of feeling that it produced in the spectator is reflected on by J.E. Gordon who writes:

Nowadays, whether we like it or not, we are stuck with one form or another of advanced technology and we have got to make it work safely and efficiently: this involves, among other things, the intelligent application of structural theory. However, man does not live by safety and efficiency alone, and we have to face the fact that, visually, the world is becoming an increasingly depressing place. It is not, perhaps, so much the occurrence of what might be described as 'active ugliness' as the prevalence of the dull and the commonplace. Far too seldom is the heart rejoiced or does one feel any better or happier for looking at the works of modern man. Yet most of the artefacts of the eighteenth century, even quite humble and trivial ones, seem to many of us to be at least pleasing and sometimes incomparably beautiful. To that extent people — all people — in the eighteenth century lived richer lives than most of us do today.[239]

An important form of Neoclassicism was the Beaux-Arts architecture which originated in the École des Beaux-Arts in Paris, particularly from the 1830s to the end of the nineteenth-century. It was very popular in the United States from 1885 to 1920, and its very last, large public projects included the Lincoln Memorial (1922), the National Gallery in Washington, D.C. (1937), and the American Museum of Natural History's Roosevelt Memorial (1936).[240]

The most important aspect of Beaux Arts architecture, aside from its study of Greek or Roman models, was its sculptural decorations with balustrades, pilasters, festoons, and cartouches, also included "statuary, sculpture (bas-relief panels, figural sculptures, sculptural groups), murals, mosaics, and other artwork, all coordinated in theme to assert the identity of the building." Neoclassicism also influenced city planning as "the grid system of streets, a central forum with city services, two main slightly wider boulevards, and the occasional diagonal street were characteristic of the very logical and orderly Roman design" as well as highlighting important public buildings.[241]

---

[239] J.E. Gordon, Structures: Or Why Things Don't Fall Down, https://www.goodreads.com/work/quotes/237710-structures-or-why-things-don-t-fall-down

[240] https://en.wikipedia.org/wiki/Beaux-Arts_architecture

[241] https://en.wikipedia.org/wiki/Neoclassical_architecture

The Romanticist reaction to republicanism and liberalism

The growing secularism and the rise of evangelicalism in the eighteenth and early nineteenth-centuries did not go unnoticed by philosophical movements associated with Catholicism and high church or Anglo-Catholic beliefs. The influence of Romanticist medievalism and anti-industrialism could be seen in the Gothic Revival that began in the late 1740s in England. Figures like the conservative architect, Augustus Pugin, believed that Christian values were being destroyed by Classicism and industrialization. These reactionary ideas took on political connotations:

> with the 'rational' and 'radical' Neoclassical style being seen as associated with republicanism and liberalism (as evidenced by its use in the United States and to a lesser extent in Republican France), the more spiritual and traditional Gothic Revival became associated with monarchism and conservatism, which was reflected by the choice of styles for the rebuilt government centres of the UK Parliament's Palace of Westminster in London, the Canadian Parliament Buildings in Ottawa, and the Hungarian Parliament Building.[242]

However, by the beginning of the twentieth century the "academic refinement of historical styles" was beginning to be perceived as the architecture of a declining aristocratic order. The move away from Gothic decoration could be seen in the Modernist architects favouring of functional details over historical references. Their designs exhibited and revealed functional and structural elements such as steel beams and concrete surfaces.[243]

Modernist architecture

As Romanticism changed into Modernism, the Romanticist interest in the decorative medieval and feudal craft form of production sud-

---

[242] https://en.wikipedia.org/wiki/Gothic_Revival_architecture
[243] https://en.wikipedia.org/wiki/Architecture

denly changed into its opposite as formalism and a minimalist aesthetic took its place instead. Modernism, in its dismissal of tradition, rejected classical notions of form in art (harmony, symmetry, and order) and, like Romanticism, rejected the 'certainty' of Enlightenment thinking. Modernism emphasized form over political content and rejected the ideology of Realism and Enlightenment thinking on liberty and progress.

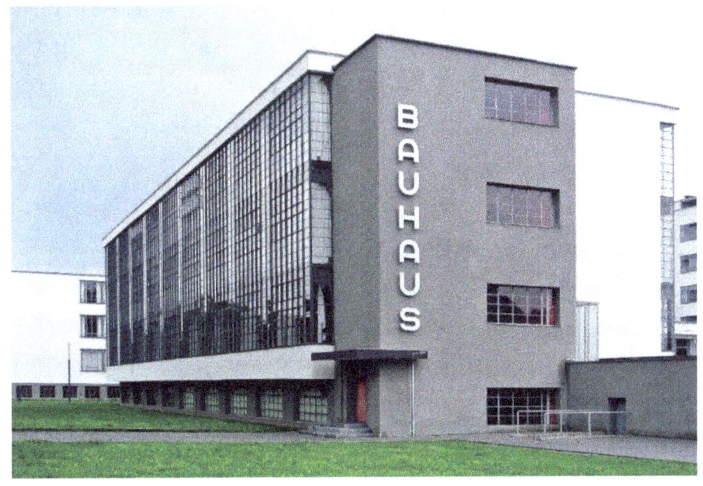

The Bauhaus building in Dessau was designed by Walter Gropius (1883–1969). It was the longest serving of the three Bauhaus locations (1925–1932)
(Spyrosdrakopoulos / CC BY-SA 4.0 / Wikimedia Commons)

The epitome of this style in architecture became most developed in the Bauhaus art and design movement that began in 1919 in Weimar, Germany. It was a style which "championed a geometric, abstract style featuring little sentiment or emotion and no historical nods", an austere aesthetic which threw the baby out with the bathwater:

The Bauhaus style of architecture featured rigid angles of glass, masonry and steel, together creating patterns and resulting in buildings that some historians characterize as looking as if no human had a hand in their creation. These austere aesthetics favored function and mass production, and were influential in the worldwide redesign of everyday buildings that did not hint at any class structure or hierarchy.[244]

The Bauhaus style (also known as the International Style) was consciously cosmopolitan in its ahistorical designs and principles of mass production. Many Germans of the time had been influenced by the cultural experimentation that was happening in the Soviet Union after the Russian Revolution, particularly Constructivism which had originated in Russia beginning in 1913.

Constructivist architecture

Constructivism was a form of Modernist architecture that developed in the Soviet Union in the 1920s and early 1930s. It emerged out of earlier broader art movements such as Futurism and Suprematism. Russian Futurism was a movement of Russian poets and artists who rejected the past and celebrated "machinery, violence, youth, industry, destruction of academies, museums, and urbanism". These ideas were based on Filippo Tommaso Marinetti's (Italian poet, editor, art theorist) Futurist Manifesto, which was written and published in 1909.[245]

Marinetti wrote: "We want to glorify war – the only cure for the world – militarism, patriotism, the destructive gesture of the anarchists, the beautiful ideas which kill",[246] and later, in 1919, co-wrote the Fascist Manifesto with Alceste De Ambris. Suprematism was "characterised by basic geometric forms, such as circles, squares, lines and rectangles, painted in a limited range of colours".[247]

Thus, we can see that Constructivism grew out of the highly individualistic, anti-historical, nihilistic, pared-down forms of Modernist art, typical of Romanticist ideas.

---

[244] https://www.history.com/topics/art-history/bauhaus
[245] https://en.wikipedia.org/wiki/Russian_Futurism
[246] https://www.theartstory.org/movement/futurism/history-and-concepts/
[247] https://www.intellectualtakeout.org/article/what-original-fascist-manifesto-said/

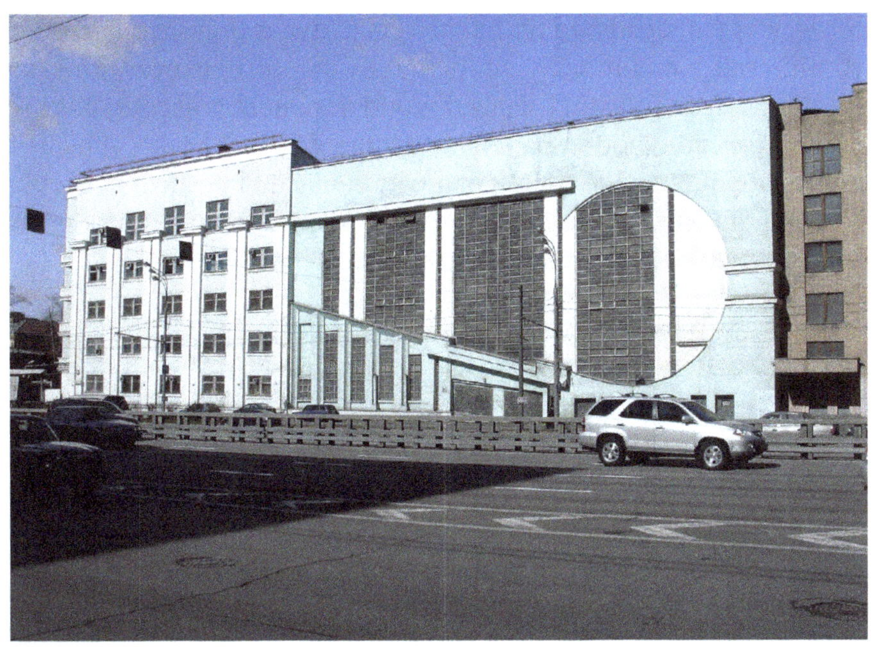

Intourist Garage by Konstantin Melnikov, 1933
(NVO / CC BY-SA 2.5 / Wikimedia Commons)

By the end of the 1920s, Constructivism was the dominant architecture of the Soviet Union. Gradually a reaction to Constructivism started with a combination of Art Deco influenced Classicism and elements of Constructivism. The move away from Constructivist pared-down forms and back to decoration and craft could already be seen in Europe and America with the introduction of Art Deco influences from the mid-1920s. Art Deco buildings featured a lot of surface decoration around windows and doors, and especially around the tops of skyscrapers. This decoration was done in low relief and combined many geometric patterns and figures.[248]

In 1932, a major competition to design the Palace of the Soviets was won by Boris Iofan in a style which became known as Stalinist Architecture or Socialist Classicism. The move to Classicism was not surprising as criticism of Modernist austerity took hold. The major projects of the time, skyscrapers, the Moscow Metro and apartment

---

[248] https://study.com/academy/lesson/art-deco-architecture-characteristics-history-definition.html

blocks, were all designed with Classical features that included much art and craft elements. These included sculpture, friezes, mosaics, molding, stucco [plaster], carved wooden panels, frescoes, bass relief, and carved wooden panels. After the death of Stalin, the 'luxurious' style of Socialist Classicism was replaced by Khrushchyovka, the name given to a type of low-cost, concrete-paneled Modernist building style supervised by Nikita Khrushchev.

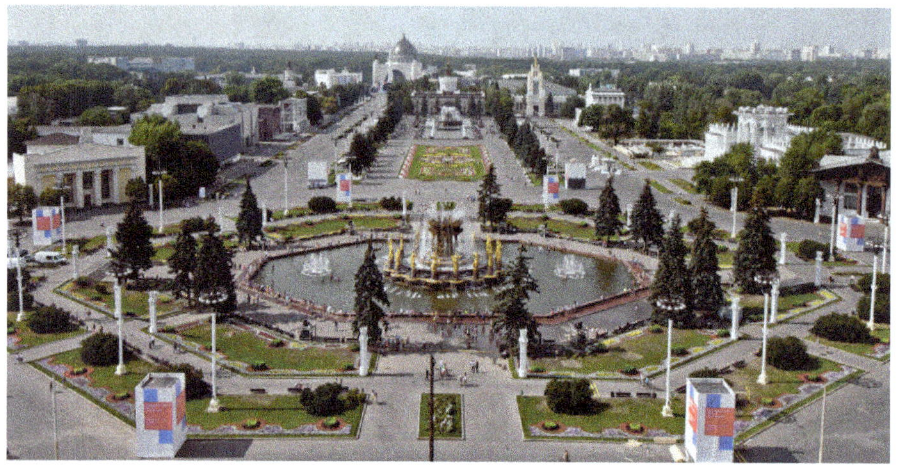

The central square. Exhibition of Achievements of
National Economy, Moscow, 1935
(Vystavka Dostizheniy Narodnogo Khozyaystva,
abbreviated as VDNKh or VDNH)
(Mos.ru / CC BY 4.0 / Wikimedia Commons)

By the late 1960s Modernism was falling out of favour in the West with many Modernist apartment blocks eventually being blown up. The harsh lines of Modernist architecture did not age well and something more artistic was in demand. The austerity, formality, and lack of variety in Modernist architecture was generally criticized for having no relation to architectural history, street plans, or the culture of individual cities. This also led to the re-introduction of craft and historical design elements into a new architectural philosophy called Postmodernism.

Postmodernist architecture

Unfortunately, Postmodernism, a late 20th-century movement characterized by broad skepticism, subjectivism, relativism, irreverence and parody, and a general suspicion of reason, was not too different from the subjectivism, relativism and general suspicion of reason in Romanticist and Modernist ideas. Postmodernist architects approached architecture with eclectic non-contextualized ideas resulting in diverse aesthetics, colliding styles, and form for its own sake producing some very self-indulgent designs. Asymmetric forms were one of the trademarks of Postmodernism as large buildings were broken into different structures and forms, 'Camp' humor was used on the basis that something could appear so bad that it was good, and the theatricality of absurd and exaggerated forms were common. As a style Postmodernist architecture has been criticized as vulgar and populist.[249]

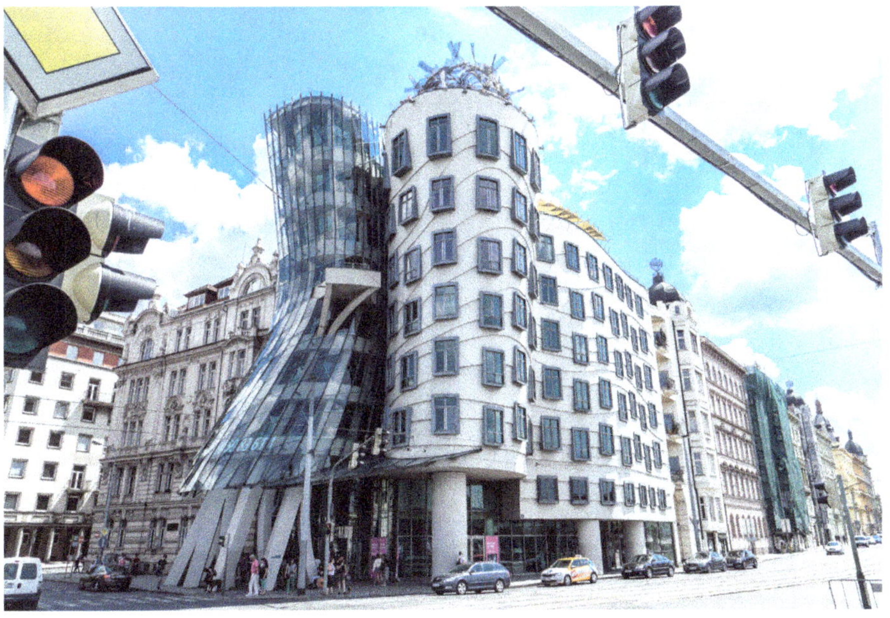

The Dancing House, Prague, Czech Republic, 1996
(Diego Robayo / CC BY-SA 2.0 / Wikimedia Commons)

---

[249] https://en.wikipedia.org/wiki/Postmodern_architecture

However, this diversification of styles subsequently led to varieties of architecture that reflect global political, economic and environmental issues with differing attitudes towards Neoliberalism, climate change, sustainability. These diverse architectural styles reflect the triumph and wealth of the 1%, but they also reflect the growing anxiety around climate chaos and they reflect those who want to design and build a better society into the future for all.

Neoliberal architecture

The influence of free market Neoliberalism on architecture globally has been critiqued by Douglas Spencer as "refashioning human subjects into the compliant figures – student-entrepreneurs, citizen-consumers and team-workers – requisite to the universal implementation of a form of existence devoted to market imperatives."[250] Spencer believes that the architecture of neoliberalism "serves mechanisms of control and compliance while promoting itself, at the same time, as progressive." It does this through the social processes these buildings enforce – "displacement of the poor, privatisation of public space, the decimation of social housing."[251]

It is not surprising that the Neoliberal privatization of the public housing stock on behalf of plutocrats could lead to a push for the privatization of all public space (including Hyde Park in London as suggested by one architect), just as when in the 18th century the aristocracy gradually enclosed the commons. As Bertrand Russell wrote:

Each enclosure required an Act of Parliament, and the aristocrats who controlled both Houses of Parliament ruthlessly used their legislative power to enrich themselves, while thrusting agricultural labourers down to the verge of starvation.[252]

---

[250] https://www.bloomsbury.com/us/the-architecture-of-neoliberalism-9781472581532/

[251] https://www.theguardian.com/books/2017/jan/12/the-architecture-of-neoliberalism-douglas-spencer-review

[252] Bertrand Russell, *A History of Western Philosophy* (Unwin, London, 1984) p 611

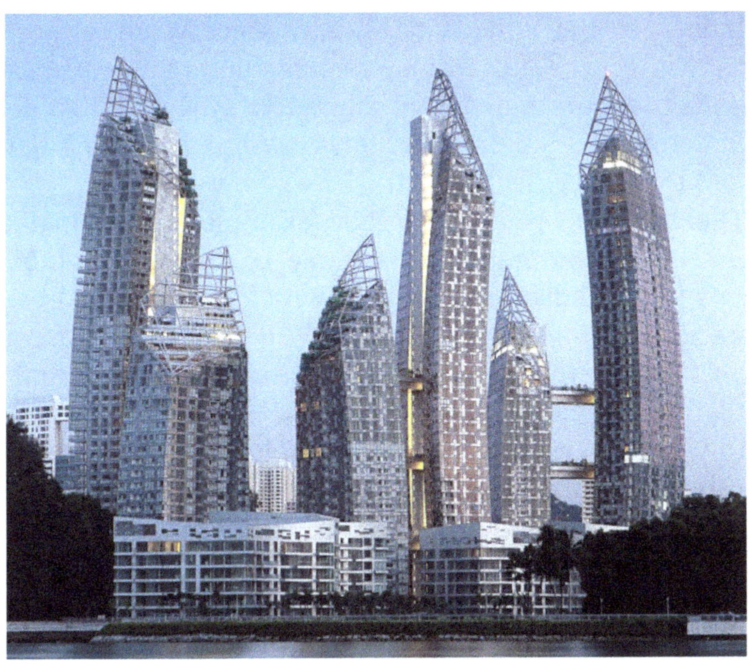

Reflections at Keppel Bay apartment complex in Keppel Bay,
Singapore by Daniel Libeskind (2011)
(Stankn / CC BY-SA 3.0 / Wikimedia Commons)

Sustainable architecture

Other forces were concerned with the negative aspects of untrammeled capitalism and the environment. The desire to bring architecture in line with other 'green' movements since the late 1980s has led to the concept of sustainable architecture:

> Sustainable architecture designs and constructs buildings in order to limit their environmental impact, with the objectives of achieving energy efficiency, positive impacts on health, comfort and improved liveability for inhabitants; all of this can be achieved through the implementation of appropriate technologies within the building [and] making the space and materials employed completely reusable.[253]

---

[253] https://www.lifegate.com/sustainable-architecture-definition-concept-projects-examples

Indeed, in the United States "a vast ecosystem of green commerce has grown" up around sustainable architecture "spurring sales in products ranging from solar panels to low-VOC [Volatile Organic Compounds] paints and low-flow toilets. "Green building is now a $1 trillion global industry,""[254]

The BedZED project is a good example of sustainable architecture in the community. It is in the London Borough of Sutton, 2 miles (3 km) north-east of the town of Sutton itself. Designed to create zero carbon emissions, it was the first large scale community to do so. The distinctive roofscape has solar panels and passive ventilation chimneys.

However, this still leaves the problem of aesthetics, as the Neoliberal designs are highly individualistic architectural enterprises generally in post-modern states which do not have, or desire to have, ultimate control of the ownership or design of such projects.

It is the public realm where the state does have the most control, despite Neoliberal desire to reduce it to nothing. The public realm generally refers to "those areas of a town or city to which the public has access. It includes streets, footpaths, parks, squares, bridges and public buildings and facilities." The public realm is a contested realm where aesthetics are lauded or criticised according to the inclination of the state or the desires of the public but at least broader integrated planning designs can be implemented, unlike Neoliberal ideology which "maintains that 'the market' delivers benefits that could never be achieved by planning." Neoliberalism also "sees competition as the defining characteristic of human relations [and] redefines citizens as consumers."[255]

Such ideology tries to naturalise the logic of capitalism by redefining people in its own image. However, it also reflects the power of elites and their political and economic grip on society as a whole. Styles of art and architecture in society also reflect elite hegemony. This can be seen in the very expensive apartments of luxury condominium towers (designed by 'starchitects') that have very little relationship with their urban neighbourhoods.

---

[254] https://psmag.com/environment/past-present-and-future-of-sustainable-architecture
[255] https://www.heritagecouncil.ie/projects/the-national-public-realm-plan-programme

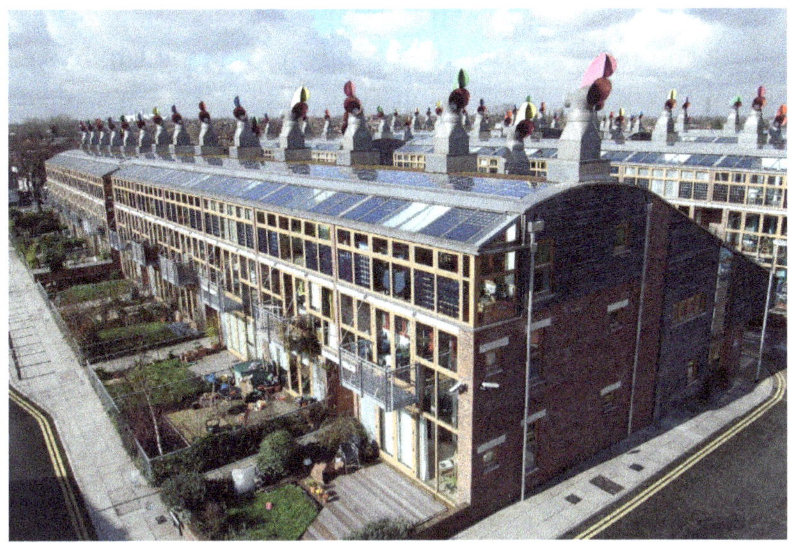

Beddington Zero Energy Development (BedZED)
is an environmentally friendly housing development in
Hackbridge, London, England 2000–2002
(Tom Chance / CC BY 2.0 / Wikimedia Commons)

It can be seen in the designs of skyscrapers for expensive hotels or headquarters of multinational companies. Contemporary designs for concert halls and art museums have had their praisers but also critics of some overwrought designs such as architecture critic Nicolai Ouroussoff's comment on the Denver Art Museum that: "In a building of canted walls and asymmetrical rooms—tortured geometries generated purely by formal considerations — it is virtually impossible to enjoy the art."[256] Frank Gehry's business school building at the University of Technology Sydney has been described as "a creased building [...] which resembles a "squashed brown paper bag".[257]

Like the earlier Modernist designs of the Bauhaus, contempo-

---

[256] 'A Razor-Sharp Profile Cuts Into a Mile-High Cityscape' Nicolai Ouroussoff. See: https://www.nytimes.com/2006/10/12/arts/design/a-razorsharp-profile-cuts-into-a-milehigh-cityscape.html

[257] 'Frank Gehry unveils 'squashed brown paper bag' building in Sydney', Jonathan Pearlman. See: https://www.telegraph.co.uk/news/worldnews/australiaandthepacific/australia/11386370/Frank-Gehry-unveils-squashed-brown-paper-bag-building-in-Sydney.html

rary architectural design can be austere and alienating (or in some cases just asinine) reflecting the confidence and egoism of wealthy elites. It also reflects the economics of our time as the wealthy get to decide the individualistic designs of their residences, work places and entertainment centres, much like the aristocracy of the eighteenth century did.

It has been suggested that the world's most popular architect is Antoni Gaudí (if measured by ticket sales for the Sagrada Família in Barcelona). As Edwin Heathcote notes, "It is not an accident that Gaudí is also the most obsessively decorative architect of modernity." Ornament and decoration in architecture has been a popular aesthetic throughout the centuries. Heathcote also writes:

Ornament is not essential to architecture but people continue to like it. Perhaps architects need to begin thinking why, after their best efforts to educate them otherwise, they still do. Perhaps the people are right and it is indispensable.[258]

Is it because people appreciate ornament, reflecting their love of applied arts and crafts, and respect for the skills that go into making them? We must not forget that decorative arts form an important part of national museum exhibitions around the world. As with any art it can be hard to understand what is popular and why, and what is considered alienating or 'human' in architecture.

The Finnish architect and former professor of architecture, Juhani Pallasmaa, goes a long way in his efforts to understand meaning in architecture. He believes that the Western obsession with sight over all the other senses has led to nihilistic and narcissistic views which have created cities of alienation at the expense of cities of participation. He notes:

The hegemonic eye seeks domination over all fields of cultural production, and it seems to weaken our capacity for empathy, compassion and participation with the world.

---

[258] 'Ornament is the language through which architecture communicates with a broader public' Edwin Heathcote. See: https://www.architectural-review.com/essays/ornament/ornament-is-the-language-through-which-architecture-communicates-with-a-broader-public

The narcissistic eye views architecture solely as a means of self-expression, and as an intellectual-artistic game detached from essential mental and societal connections, whereas the nihilistic eye deliberately advances sensory and mental detachment and alienation. Instead of reinforcing one's body-centred and integrated experience of the world, nihilistic architecture disengages and isolates the body, and instead of attempting to reconstruct cultural order, it makes a reading of collective signification impossible. The world becomes a hedonistic but meaningless visual journey.[259]

Pallasmaa believes that the impossibility of collective signification is related to various different factors. He believes that the avant-garde is more engaged with architectural discourse *itself* than with human experience.[260] He argues that architecture has little relationship with society, and we are made to experience another's feelings instead of our own. Moreover, the twin problems of complex regulations and the pursuit of profit have severely diminished what he calls 'real architectural qualities'. His overall view is a succinct description of what a human architecture should entail: "I believe in architecture that is relational and which is in a dialog with history, time, setting, existing buildings, and life in general. I think that this is the essence of architecture; its relational and mediating nature."[261]

It does seem that the Greeks and Romans hit on something in their combinations of art and architecture that has struck a chord with many people over time. As Rebecca Solnit writes:

Italian cities have long been held up as ideals, not least by New Yorkers and Londoners enthralled by the ways their architecture gives beauty and meaning to everyday acts.[262]

---

[259] Juhani Pallasmaa, *The Eyes of the Skin: Architecture and the Senses* (1996) p22

[260] Juhani Pallasmaa, *The Eyes of the Skin: Architecture and the Senses* (1996) p32

[261] https://architectureau.com/articles/architecture-is-choreography-in-conversation-with-juhani-pallasmaa/

[262] Rebecca Solnit, *Wanderlust: A History of Walking*

Chapter 11
Cinema

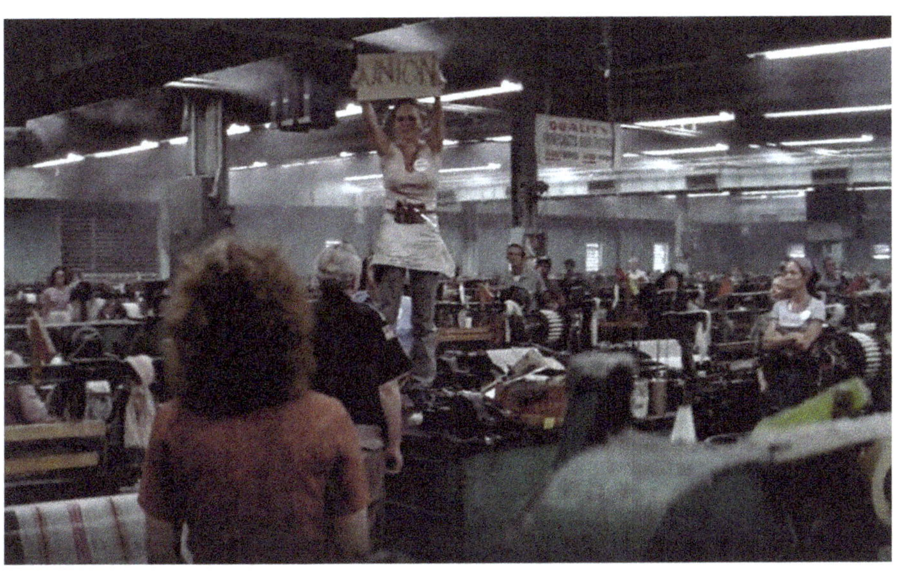

Sally Field in *Norma Rae* (1979)
(Screenshot)

Power revealed is power sacrificed. The truly pow-
erful exert their influence in ways unseen, unfelt. Some
would say that a thing visible is a thing vulnerable.
Guillermo del Toro

To reveal is to change
Jean-Paul Sartre

Individual and Collective Struggles in Cinema

The Fascist regime's strict control over the national cultural production and consumption invested post-war Italian cinema with profound political connotations. Mere entertainment and escapism were known as suspect ploys. Consequently, several post-war film directors—whether politicised intellectuals or not—felt that their work ... bore an inherent political responsibility.
Giorgio Bertellini

Ever since ROME, OPEN CITY, I have maintained a conscious, determined endeavor to try to understand the world in which I live, in a spirit of humility and respect for the facts and for history. What is the meaning of ROME, OPEN CITY? We were emerging from the tragedy of the war. We had all taken part in it, for we were all its victims. I sought only to picture the essence of things. I had absolutely no interest in telling a romanticized tale along the usual lives of film drama. The actual facts were each more dramatic than any screen cliche.
Roberto Rossellini

Throughout the last 100 years of cinema we have seen the influence of Enlightenment and Romanticist ideas in a medium ideally suited for popular criticism and resistance, as well as mass diversion and escapism. The scale of its form in terms of image size, sound volumes, and production costs have no equal in the arts. This of course can also be its downfall as the more money that is required to produce a film, the more it is ideologically controlled by those providing the cash. As the Dutch actor Rutger Hauer stated: "In my experience there are billions of dollars available for pieces of shit. As soon as the material distinguishes itself by something interesting, financing becomes a problem."[263]

However, there have been periods in cinema history when Realist or progressive films were popular such as the films of Frank Capra in the USA (1930s) and the neorealist cinema in Italy (1943 to 1950). Since then progressive films do surface but sporadically. In recent decades we have seen the rise and rise of Romanticist inspired superhero movies especially as advances in technology have allowed for a huge increase in production values.

In this chapter I will look at the history and origins of superheroes in Romanticist ideology and cinema, comparing them to an opposing ideology of working-class heroes who compete with superheroes for the attention of the oppressed masses who are to be 'freed' and/or saved, especially in the 20th century. Such working-class themes of freedom and solidarity were the mainstay of the films of Frank Capra which I will examine in terms of individual and collectivist narratives that almost cost Capra his career.

The rise of the superheroes

The rise of the superheroes in cinema is demonstrated by the proliferation of superhero films today and is a phenomenon that is unprecedented in culture. Many superhero films are based on superhero comics while some are original for the screen, some are based on animated television series, and others are based on Japanese manga and television shows.[264] According to Cooper Hood in Screen Rant:

2019 will be the year of superhero movies, seeing the release of a record-setting amount: a whopping eleven films. As the superhero movie craze continues, next year looks poised to

---

[263] https://medium.com/@michaelbrakemeyer/the-future-so-dim-the-evolution-of-blade-runner-fccd9945e72d

[264] https://en.wikipedia.org/wiki/Superhero_film

be the prime example of how invested Hollywood as a whole really is. There's the usual amount of Marvel movies, but increased output from Warner Bros. and DC, as well as some final Fox X-Men titles. All of these make up an astonishing ten confirmed 2019 superhero movies.[265]

This is nearly double the 2018 output of six live-action superhero movies: Black Panther, Avengers: Infinity War, Deadpool 2, Ant-Man & the Wasp, Venom and Aquaman.[266]

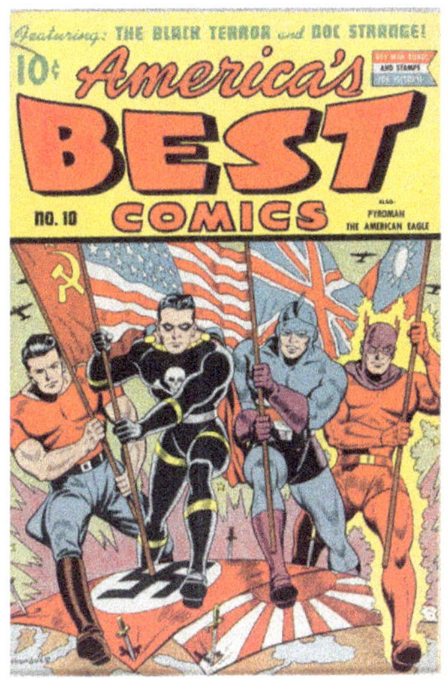

America's Best Comics #7 October 1943
(Alex Schomburg / Public domain / Wikimedia Commons)

Superheroes take their inspiration from earlier heroes such as Robin Hood and the Scarlet Pimpernel but the idea originates in Romanticist ideas about heroes that save the world and the powers of the superhero. Despite their designation as science fiction, superheroes have their ideological roots in anti-science, individualistic Romanticism.

---

[265] '2019 Will Have The Most Superhero Movies Ever Released', Cooper Hood. See: https://screenrant.com/2019-superhero-movies/

[266] '2019 Will Have The Most Superhero Movies Ever Released', Cooper Hood. See: https://screenrant.com/2019-superhero-movies/

In *The Roots of Romanticism*, Isaiah Berlin discusses the Romanticist's negative view of science:

> The only persons who have ever made sense of reality are those who understand that to try to circumscribe things, to try to nail them down, to try to describe them, no matter how scrupulously, is a vain task. This will be true not only of science, which does this by means of the most rigorous generalisations of (to the Romantics) the most external and empty kind, but even of scrupulous writers, scrupulous describers of experience – realists, naturalists, those who belong to the school of the flow of consciousness, [e.g. Proust and Tolstoy] labour under the illusion that it is possible once and for all to write down, to describe, to give any finality to the process which they are trying to catch, which they are trying to nail down, unreality and fantasy will result.[267]

Thus, the Romanticists fundamentally oppose the general values and objectives of science and in particular Realist and Naturalist artists who use scientific knowledge or methods to develop their art. It goes without saying then that on a philosophical level, scientific ideas about the progress of mankind are also rejected by the Romanticists.

This is because for the Romanticists, "new abysses open, and these abysses open to yet other abysses."[268] However, scientists understand that new abysses open as they dig deeper into new levels of understanding. Yet, they are not afraid and they don't throw up their hands in frustration or despair: they see these discoveries as new paths and concepts also to be explored fearlessly.

Isaiah Berlin believes that one of the most influential writers against the science-based Enlightenment and who began the Romanticist backlash was Johann Georg Hamann who believed, acording to Berlin, that "the sciences were very well for their own pur-

---

[267] *The Roots of Romanticism*: Second Edition (The A. W. Mellon Lectures in the Fine Arts) (Princeton Uni Press, Princeton, 2013) by Isaiah Berlin (Author), Henry Hardy (Editor), John Gray (Foreword), p140

[268] *The Roots of Romanticism*: Second Edition (The A. W. Mellon Lectures in the Fine Arts) (Princeton Uni Press, Princeton, 2013) by Isaiah Berlin (Author), Henry Hardy (Editor), John Gray (Foreword), p140

poses" but that:

> this is not what men ultimately sought. If you asked yourself what were men after, what did men really want, you would see that what they really wanted was not at all what Voltaire supposed they wanted. Voltaire thought that they wanted happiness, contentment, peace, but this was not true. What men wanted was for all their faculties to play in the richest and most violent possible fashion. What men wanted was to create, what men wanted was to make, and if this making led to clashes, if it led to wars, if it led to struggles then this was part of the human lot.

This view of violence and war as irrational chaos that cannot be controlled is also an element of superhero narratives which the superhero tries to overcome.[269]

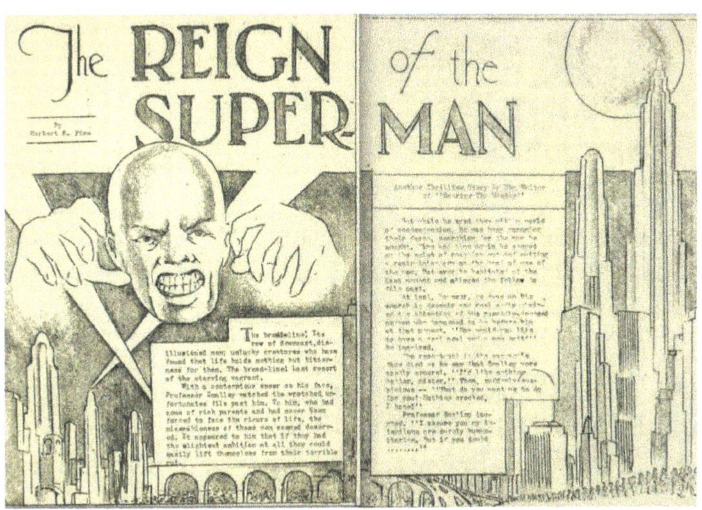

"The Reign of the Superman", short story by Jerry Siegel
(January 1933)
(Herbert S. Fine (Jerry Siegel) and Joe Shuster / Public domain / Wikimedia Commons)

---

[269] *The Roots of Romanticism*: Second Edition (The A. W. Mellon Lectures in the Fine Arts) (Princeton Uni Press, Princeton, 2013) by Isaiah Berlin (Author), Henry Hardy (Editor), John Gray (Foreword), p50

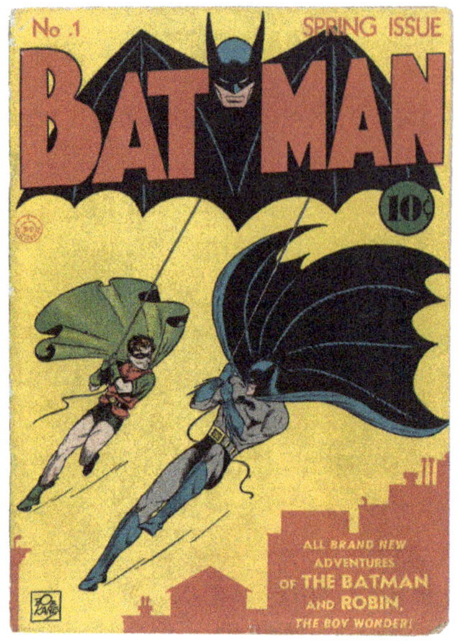

Cover of Batman #1
(National Archives and Records Administration /
Public domain / Wikimedia Commons)

Superheroes: emotions over logic

These ideas of individualism, emotion, personalised motivations and cynicism towards the concept of a progressive society are all part of the Superhero psyche. Mason Woodard writes:

> One of the first Romantic elements of Batman is his motivation. He is a vigilante, sometimes hunted by Gotham Police. But the reason Bruce fights crime even in face of the law is because a common criminal murdered his parents when Wayne was just a boy. The emotion of avenging his parents and stopping this from happening drives him far more. This is an example of emotions over logic, a Romantic idea. [...] One component of Romanticism embodied by Superman is to trust your instincts and emotions before logic and reasoning. Superman will often be seen saving his love, Lois Lane, or a group of kids in the midst of a massive fight, even when a

logical analysis tells you to sacrifice the people and finish off the baddie (even though Superman does win in the end).[270]

Thus, the personalised empathy of the superhero covers over the narcissism of a costumed attention-seeker.

The Golden Age and the Warrior

The Romanticists looked back to the Golden Age of the autonomous, powerful warrior who looks after his tribe and is the earliest version of this idea – the peasant as 'noble savage'. This Romanticisation of the Golden Age was very different from the Renaissance emphasis on the alignment of nature and reason as a positive conception of man. The Golden Age denotes "a period of primordial peace, harmony, stability, and prosperity. During this age peace and harmony prevailed, people did not have to work to feed themselves, for the earth provided food in abundance. They lived to a very old age with a youthful appearance, eventually dying peacefully, with spirits living on as 'guardians'."[271]

The idea of a Fall, the end of a Golden Age, is a common theme in many ancient cultures around the world. Richard Heinberg, in *Memories and Visions of Paradise*, examines various myths from around the world and finds common themes such as sacred trees, rivers and mountains, wise peoples who were moral and unselfish, and in harmony with nature and described heavenly and earthly paradises,[272] i.e. not savages.

The Romanticist view of the Golden Age was a reaction to the contemporary slave-like conditions of the working class in factories and mills. Romanticist rejection of modernity was rooted in this over-rationalisation of the worker and its effect on the human spirit. This rationalisation could be seen as the continuation of earlier slavery but in a modern-day form as 'wage slavery'.

---

[270] 'Romanticism in Superheroes' http://romanticismsuperhero.blogspot.com/
[271] https://en.wikipedia.org/wiki/Golden_Age
[272] Richard Heinberg, in *Memories and Visions of Paradise*

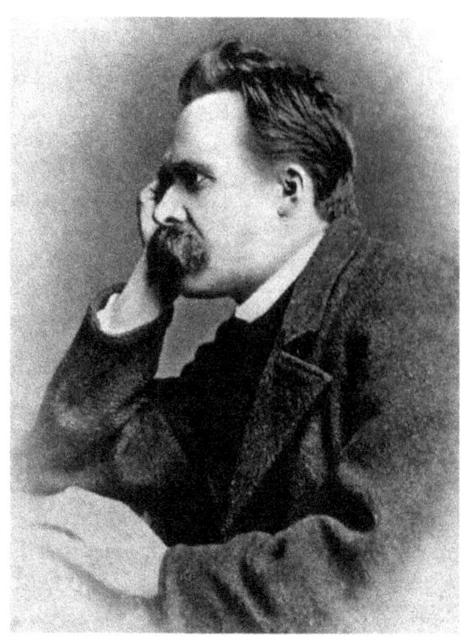

Friedrich Nietzsche (1844–1900)
(Gustav-Adolf Schultze (d. 1897) / Public domain / Wikimedia Commons)

'Supermen' or 'Übermensch [Overmen]'

This modern slavery had a profound affect on Friedrich Nietzsche (1844–1900) who defined the first 'Supermen' or 'Übermensch [Overmen]' (super – Latin: over/beyond) as a goal humanity can set for itself. The Overman would be a new human who was to be neither master nor slave and all human life would be given meaning by how it advanced a new generation of human beings. Like Marx, Nietzsche recognised the social uses of religion to divert attention and action away from the exploitative nature of the social and economic system itself. The individualism of Nietzsche's ideas attracted the anarchists. According to Spencer Sunshine:

> There were many things that drew anarchists to Nietzsche: his hatred of the state; his disgust for the mindless social behavior of 'herds'; his anti-Christianity; his distrust of the effect of both the market and the State on cultural production; his desire for an 'overman' — that is, for a new human who was to be neither master nor slave; his praise of the ecstatic

and creative self, with the artist as his prototype, who could say, 'Yes' to the self-creation of a new world on the basis of nothing; and his forwarding of the 'transvaluation of values' as source of change, as opposed to a Marxist conception of class struggle and the dialectic of a linear history.[273]

While Marx and the Anarchists had opposing views on the role of the state, what Marx did have in common with anarchist thinkers like Mikhail Bakunin and Peter Kropotkin was the belief that wage slavery was a class condition in place due to the existence of private property and the state. This class situation was based on the lack of direct access to, or ownership by workers of, the means of production.

Henceforth, the working class took to the stage as social classes and started lifting themselves up, particularly in the aftermath of the revolutions in the nineteenth and twentieth centuries.

In the twentieth century the battle was on for who would become the saviours of the oppressed – the fictional superheroes who fought crime in western culture or working-class leaders who advocated social change? On a philosophical level the battle between Romanticism and Enlightenment ideas resurfaced between elite Nietzschean individualism and the opposing collectivist historical materialism of Marx.

In Ireland, for example, the changing relationship between the master and the slave could be seen in the formation of the Irish Citizens Army (ICA) by James Larkin, James Connolly and Jack White on 23 November 1913. Connolly wrote of the ICA in Workers' Republic in 1915:

An armed organisation of the Irish working class is a phenomenon in Ireland. Hitherto the workers of Ireland have fought as parts of the armies led by their masters, never as a member of any army officered, trained and inspired by men of their own class. Now, with arms in their hands, they propose to steer their own course, to carve their own future.[274]

---

[273] https://en.wikipedia.org/wiki/%C3%9Cbermensch
[274] https://en.wikipedia.org/wiki/Irish_Citizen_Army

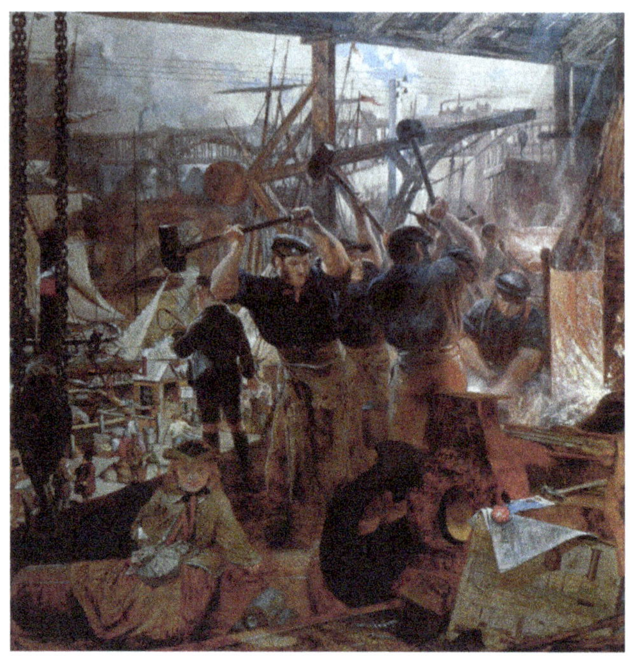

Iron and Coal (1855–60) by William Bell Scott (1811–1890). National Trust, Wallington, Northumberland
(Public domain / Wikimedia Commons)

James Connolly, an Irish working-class hero, led the ICA into a failed uprising against British colonialism in 1916 and was executed by the British not long after. He was a self-taught scholar, a socialist, and an outstanding Labour leader of Ireland. While some may see the uprising as a failed Romantic gesture this could not be further from the truth from Connolly's philosophical and ideological perspective of ridding the country of colonialism before the question of governance could be decided.

Superhero reified

Ultimately the question has to be asked – do superheroes 'save' the people? Of course, they are symbolic heroic figures and so do not save anyone. Is it possible then to become a real life 'superhero'?

This idea is developed in the film Kick-Ass where a fictional 'reification' of the superhero concept happens. Kick-Ass "tells the story of an ordinary teenager, Dave Lizewski (Aaron Johnson), who sets out to become a real-life superhero, calling himself "Kick-Ass". Dave gets caught up in a bigger fight when he meets Big Daddy (Nicolas Cage), a former cop who, in his quest to bring down the crime boss Frank D'Amico (Mark Strong) and his son Red Mist (Christopher Mintz-Plasse), has trained his eleven-year-old daughter (Chloë Grace Moretz) to be the ruthless vigilante Hit-Girl."[275]

While initially Kick-Ass is constantly getting his ass kicked by thugs precisely because he does not have super powers, he eventually saves the day by arriving on the scene strapped to a jet pack fitted with miniguns and kills the remaining thugs. Thus, in the 'real world' Kick-Ass has to resort to 'real weapons' and falls into the normal superhero (as opposed to working class hero) pattern of solving crimes with the usual extra-juridical killing and cathartic ending (and without any questioning of the ownership of the means of production).

Problems of Romanticism

Overall then, there are three different problems associated with superheroes, particularly from the point of view of the very people to be saved.

At first, in an era of socio/political cynicism and helplessness in the face of poverty, corruption and crime, superheroes are cathartic as we purge our emotions watching the difficulties they have 'solving' our problems. In this way action is shifted sideways as we wait for a hero to arrive rather than being active ourselves.

Secondly, the ideology of superheroes comes from above, from elites, and not from below, from the masses themselves and therefore is directed towards the agendas of elites. Superheroes are bourgeois vigilantes who ultimately do not question the structure of society itself but merely try and solve the problems created by structural inequality. Emotions are poured into superhero indi-

---

[275] https://en.wikipedia.org/wiki/Kick-Ass_(film)

vidualists who battle against crime while diverting attention away from questions of collective control of society and progress.

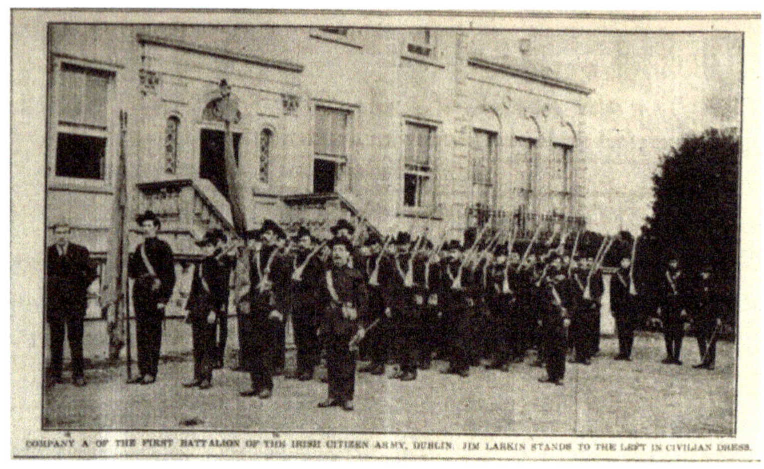

Jim Larkin with Company A of the Irish Citizen Army outside
of Liberty Hall
(The Gaelic American / Public domain / Wikimedia Common)

Thirdly, they represent the anti-logical emotionalism of Romanticism, itself a reaction to science and enlightenment. While described as science fiction, superheroes are given fanciful powers that have more in common with the ancient Greek gods than modern science.

To give them credibility in providing results for the struggling oppressed, superheroes must have super powers (as people know you need more than an individual poor-man's resources to battle against the system itself), *ergo*, the need ultimately for the superpower of working-class solidarity and collectivist action to bring about real changes in society.

Enlightenment traditions – Frank Capra's cinema

The Enlightenment intellectual and philosophical movement arose out of Renaissance humanism and centered on reason and science as the basis of knowledge and promoted ideals of progress and liberty. How did Enlightenment artists and philosophers do this? They tended to focus on the psyche and conditions of everyday life, including poverty, oppression, injustice, and desperation, for example, the writers Thomas Paine (1737-1809), Alexander Pope (1688-1744), Jean-Jacques Rousseau (1712-1778), Jonathan Swift (1667-1745), Voltaire (1694-1778) and Mary Wollstonecraft (1759-1797).

These traditions continued on to the nineteenth century with Auguste Comte (1798–1857) in France, John Stuart Mill (1806–73) in England, and through liberal (Mill) and radical (Marx) social theories. Enlightenment ideas of progressive change crossed all the arts and could be seen in literature, music, art, poetry, architecture and theatre where they would have definite effects on form and content. The new art of cinema in the twentieth century was no different. Directors like Frank Capra used cinema to highlight poverty and injustice, but also the positive social effects of individual acts of courage.

Capra exposes the negative behaviour and manipulations of society elites and tries to educate people into ways of dealing with these problems through solidarity and political means. Although Capra's own politics may have been more conservative, Capra was in a very difficult position that meant he had to resort to an almost Machiavellian approach of appearing to do one thing but actually doing another. This made Capra's films very progressive for their time and few directors have managed to do the same since, except, for example, the English director Ken Loach. Through the use of various different types of plot lines Capra turned cinema into a progressive socio-political vehicle for encouraging societal and community unity. I will look at some of Capra's main films to explore how he achieved this, while at the same time struggling to maintain his career against conservative political forces who were not happy with his popularity.

Frank Capra's main films *Mr. Smith Goes to Washington* (1939), *American Madness* (1932), *Mr. Deeds Goes to Town* (1936), *Platinum Blonde* (1931), *State of the Union* (1948), *Meet John Doe* (1941), and *It's a Wonderful Life* (1946), all show a commitment to progress and social change. Capra used some of the techniques later developed in the Italian Neorealist cinema of the 1940s and 1950s such as a definite social context, a sense of historical actuality and immediacy and a documentary style of cinematography.

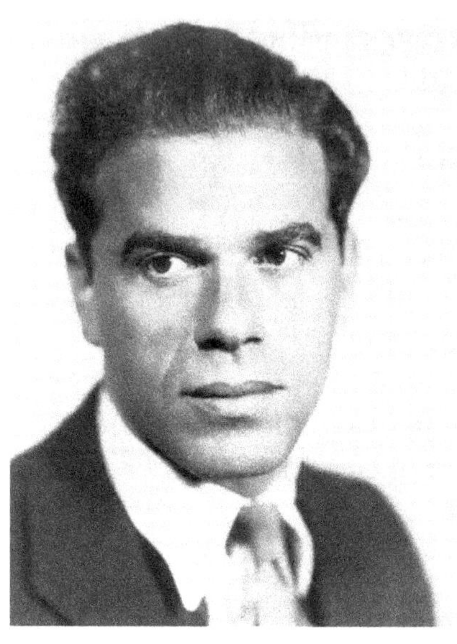

Frank Capra (1897–1991) circa 1930s
(Columbia Pictures / Public domain / Wikimedia Commons)

Capra depicts two separate social worlds which rarely come together except to show how different their values and moral systems are. Their relations are depicted two main ways:

(1) Failed attempts to corrupt a good man [*Mr. Smith Goes to Washington* (1939), *Platinum Blonde* (1931), *Mr. Deeds Goes to Town* (1936), *Meet John Doe* (1941), *State of the Union* (1948)]

(2) Working class solidarity or victory [*American Madness* (1932), *It's a Wonderful Life* (1946)]

Capra's themes – (1) Failed attempts to corrupt a good man

Capra liked to show individuals who are human and have their own problems yet are courageous and morally upstanding. These individuals are bullied, offered well-paid jobs or the chance to retire wealthy but refuse to sell out their friends, class and/or family.

Mr. Smith Goes to Washington (1939)

In 1939 Frank Capra released *Mr. Smith Goes to Washington*, a film that was nominated for eleven Academy Awards, winning for Best Original Story, and turned James Stewart into a major star. Stewart plays Junior Senator Jefferson Smith in Washington who launches into a filibuster talking non-stop for 25 hours and reaffirms American ideals of freedom. Capra's depiction of manipulating elites is carried out in fine detail as Smith quickly learns the ropes on the Senate floor. This representation of the upper echelons of society is the common link between all of Capra's major films of the 1930s and 1940s.

There are many scenes in *Mr. Smith Goes to Washington* where Capra shows how corruption and collaboration with the media push through the agenda of corrupt elites on the make. Capra uses an almost documentary style of having characters explaining in detail how they operate while at the same time giving out lots of information on how progressive-minded individuals can resist.[276]

Smith is working on a bill to authorize a federal government loan to buy some land in his home state for a national boys' camp but the proposed campsite is already part of a dam-building graft scheme included in an appropriations bill framed by Taylor and supported by Senator Paine. Paine is concerned about Smith's reaction to all this and suggests they drop the bill. Jim Taylor (Edward Arnold), responds:

> We can't drop it now, Joe. We bought the land around this Dam and we're holding it in dummy names. If we drop it or delay it – we are going to bring about investigations, and investigations will show that we own that land and are trying to sell it to the State under phoney names. No, Joe, in my judgment the only thing to do is push this Dam through–and get it over with.[277]

In the meantime, Clarissa Saunders (Jean Arthur), who was the aide to Smith's predecessor and had been around Washington and

---

[276] https://en.wikipedia.org/wiki/Mr._Smith_Goes_to_Washington
[277] https://www.dailyscript.com/scripts/Mr%20Smith%20Goes%20To%20Washington.txt

politics for years explains in detail to Smith how the system in the Senate operates:

> Yes. House. More amendments – more changes – and the Bill goes back to the Senate – and waits its turn on the calendar again. The Senate doesn't like what the house did to the Bill. They make more changes. The House doesn't like those changes. Stymie. So they appoint men from each house to go into a huddle called a conference and battle it out. Besides that, all the lobbyists interested give cocktail parties for and against – government departments get in their two cents' worth – cabinet members – budget bureaus – embassies. Finally, if the Bill is alive after all this vivisection, it comes to a vote. Yes, sir – the big day finally arrives. And – nine times out of ten, they vote it down. (Taking a deep breath) Are you catching on, Senator?[278]

Capra even goes so far as to have Smith (on the directions of Saunders) give direct quotes from the Senate Manual itself:

> Uh – Mr. President – you and I are about to be alone in here, sir. I'm not complaining for social reasons, but it'd be a pity if the gentlemen missed any of this. (Then, referring to his manual – in a business-like tone) Mr. President – I call the chair's attention to Rule Five of the Standing Rules of the Senate Section Three. 'If it shall be found that a quorum is not present, a majority of the Senators present –,' and that begins to look like me – 'may direct the Sergeant-at-arms to request, and if necessary compel the attendance of the absent Senators.' (Then - stoutly) Mr. President–I so direct.[279]

As the filibuster starts to attract the reporters' attention Taylor ups the ante and grabs the phone:

> Hendricks! Line up all the papers in the State! Don't print a

---

[278] https://www.dailyscript.com/scripts/Mr%20Smith%20Goes%20To%20Washington.txt
[279] https://www.dailyscript.com/scripts/Mr%20Smith%20Goes%20To%20Washington.txt

word of what Smith says – not a word of any news story coming out of Washington! Understand? Defend the machine. Hit this guy! A criminal – convicted by Senate – blocking relief bill – starving the people. Start protests coming. Wires. Buy up every minute you can on every two-watt radio station in the State. Keep 'em spouting against Smith! McGann's flying out – be there in five hours. Stop your presses – yank out the stories you got in 'em now – and get going – get that whole State moving –![280]

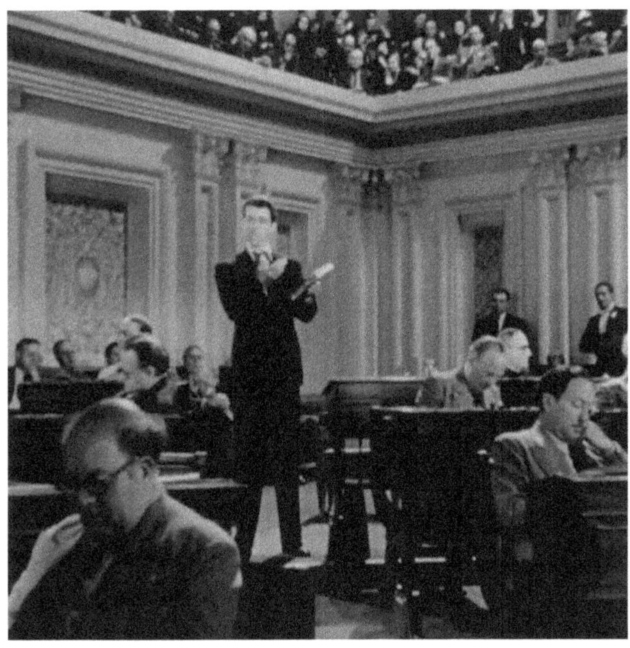

Senator Jefferson Smith pursues his filibuster
before inattentive Senators
(Trailer screenshot / Public domain / Wikimedia Commons)

Meanwhile, in another documentary-style verbatim moment Smith reads out the United States Declaration of Independence:

'– certain Unalienable Rights – that among these are Life, Liberty and the Pursuit of Happiness. That to secure these

---

[280] https://www.dailyscript.com/scripts/Mr%20Smith%20Goes%20To%20Washington.txt

rights, Governments are instituted among Men, deriving their just powers from the consent of the governed, that whenever any form of government becomes destructive of these ends, it is the Right of the People to alter or to abolish it, and to institute new government, laying its foundation on such principles and organizing its powers in such form, as to them shall seem most likely to effect their Safety and Happiness' – (Finishing with a flourish and putting the book down) Now, that's pretty swell, isn't it? I always get a great kick outa those parts of the Declaration – especially when I can read 'em out loud to somebody.[281]

Of course, The United States Declaration of Independence was drafted by Thomas Jefferson and the irony of his namesake reading it out loud in the Senate was not lost on the audiences of the time. Moreover, the name Smith, a common pseudonym, implies that any Joe Soap could do the same. Thus, in a few short scenes, Capra shows how the Senate is manipulated, the power of the media and how filibusters work.

Platinum Blonde (1931)

Capra's film *Platinum Blonde* shows an ordinary person thrown into a rich millieu as a vehicle to show the lives and attitudes of society elites. Stewart "Stew" Smith (Robert Williams) an ace reporter for the Post meets Anne (Jean Harlow) the sister of a rich playboy Michael Schuyler (Donald Dillaway) he is sent to report on. Stew falls for Anne and they get married.[282] However, while Anne tries to turn him into a 'gentleman', his workmates make fun of him:

Conroy: (singing) 'For he's only a bird in a gilded cage, a beautiful sight to see —' (he waves his hand) Tweet, tweet – ha, ha —[283]

---

[281] https://www.dailyscript.com/scripts/Mr%20Smith%20Goes%20To%20Washington.txt
[282] https://en.wikipedia.org/wiki/Platinum_Blonde_(film)
[283] https://www.scripts.com/script.php?id=platinum_blonde_499&p=8

Eventually Stew has enough of his new valet, and being pressurised into behaving according to the social norms of the upper class. He refuses to conform and gives it straight to Anne:

Stew: Yes, I'll tell you – for the same reason I've never wanted to go out with those social parasites, those sweet-smelling fashion plates. I don't like them. They bore me. They give me the jitters.

Anne's Voice: Do you know you're talking about my friends?

Stew: Yes, I'm talking about your friends, and they still give me the jitters.[284]

He eventually decides to leave Anne and refuses to take money (she offers him alimony) which depicts his incorruptible nature and his working-class allegiances.

Mr. Deeds Goes to Town (1936)

In *Mr. Deeds Goes to Town*, Longfellow Deeds (Gary Cooper), the co-owner of a tallow works and part-time greeting card poet inherits 20 million dollars from his late uncle, Martin Semple, during the Great Depression. Semple's scheming attorney, John Cedar (Douglass Dumbrille) tries to get Deeds' power of attorney in order to keep his own financial misdeeds secret.

However, Deeds is not easily manipulated and fends off all greedy opportunists. His sincerity also charms minder Cornelius Cobb (Lionel Stander) and star reporter Louise 'Babe' Bennett (Jean Arthur) who writes popular articles about him with the nickname 'Cinderella Man'. When Deeds meets a dispossessed farmer (John Wray) who comes at him with a gun, Deeds calms him down and decides to give fully equipped 10-acre (4-hectare) farms free to thousands of homeless families. He is taken to court but wins over the people and the judge in the end.[285]

---

[284] https://www.scripts.com/script.php?id=platinum_blonde_499&p=8

[285] https://en.wikipedia.org/wiki/Mr._Deeds_Goes_to_Town

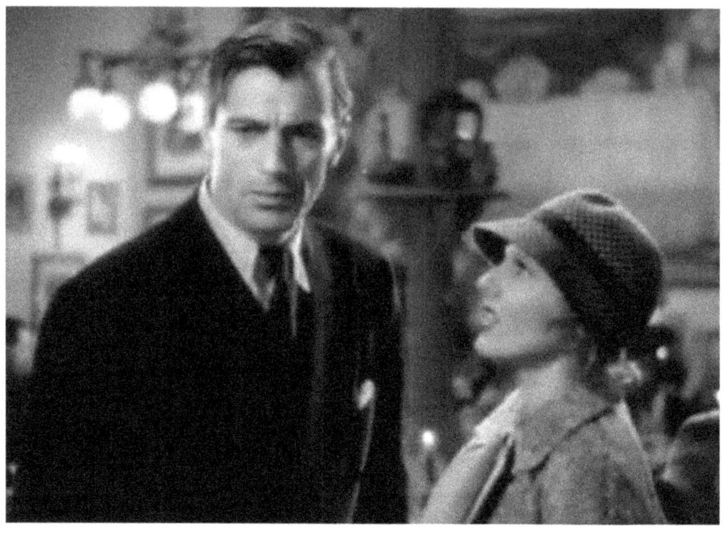

Gary Cooper and Jean Arthur in *Mr. Deeds Goes to Town*
(Columbia Pictures / Public domain / Wikimedia Commons)

Meet John Doe (1941)

In *Meet John Doe* Ann Mitchell, a newspaper reporter, prints a letter from a fictional unemployed 'John Doe' threatening suicide on Christmas Eve in protest of society's ills. The letter gets much attention and Ann is rehired to exploit the fictional John Doe. She gets John Willoughby, a former baseball player, hired to play the role of John Doe. Ann then writes a series of letters exposing society's disregard for people in need inspiring ordinary people to start 'John Doe clubs' with the slogan 'Be a better neighbor'.

This philosophy develops into a movement. Willoughby himself becomes inspired by the movement which the newspaper's publisher, D. B. Norton decides to manipulate to have himself endorsed as a presidential candidate. After Norton exposes the letter fraud John decides to kill himself as the original letter had stated (by jumping from the roof of the City Hall) but the people change his mind when they tell him that they planned to restart the John Doe clubs anyway. As John leaves, the editor Henry Connell turns to Norton and says, "There you are, Norton! The people! Try and lick that!"[286]

---

[286] https://en.wikipedia.org/wiki/Meet_John_Doe

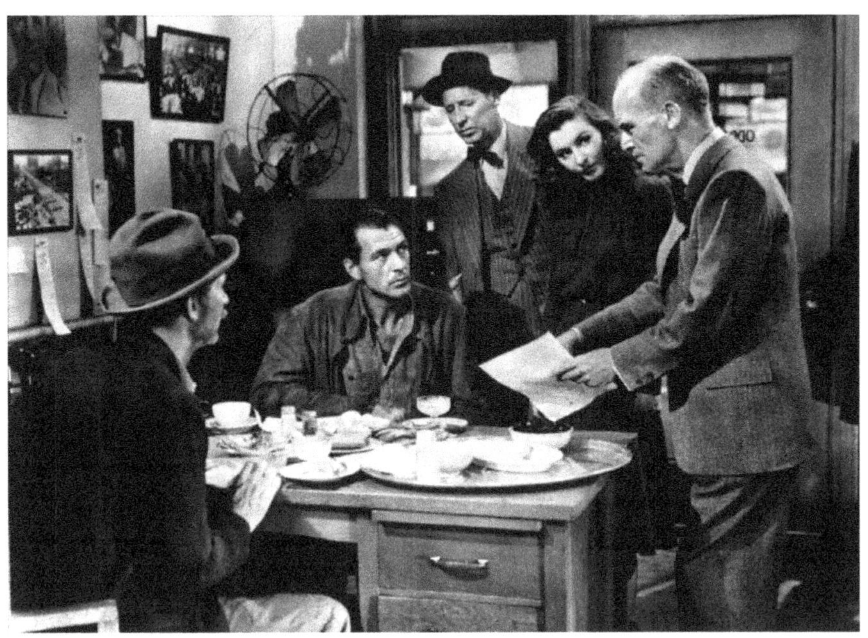

Walter Brennan, Gary Cooper, Irving Bacon, Barbara Stanwyck,
and James Gleason in *Meet John Doe*
(Film screenshot (Frank Capra Prod. / Warner Bros.)
/ Public domain / Wikimedia Commons)

State of the Union (1948)

In *State of the Union* Kay Thorndyke (Angela Lansbury), Republican
newspaper magnate, plans to make her lover, aircraft tycoon Grant
Matthews (Spencer Tracy), president, a power which she can then
manipulate. Matthews's wife Mary agrees to support him in public
because of his idealism and honesty. Matthews is a powerful speak-
er and appeals to ordinary people and their trade unions ("audience was full of cheering union men").[287] He is a progressive:

> I'm going to tell them that the wealthiest nation in the world
> is a failure unless it's also the healthiest nation in the world.
> That means the highest medical care for the lowest income
> groups. And that goes for housing, too. [...] And I'm going to

---

[287] https://en.wikipedia.org/wiki/State_of_the_Union_(film)

tell them that the American Dream is not making money. It is the well-being and the freedom of the individual throughout the world from Patagonia to Detroit.[288]

Elite manipulation of the economy itself is indicated:

Now, look here, Jim, you know just as well as I do that there are men at that banquet who'll be rooting for a depression, just so they can slap labor's ears back.[289]

Capra exposes elite methods of divide and rule ("They've carried hatreds around for centuries. The trick is to play on these hatreds, one nationality against the other, keep them voting as blocks.") and shows how the people can get their voice heard on the monopolised media:

Ladies and gentlemen, this is a paid political broadcast. Paid for, not by any political group or organization, but by thousands of public-spirited citizens who have taken this method of insuring that their voice, the voice of the people shall be heard.[290]

When Matthews discovers the political manipulations going on behind his back, "He steps to the microphone before the cameras, and confesses to the American people. While promising to seek bipartisan reform — and challenging the voters to vote — he denounces as frauds both his backers and himself and withdraws as a candidate for any political office."

Capra's themes – (2) Working class solidarity or victory

In these films the main theme is the machinations of elites to gain control, monopolise and increase profits. The developing aware-

---

[288] https://www.scripts.com/script-pdf/18829
[289] https://www.scripts.com/script-pdf/18829
[290] https://www.scripts.com/script-pdf/18829

ness of ordinary people that they will be the ones most affected if these plans are successful forms the basis of solidarity action.

American Madness (1932)

Set during the Great Depression, the Board of Directors of Thomas Dickson's bank want Dickson (Walter Huston) to merge with New York Trust and resign. Dickson refuses as he believes that the merger will exclude many of his ordinary clients in the drive for profits. When the bank is robbed of $100,000 different aspects of this morality story relating to extra-marital affairs, gambling and staff loyalty are played out. As word of the robbery gets out a huge crowd of clients arrive panicked about their savings and a run on the bank starts.

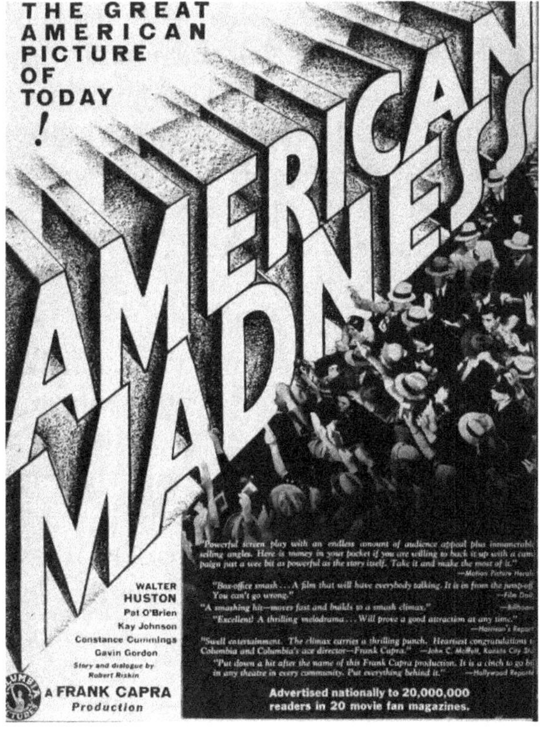

American Madness ad from *The Film Daily*, 1932
(New York, Wid's Films and Film Folks, Inc. / Public domain / Wikimedia Commons)

However, the long-held policy of Dickson to help people when they were down produces positive results as favours are called in. Clients who did well arrive at the bank holding up wads of cash declaring that they were depositing money, not taking it out. This action of solidarity with Dickson calms the queues and people start putting their money back in or going home thus saving the bank from the vulture Board of Directors.[291]

It's a Wonderful Life (1946)

38-year-old George Bailey postpones his plans to tour the world before college to sort out the family business, Bailey Brothers' Building and Loan. George's father suffers a stroke and dies but the board votes to keep it open, provided that George runs it. George marries Mary Hatch but they end up using their $2,000 honeymoon savings to stop a run on the bank and keep it solvent. George sets up Bailey Park, a housing development financed by the Building and Loan, in contrast to his competitor Henry F. Potter's overpriced slums. Due to a mistake by his forgetful uncle a large sum of cash goes missing which threatens the future of Bailey Brothers' Building and Loan. George becomes desperate and contemplates suicide. However, an angel appears on the bridge he is about to jump off and shows him what the town would have looked like without his efforts.

This idea is a stroke of genius in the film as the angel shows him that his town Bedford Falls has been renamed Pottersville, "a seedy town occupied by strip clubs, swing halls, and cocktail lounges" thus depicting the reality and desperation of many places in the United States at the time (gritty social realism under the cover of a 'spiritual' sequence). George has a change of heart and begs the angel for his life back. He runs home to discover that the townspeople had rallied and donated enough money to save the bank.

Frank Capra released *It's a Wonderful Life* in 1946, a film which is still shown every year in cinemas and on TV, thus maintaining its popularity. Yet when first released it performed poorly at the box

---

[291] https://en.wikipedia.org/wiki/American_Madness

office mainly due to the sheer quantity of films released that year. Despite the rough start the film went on to become voted as one of the best films ever made. Though often perceived as a sentimental movie, a more recent analysis describes the story line as "a terrifying, asphyxiating story about growing up and relinquishing your dreams, of seeing your father driven to the grave before his time, of living among bitter, small-minded people."[292] Yet Capra shows how good examples can break down bitterness and turn into its opposite.

The individual and the collective

In these films Capra operates on two levels (sometimes at the same time) — the individual and the collective. He exhorts the individual to stand strong in the face of extreme pressure, and shows the power of collective action, even if it does take some time to form. However, this is an important point in itself as changing beliefs and ideas lead to a new understanding and self-awareness within the group. The success of collective action then gives the group a feeling of self-worth and power which becomes an important element in future struggles. In a way, Capra takes on a similar role as Nicolo Machiavelli (1469-1527), the author of the 16th century book *The Prince*. While many would see Machiavelli as a self-serving immoral opportunist writing a book advising elites on the craft of ruling and exploiting the exercise of power, this may not have been the case. Erica Benner writes:

> Just a year before he finished the first draft of his 'little book', the Medici swept into Florence in a foreign-backed coup after spending years in exile. They were deeply suspicious of his loyalties, dismissed him from his posts, then had him imprisoned and tortured under suspicion of plotting against them.[293]

---

[292] https://en.wikipedia.org/wiki/It%27s_a_Wonderful_Life

[293] 'Have we got Machiavelli all wrong?', Erica Benner. See: https://www.theguardian.com/books/2017/mar/03/have-we-got-machiavelli-all-wrong

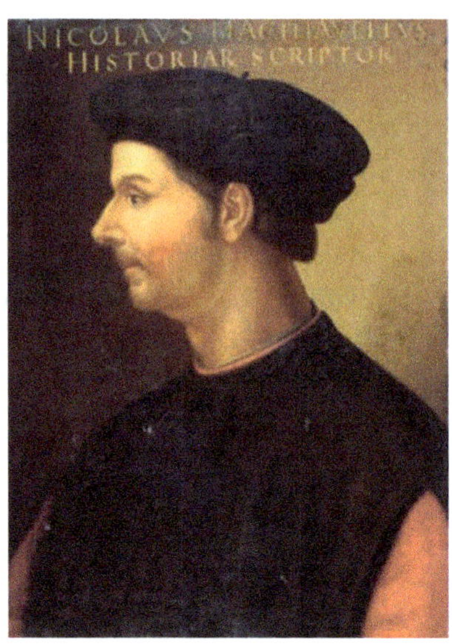

Oil painting of Niccolò Machiavelli (1469–1527)
by Cristofano dell'Altissimo (c. 1525–1605)
(Public domain / Wikimedia Commons)

She notes that "Machiavelli's writings speak in different voices at different times" and that "Francis Bacon, Spinoza and Rousseau – had no doubt the book was a cunning exposé of princely snares, a self-defence manual for citizens. 'The book of republicans,' Rousseau dubbed it."[294]

Benner describes the benefits of seeing Machiavelli in a positive light:

His city's tempestuous history taught Machiavelli a lesson he tries to convey to future readers: that no one man can overpower a free people unless they let him. [...] Citizens need to realise that by trusting leaders too much and themselves too little, they create their own political nightmares. [...] So what can citizens can do to preserve their freedoms? For one thing, they can train themselves to see through the various ruses in the would-be tyrant's handbook. Machiavelli's *The*

---

[294] 'Have we got Machiavelli all wrong?', Erica Benner. See: https://www.theguardian.com/books/2017/mar/03/have-we-got-machiavelli-all-wrong

Prince describes most of them, in ways that mimic their disorienting ambiguity.[295]

Capra, like Machiavelli, shows in detail how elites manipulate in many different ways, through friends, bought-off individuals and their use of the media. Capra also shows people the negative effects of trusting their leaders too much and how they can resist being overpowered by developing awareness and solidarity.

However, Capra, like Machiavelli, also experienced suspicion and rebukes from the elites he was depicting. *Mr. Smith Goes to Washington* had been attacked as a film that showed America in a bad light, the sort of things that "unfriendly" people were saying "in and out of America" about "the institution of these United States".[296] The film *State of the Union* was criticized by the Hollywood columnist Lee Mortimer of Hearst's New York Daily Mirror as:

stuff slipped through the customers by one of the oldest dodges in the game, 'Sure I'm against communism, but' - The big 'but' here seem to be a deep-seated dislike for most of the things America is and stands for ... The indictment against this country, its customs, manners, morals, economic and political systems, as put in the mouths of Tracy and Miss Hepburn, would not seem out of place in Izvestia [Russian newspaper].[297]

The implications of being anti-American and pro-Soviet Union were very serious for Capra as they attracted the attention of HUAC (House Un-American Activities Committee) which could lead one to be black listed and effectively unemployed. As Capra himself stated: "Courage made me a champion ... But the world was full of ex-champions."[298]

Capra urged respect for American traditions of free speech and political dissent invoking the names of Jefferson, Paine, Emerson

---

[295] 'Have we got Machiavelli all wrong?', Erica Benner. See: https://www.theguardian.com/books/2017/mar/03/have-we-got-machiavelli-all-wrong

[296] Joseph McBride, *Frank Capra: The Catastrophe of Success* (Simon and Schuster: New York, 1992), p.422

[297] McBride, *Frank Capra*, p.547

[298] McBride, *Frank Capra*, p.543

and Thoreau and tried briefly to organise a petition of support for Hollywood writers, including the ones he had worked with who had been subpoenaed and black-listed. However, this fell through and Capra abandoned the protest. (Capra replied to criticism by saying he was a Catholic and wanted to present a Christian doctrine). As it happened Capra was never criticized by name in the hearings "nor were [his] films such as *Mr Deeds* and *Mr Smith*".[299] As Capra saw his colleagues being forced out of Hollywood he "set about purging his work of any elements he could anticipate that anyone, anywhere, present or future, might find 'un-American'".[300] Sadly, this action resulted in his later films becoming ever more saccharine and innocuous.

The 1930s and 1940s were an extraordinary time for progressive cinema and Frank Capra became one of America's most influential directors. He won three Academy Awards for Best Director from six nominations and was active in various political and social activities in the industry. His social realist depictions of society depicting the conflict of groups with very different economic and political agendas is a far cry from much cinema today.

By the 1950s the pressure against film producers and directors was stepped up. The film *Salt of the Earth* is a good example of the difficulties face by black-listed and jailed directors.

Born in controversy but then ignored in its youth, the film *Salt of the Earth* (1954) has now matured beautifully into a classic film in the neorealist style. Set in Zinc Town, New Mexico, a mining community with a majority of Mexican-Americans strike for working conditions equal to those of the white, or "Anglo" miners.[301]

The origin of the film's woes stretched back some years when the director Herbert Biberman refused to answer the House Committee on Un-American Activities in 1947 on questions of affiliation to the Communist Party USA, and he became known as one of the Hollywood Ten who were cited and convicted for contempt of Congress and jailed.[302] This meant that Biberman (as well as actors, screenwriters, directors, and musicians) were denied employment

---

[299] McBride, *Frank Capra*, p.542

[300] McBride, *Frank Capra*, p.543

[301] https://en.wikipedia.org/wiki/Salt_of_the_Earth_(1954_film)

[302] https://en.wikipedia.org/wiki/Hollywood_blacklist

in the entertainment industry for years after. During the making of *Salt of the Earth* Biberman was hounded by Roy Brewer. Roy Martin Brewer (1909–2006) was an American trade union leader who was prominently involved in anti-communist activities in the 1940s and 1950s. He accompanied Ronald Reagan on his first visit to the Whitehouse.[303]

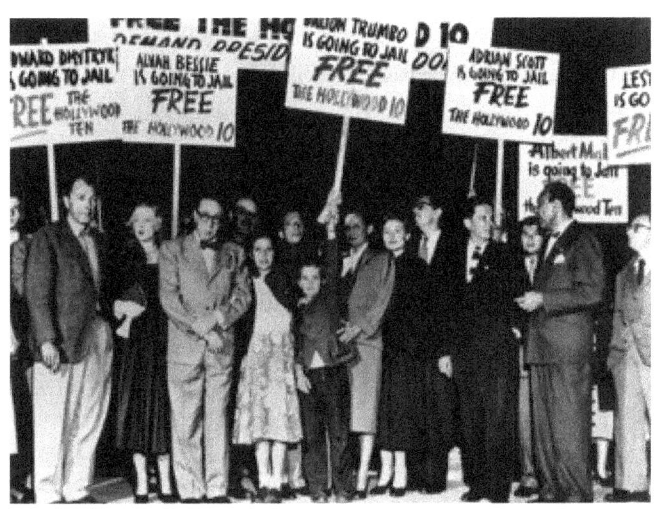

Members of the Hollywood Ten and their families in 1950, protesting the impending incarceration of the ten.
(Judy Chaikin / Legacy of the Hollywood Blacklist)

Brewer tried many times to stop the production of *Salt of the Earth*. He believed that "officers of the Writers' Guild were under the domination of the Communist Party until the hearings of 1947. During that time, they began to change the mind, the creative minds, of the people who made these pictures and they didn't do it by selling them communism. They got them to accept the idea that it was the obligation of a writer to put a message in the film."[304]

Paul Jarrico (1915–1997) the blacklisted American screenwriter and film producer of *Salt of the Earth* commented on Brewers statements:

---

[303] https://en.wikipedia.org/wiki/Roy_Brewer

[304] https://archive.org/details/clcop_000371

The studio reluctance to make message movies started long before the blacklist and Brewer's attribute to our cleverness in manipulating the culture of America is undeserved. We were unable to get anything more than the most moderate kind of reform messages into our films and if we thought we got some women treated as human beings rather than as sex objects we thought it was a big victory, and in fact, one of the reasons we made *Salt of the Earth* after we were blacklisted was to commit a crime worthy of the punishment having already been punished for subverting American films, it was all ridiculous.[305]

To make matters more difficult, *Salt of the Earth* had been sponsored by a Union (the International Union of Mine, Mill and Smelter Workers) and many blacklisted Hollywood professionals helped produce it. The production of *Salt of the Earth* faced many difficulties from locations, cameramen to actors. A small plane buzzed overhead and anti-communists fired at the sets. They eventually found a documentary cameraman who was willing to take the risks involved with working on the project. Later, Rosaura Revueltas (Esperanza Quintero) the lead actor, was deported to Mexico and the editors had to cut in previously filmed footage to finish the narrative. After editing in secret, the release of the film was met with an American Legion call for a nationwide boycott and the majority of theaters refused to show it. For ten years the film was ignored in the USA while finding an audience and accolades in Eastern and Western Europe. By the 1960s the film was seen by larger audiences in union halls, women's associations, and film schools.[306]

In the years thereafter the controversies surrounding *Salt of the Earth* had died down or were largely forgotten, more films depicting working class life and struggles were produced, for example, *The Organizer* (1963) (Italian), *The Battle of Algiers* (1966) (Italian-Algerian), *Blue Collar* (1978) (USA), *Norma Rae* (1979) (USA), *Vera Drake* (2004) (UK), *I, Daniel Blake* (2016) (UK), *The Young Karl Marx* (2017) (French-German-Belgian), *Sorry We Missed You* (2019)

---

[305] https://archive.org/details/clcop_000371

[306] https://en.wikipedia.org/wiki/Salt_of_the_Earth_(1954_film)

(UK), *Parasite* (2019) (Korean).

It is no coincidence in these neoliberal, monopolizing, plutocratic times that there has been a huge rise in the Romanticist cinema culture of Superheroes at the expense of progressive cinema and directors who would like to emulate Frank Capra's *oeuvre*. It is far better (and safer) for elites to encourage a cinema of hero worship of saviours and superheroes, than one that inspires ordinary people to become politically conscious enough to make a commitment to progress and social change.

Chapter 12

Television

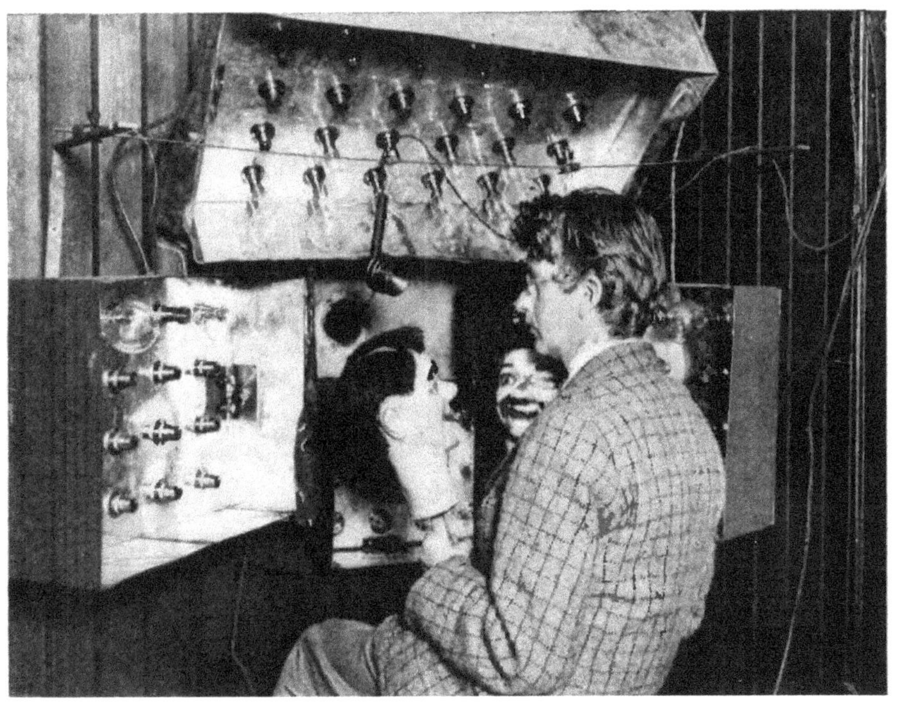

John Logie Baird FRSE (1888–1946)
'James' and 'Stooky Bill'
(Orrin Dunlap, Jr. / Public domain / Wikimedia Commons)

*People often claim to hunger for truth, but seldom
like the taste when it's served up.*
George R.R. Martin

Game of Thrones: Olde-Style Catharsis or Bloody Good Counsel?

> *"You have been too clever for your own good, O human na-*
> *ture (hominen natura)! and gifted beyond measure to your*
> *ruin. Of what avail to you to gird cities with turreted walls?*
> *Of what avail to arm hands in strife? What had you to do*
> *with the sea - you might have been satisfied with the land!*
> *Why do you not seek the sky as well - a third kingdom? In*
> *so far as you may, you do annex the sky also - Quirinus has*
> *his temple, and Liber and Alcides, and now Caesar. We draw*
> *from the earth solid gold instead of grains. The soldier pos-*
> *sesses riches made from his blood. The curia is closed to the*
> *poor - a man's rating in the tax assessors' books procures him*
> *public office; from that come the*
> *grave judge and the stern knight!"*
> Ovid, *Amores*, III, viii, 35-56

Game of Thrones is a television series based on the storylines of *A Song of Ice and Fire*, set in the fictional Seven Kingdoms of Westeros and the continent of Essos. The series chronicles the violent dynastic struggles among the realm's noble families for the Iron Throne, while other families fight for independence from it. The final season depicts the culmination of the series' two primary conflicts: the Great War against the Army of the Dead, and the Last War for control of the Iron Throne. Game of Thrones is not typical of contemporary fantasy, with more emphasis on battles and political intrigue

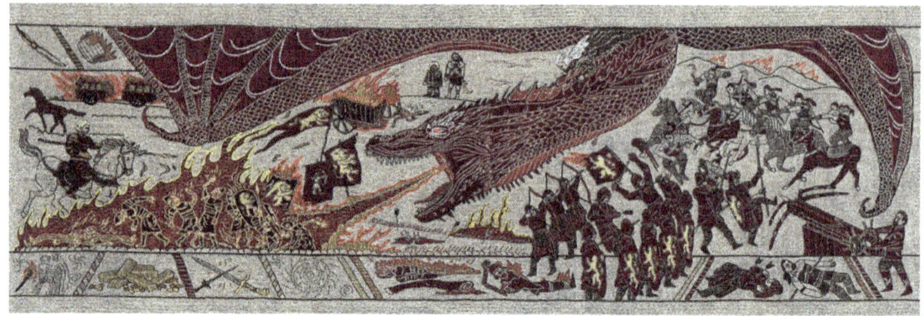

Battle of the Goldroad from *Game of Thrones* - Season 7 Episode 4 on the official tapestry produced in Northern Ireland
(Kal242382 / CC BY-SA 4.0 / Wikimedia Commons)

and less emphasis on magic and sorcery.[307]

As the series drew to a conclusion many fans of the show complained bitterly about the final season and finale. As Ien Ang wrote in *Watching Dallas: Soap Opera and the Melodramatic Imagination*, another show with a huge worldwide viewership in the 1970s:

> It is wrong, however, to pretend that the ideology of mass culture exercises dictatorial powers. The discourses of this ideology are very important, culturally legitimized organizers of the way in which the social meaning of Dallas is constructed, but alternative discourses do exist which offer alternative points of identification for lovers of Dallas.[308]

People construct their own meanings which the show's producers have no control over. They may agree or disagree with the decisions of the producers but they will still find a meaning that is satisfactory for them. Even the violence and bleakness of the show can be interpreted in a positive way. I will take *Game of Thrones* at face value and look at what was actually produced and transmitted and examine possible meanings. I will argue that the series has subconscious elements which satisfy audiences frustrated with modern society, and even though good forces generally prevail, ultimately

---

[307] https://en.wikipedia.org/wiki/Game_of_Thrones

[308] Ien Ang, *Watching Dallas: Soap Opera and the Melodramatic Imagination* (Routledge: London, 1991) p.111

the moral of the tale is that one should not hand one's destiny over to 'great' leaders. The series has Enlightenment and Romanticist elements which are an important aspect of the storyline that has been overlooked.

I will look at three questions: why do people watch *Game of Thrones*? is *Game of Thrones* an historical allegory? and, does *Game of Thrones* rise above being pure fantasy?

Why do people watch Game of Thrones?

One friend with the *Game of Thrones* box set revealed to me that she cried after watching the first episode of Season One because of its unremitting bleakness and didn't watch any more episodes after that. She couldn't find anything positive in the show, yet millions of people all over the world watched the show apparently finding it a worthwhile experience. The interest in *Game of Thrones* is similar to the interest in Romanticism in the mid nineteenth century. Disillusionment with society, a desire for a simpler life and a closer relationship with nature became the basis of a new Romantic culture and philosophy that spread across Europe.

What could a modern audience find positive in *Game of Thrones* in an era of mass production and international trade, alienation, disillusionment, ennui, gender confusion, and general dissatisfaction with governments, politicians and legal systems? In other words, in a world which is depressing enough already.

While the dramatic and sometimes very violent narrative holds the audience's attention, there are subconscious elements that add to the fascination with the show. These are taken-for-granted elements which add to the background authenticity of the drama. And authenticity seems to have been high up in the objectives of the show runners. There is an earthiness in the production values that make one constantly aware of faeces, dung, dirt, urine, blood and mud. Indeed, some scenes seem to try and incorporate all these aspects in to one scene (like when Jaime is tied to a pole in captivity). These elements I will look at under the headings of (1) small scale 'artisan' production, (2) gender roles, and (3) justice and politics.

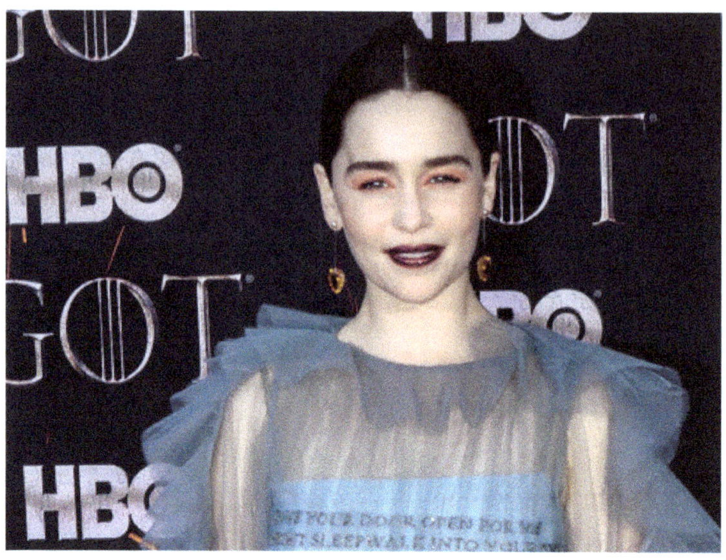

Emilia Clarke plays Daenerys Targaryen
(Sachyn / CC BY-SA 3.0 / Wikimedia Commons)

Small scale production -
('yesterday's bread and a "bowl o' brown"')

We are slowly drawn in and made aware that nothing in *Game of Thrones* can be taken for granted. There are no supermarkets or hardware stores. Small scale production is everywhere. Everything is made, grown, baked, forged, sewn, cooked, brewed or built before our eyes. This produces joy when made well and disgust when done badly (wine, bread, clothes, swords etc.) in the characters in the drama. However, when the characters are used to something bad they appreciate when something is good. In modern society the skills necessary to make things are taken out of our hands as production becomes more complex, standardised and automated.

We are alienated from production and are becoming more and more distant from the harvesting, gathering and production of our food and manufacture of our goods. It is really only at Christmas time that some of that sense of medieval production operates with baking, setting the fire, decorating the tree, wrapping presents and family games. Even then, consumption still plays a much larger role than production. However, the Romanticist desire for a closer relationship with Nature and indigenous production is still strong and reveals itself generally in the burgeoning interest in nationalist ideas and politics.

Gender roles - ("I'm no Lady" - Brienne)

While the World Health Organization (WHO) defines gender roles as "socially constructed roles, behaviors, activities and attributes that a given society considers appropriate for men and women", we live in a society where traditional roles have been breaking down and definitions of masculinity and femininity are constantly changing. In *Game of Thrones* we follow the actions of men training, fighting and dying for 'causes'. We see women training and fighting too (Brienne and Arya), as exceptions, but in the main women are there to be protected, or in particular, through oaths taken by knights.

Again, a simple and Romanticist notion but one that is obviously appealing on a subconscious level as it is a consistent theme throughout all eight seasons. The main characters also have a sense of destiny, objectives and direction in their lives. In our society unemployment, alienation and high suicide rates among men, show that at the very least something is broken and people do not have the same sense of control over their own lives.

Justice and politics - (serving up oats and oaths)

Oaths are a big thing in the *Game of Thrones*. The taking and breaking of oaths will get you lauded (Brienne of Tarth) or hated by everyone (Jaime the Kingslayer). The seriousness with which oaths are taken is a sign of the importance given to personal integrity in the show. In real life oaths are also taken, e.g. in the USA members of parliament 'solemnly swear (or affirm) that I will support and defend the Constitution of the United States' and in the UK members 'swear by Almighty God that I will be faithful and bear true allegiance to Her

Majesty'. However, we live in a society where MPs, committees, and task forces, do not take oaths seriously and are constantly found to be diluting bills, lying, and abusing the political system for self-gain. This breeds much cynicism with politics and politicians especially as the justice system also seems to be loaded in their favour.

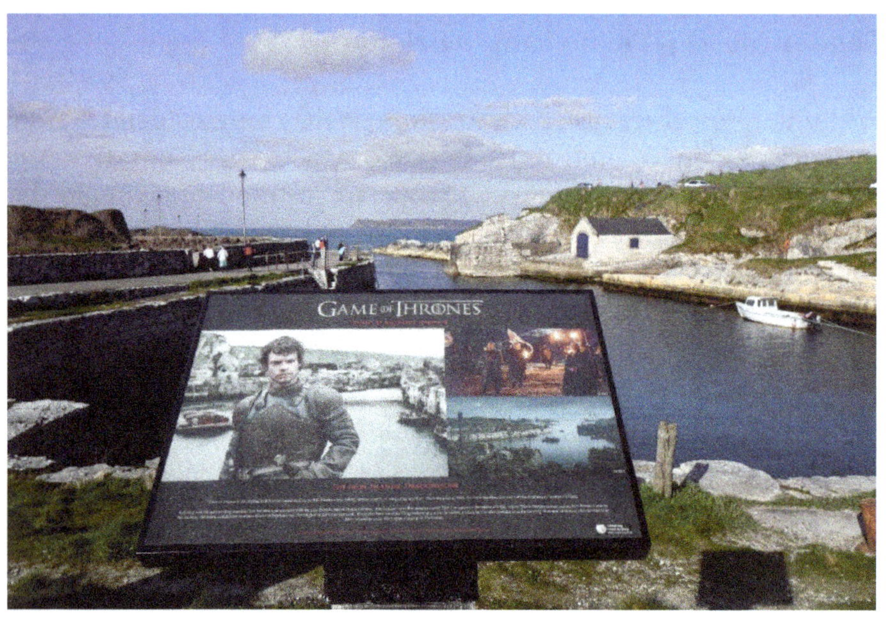

Ballintoy Harbour was Lordsport on the Iron Islands in
Game of Thrones
(Sonse / CC BY 2.0 / Wikimedia Commons)

Not so, however, in the Game of Thrones, where justice is often meted out deftly and swiftly at the pointy end of a sword. Instant justice here may seem refreshing and satisfying compared to the real world of procrastinating judicial systems which breed cynicism regarding the 'lack of a death penalty', sentences perceived to be 'too light', or never-ending court cases.

Thus, *Game of Thrones* has many pared down and simplified aspects that give a temporary relief from complex, modern society. In *Game of Thrones* everyone is an artisan because everything has to be done or learned directly (swordsmanship, horse riding, copying books) or got from somebody with the necessary skills (wine, bread, smith).

Is *Game of Thrones* an historical allegory?

While it is known that Martin takes examples from history such as "Hadrian's Wall (which becomes Martin's Wall), the Roman Empire, and the legend of Atlantis (ancient Valyria), Byzantine Greek fire ('wildfire'), Icelandic sagas of the Viking Age (the Ironborn), the Mongol hordes (the Dothraki), the Hundred Years' War, and the Italian Renaissance", *Game of Thrones* is not a mish-mash of historical dramatic incidents.

A certain logic is imposed on the narrative of *Game of Thrones* which is similar to a broad overview of human history. At first, we have primitive society, then a combination of feudalism and slavery, then Enlightenment and bourgeois concepts of freedom and democracy with the future being left open to speculation.

Primitive society - ("We don't kneel for anyone beyond the Wall." - Mance Rayder)

The people who live north of the wall, called Wildlings, worship the Old Gods of the Forest which consist of nature spirits. Their sacred places were 'weirwood' trees, a deciduous tree similar in shape to the Oak tree. In *Game of Thrones* many of the weirwood trees were cut down during the violent invasion of the Andals who killed and replaced the First Men. These ideas are similar to the ancient traditions of the Celtic and Germanic people who worshipped sacred oaks in consecrated groves or on islands on lakes with perpetual fires. The Celtic and Germanic peoples believed in the spiritual connection with the natural environment around them.

One story focuses on Saint Boniface, an Anglo-Saxon missionary, who cut down a sacred tree of the Germanic pagans, Donar's Oak. To add insult to injury the wood from the oak was then used to build a church at the site dedicated to Saint Peter.

These early communities were destroyed but their culture survived down the centuries in remnants of nature-based traditions, stories and mythology. In *Game of Thrones*, the awareness of the Old Gods survives as an active religion ("I swear it by the old gods and the new") whereas in real life the old gods are relegated to mythology and their nature-based rites have survived to today as traditions (e.g. wassailing the apple trees, the Christmas tree, festivals of light, Easter eggs, bonfires etc.).

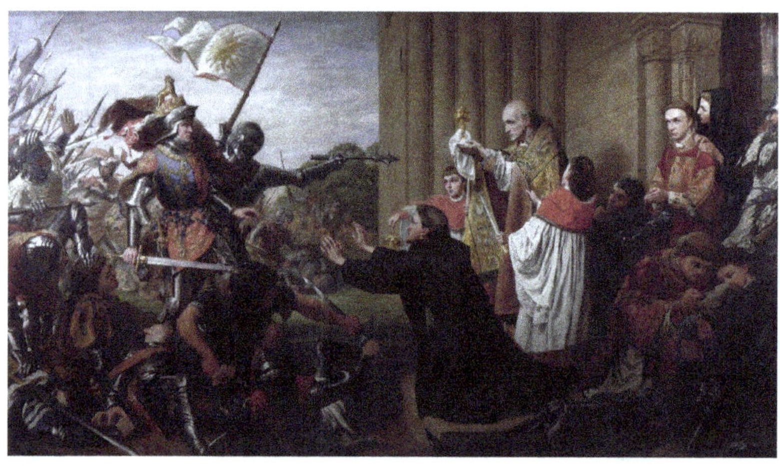

A Song of Ice and Fire series was partly inspired by the Wars of the Roses, a series of dynastic civil wars for the throne of England. This painting by Richard Burchett portrays Edward IV demanding that his defeated enemies be taken from Tewkesbury Abbey
(Guildhall Art Gallery / Public domain / Wikimedia Commons)

Feudalism and slavery -

("No man wants to be owned" - Daenerys Targaryen)

The Wildlings described themselves as free folk, not bound by the oaths and loyalties of the feudal hierarchical structure of society in the Seven Kingdoms. The 'turreted walls' described by Ovid above became associated with ideas of 'honourable' monarchies and chivalry throughout feudal Europe. Yet these elites were essentially the descendants of the earlier hostile invaders. In *Game of Thrones*,

Bronn breaks this Romanticist vision of honour with more than a touch of historical realism when Jaime reacts to his request for Highgarden castle:

> Jaime Lannister: Highgarden will never belong to a cutthroat.
> Bronn: No? Who were your ancestors, the ones who made your family rich? Fancy lads in silk? They were fucking cutthroats. That's how all the great houses started, isn't it? With a hard bastard who was good at killing people. Kill a few hundred people, they make you a lord. Kill a few thousand, they make you king. And then all your cocksucking grandsons can ruin the family with their cocksucking ways.[309]

Bronn's view of the rich echoes Jean Jacques Rousseau's Enlightenment analysis on the origins of inequality in society. In *Discourse on Inequality*, Rousseau writes:

> The rich, in particular, must have felt how much they suffered by a constant state of war, of which they bore all the expense; and in which, though all risked their lives, they alone risked their property. Besides, however speciously they might disguise their usurpations, they knew that they were founded on precarious and false titles; so that, if others took from them by force what they themselves had gained by force, they would have no reason to complain.[310]

The *Game of Thrones* essentially echoes the medieval battles of different families in Europe for power and supremacy: forming alliances and borrowing money, as well as risking the perils of getting the church involved, as the Inquisition-like 'sparrow' movement in *Game of Thrones* demonstrated, working its way up the hierarchy to the very top for power.

Having the Iron Bank, 'the most powerful financial institution in the Known World', backing you is also extremely important for survival. As Tywin Lannister states:

---

[309] *Game of Thrones* – Season 8 Episode 4: 'The Last Of The Starks'
[310] Jean Jacques Rousseau, *Discourse on Inequality* (Oxford Uni Press: Oxford, 1994) p.67

One stone crumbles and another takes its place and the temple holds its form for a thousand years or more. And that's what the Iron Bank is, a temple. We all live in its shadow and almost none of us know it. You can't run from them, you can't cheat them, you can't sway them with excuses. If you owe them money and you don't want to crumble yourself, you pay it back.[311]

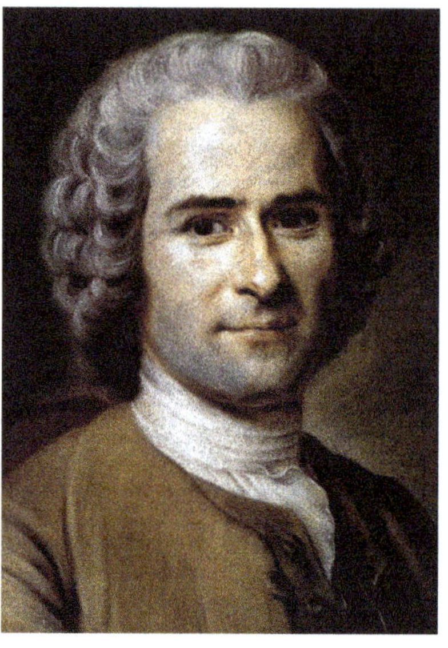

Jean-Jacques Rousseau (1712–1778) (1753)
by Maurice Quentin de La Tour (1704–1788)
(Public domain / Wikimedia Commons)

The Iron Bank always gets its due by switching sides to new kings who pay back the previous debt as well as the new loans given to them when claiming power. Similarly, the central banks and the BIS (Bank for International Settlements) are looked after with bail-outs and bail-ins by generation after generation of politicians.

Like the rise of humanism through the Renaissance and groups like the Florentine Camerata, in *Game of Thrones* Samwell Tarly goes to the ancient libraries and books for knowledge to solve fundamental problems in the face of dogma and ignorance. While in Europe the Enlightenment came through the ancient Greek texts, in

---

[311] https://gameofthrones.fandom.com/wiki/Iron_Bank_of_Braavos

the *Game of Thrones*, Enlightenment comes literally from the warm light of the south in the form of Daenerys Targaryen (who is known as the Breaker of Chains) as she brings Enlightenment mercy and freedom from slavery northwards, one town at a time. Known also as the Mother of Dragons, she has in her control an awesome source of power which aided her rise to power but was also her undoing: her three fire-breathing dragons.

Thus, throughout the chronology of *Game of Thrones* we see the almost socialist continuum of: the primitive communal ('old free') free folk, slavery, serfdom, and then the newly liberated ('new free') freed slaves who scrawled 'Death to the Masters' on their city walls in a reflection of the ideology of the French Revolution.

Enlightenment and democracy -
("Chaos is a ladder" - Petyr Baelish)

Victory comes to Daenerys in the battle for King's Landing as she uses the dragons to destroy the city and burn the inhabitants alive even though the city had surrendered to her. Her liberated slave army also killed many citizens under her orders. When the war is finished she rallies her troops "proclaiming that they will continue to 'liberate' the rest of the world as they did for King's Landing and 'break the wheel' to free all the common folk from their rulers, whom she perceives as tyrants."[312]

Daenerys Targaryen's black leather costume and blond hair are reminiscent of the Nazi leaders' uniforms and Aryan ideology (Targ-Aryan?). After her triumphant speech she is confronted by Jon (lover, nephew and competitor for the Iron Throne) about the genocide she has carried out. They disagree on what is good: to build a new world, Daenerys wants to destroy the old one, while Jon argues for mercy and forgiveness. Realising she was not going to change, Jon plunges a knife in her heart and kills her. The burning of the city using overwhelming firepower is reminiscent of Hitler's bombing campaign against the United Kingdom in 1940 and 1941.

However, the 'democratic' countries were not immune to simi-

---

[312] https://gameofthrones.fandom.com/wiki/Daenerys_Targaryen

lar strategies as the British/American aerial bombing attack on the city of Dresden in 1945 - 3,900 tons of high-explosive bombs and incendiary devices were dropped on Dresden killing an estimated 22,700 to 25,000 people.[313] Thus, it is shown that in the real world even the 'good' can be guilty of extreme measures to achieve political aims, but, unlike in *Game of Thrones*, do not receive retribution for war crimes.

The surviving main leaders of the Kingdoms gather and Tyrion proposes that all future monarchs be chosen by Westerosi leaders. They elect Bran the Broken to be leader as he cannot have children, thus finally breaking the wheel of hereditary titles and bringing in democracy of the nineteenth century type where only the elites can vote. Samwell Tarly suggests a much broader democratic base for the voting:

> 'Maybe the decision about what's best for everyone should be left to ... well, everyone.'
> 'Maybe we should give the dogs a vote as well,' laughs Bronze Yohn Royce.[314]

This disrespect for universal adult suffrage echoes modern democracy whereby the gap between the people's desires and their elected representatives' promises always remains very wide. The series ends with the new cabinet squabbling, while Jon heads north and the Danaerys' Unsullied army sails away.

Does *Game of Thrones* transcend fantasy?

The constant push for shocking drama in each episode, especially as the series headed for its grand finale could lead one to believe that the overriding mantra of the show was that *effect* was more important than *affect*. Much science fiction and fantasy literature stays within the narrow worlds created, and encourages never-ending

---

[313] https://en.wikipedia.org/wiki/Bombing_of_Dresden_in_World_War_II

[314] https://www.hollywoodreporter.com/tv/tv-news/game-thrones-series-finale-iron-throne-best-quotes-explained-1213276/

adolescence and nerd-like awareness of every detail, accompanied by board games and comic cons.

Storytelling - (Stark raven madness)

While effect is an important aspect to the excitement generated by *Game of Thrones*, Martin believes in the power of storytelling. Within the narrative many of the characters tell stories to explain their ideas or situation. There is also a meta element to the narrative as Martin uses the idea of storytelling in three different ways. At first, there is the play-within-a-play, with the medieval retelling of the poisoning of Joffrey and Tyrion's patricide by strolling players, and called The Bloody Hand.

The play is a farce and Arya, who happens upon the play, is disgusted at the humorous portrayal of the beheading of her father. The play allows Martin to have a little bit of fun with his own serious narrative, while at the same time showing how recent elite events can be satirised 'from below' by rebellious commoners, or become 'false news' propagated by elite competitors. It is also possible he is satirising the po-faced pretentiousness and egoism of many fantasy and science fiction narratives.[315]

Secondly, Martin has Tyrion extol the importance of storytelling as the memory of society itself:

Tyrion Lannister: What unites people? Armies? Gold? Flags? Stories. There's nothing more powerful than a good story. Nothing can stop it. No enemy can defeat it. And who has a better story than Bran the Broken? The boy who fell from a high tower and lived. He knew he'd never walk again, so he learned to fly. He crossed beyond the Wall, a crippled boy, and became the Three-Eyed Raven. He is our memory, the keeper of all our stories. The wars, weddings, births, massacres, famines. Our triumphs, our defeats, our past. Who better to lead us into the future?[316]

---

[315] https://gameofthrones.fandom.com/wiki/The_Bloody_Hand
[316] https://en.wikiquote.org/wiki/Game_of_Thrones/Season_8

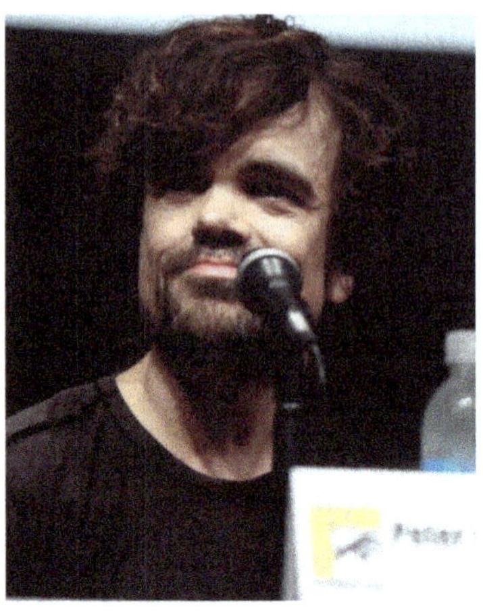

Peter Dinklage by Gage Skidmore at the 2013 San Diego Comic-Con.
Dinklage plays Tyrion Lannister in *Game of Thrones*
(Gage Skidmore / CC BY-SA 3.0 / Wikimedia Commons)

Thirdly, the power of storytelling is also demonstrated by the power of inclusion or exclusion in the narrative in a funny scene where Tyrion is presented with a large book describing recent history (and an ad for the Martin's book, *A Song of Ice and Fire*):

Tyrion Lannister: [sees a large book placed in front of him] What's this?

Samwell Tarly: *A Song of Ice and Fire.* Archmaester Ebrose's history of the wars following the death of King

Robert. I helped him with the title.

Tyrion Lannister: [flips through pages] I suppose I come in for some heavy criticism.

Samwell Tarly: Oh, I wouldn't say that.

Tyrion Lannister: Oh, he's kind to me. Never would've guessed. [Sam doesn't reply] He's not kind?

Samwell Tarly: He ...

Tyrion Lannister: He what? What does he say about me?

Samwell Tarly: ... I don't believe you're mentioned, ahem.[317]

---

[317] https://en.wikiquote.org/wiki/Game_of_Thrones/Season_8

Genocide - ("the true horrors of human history")

In *Game of Thrones* the tragic ending for Daenerys Targaryen, who audiences believed to be good, was an important moment for George R.R. Martin's views on good storytelling. Martin talked about fellow writer Tolkien's less than critical attitude towards his own characters:

> George RR Martin pointed out that Tolkien believed if there was a good ruler, like King Aragorn at the end of *The Lord of the Rings*, then things would be okay. However, Martin disagreed saying: "You can be a really decent human being … you can have the noblest of intentions, and your reign can still be horribly screwed up. He did what he wanted to do very brilliantly but … I look at the end and it says Aragorn is the king and he says, 'And Aragorn ruled wisely and well for 100 years'. It's easy to write that sentence … but I want to know what was his tax policy and what did he do when famine struck the land. And what did he do with all those Orcs? A lot of Orcs left over. They weren't all killed, they ran away into the mountains. Did Aragorn carry out a policy of systematic Orc genocide?[318]

Martin believes that "the true horrors of human history derive not from orcs and Dark Lords, but from ourselves."[319] He writes in a genre in which there is the constant, predictable battle between good and evil. However, in *Game of Thrones* we see, among others, the demonisation of (the good) Daenerys and the valorisation of (the bad) Jaime, demonstrating that questions of redemption and character change are an important part of Martin's stories. The changes we see in the main heroine of the show demonstrate Martin's reluctance to have only worn-out black and white, good and evil depictions of morality and instead he depicts the human psyche in all its dialectical processes.

---

[318] https://www.express.co.uk/entertainment/books/1190177/Game-of-Thrones-George-RR-Martin-Lord-of-the-Rings-ending-JRR-Tolkien-King-Aragorn-ASOIAF

[319] https://en.wikipedia.org/wiki/Game_of_Thrones

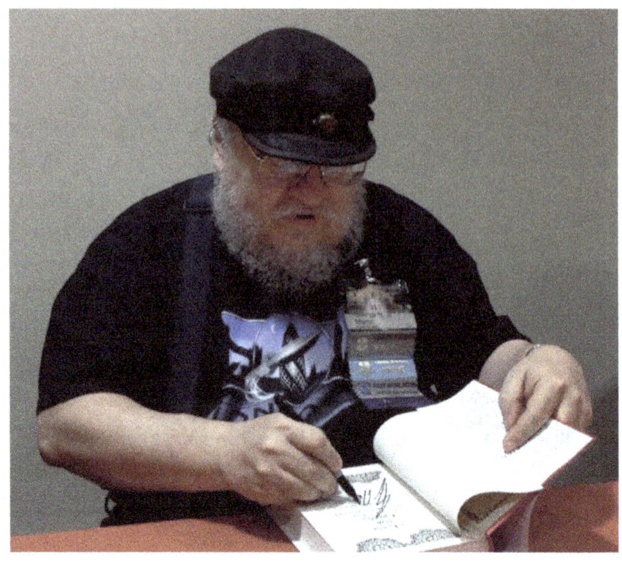

Martin at LoneStarCon 3
(the 71st World Science Fiction Convention), 2013
(User:dravecky / CC BY-SA 3.0 / Wikimedia Commons)

This makes the series ending narrative perfectly logical, except for the fans who invested too much in the concept of a 'good' leader. Our leaders promise everything from employment and better social welfare to resolving the climate change crisis, yet when elected, continue with economic and political agendas which benefit only a tiny elite. George R.R. Martin's point is to get the legions of superhero fans to stop looking for a 'saviour' and start looking to themselves to solve society's problems. How much more plainly can it be put?

Martin demonstrates the harsh reality behind Romanticist ideas about medievalism, chivalry, monarchies, banks and hero worship, while at the same time perfectly reflecting the Enlightenment's origins in bourgeois claims to universality in freedom and democracy which are never fully implemented, especially when it is realized that they would only compromise the new elites *complete* grasp of control and power.

Chapter 13

Culture

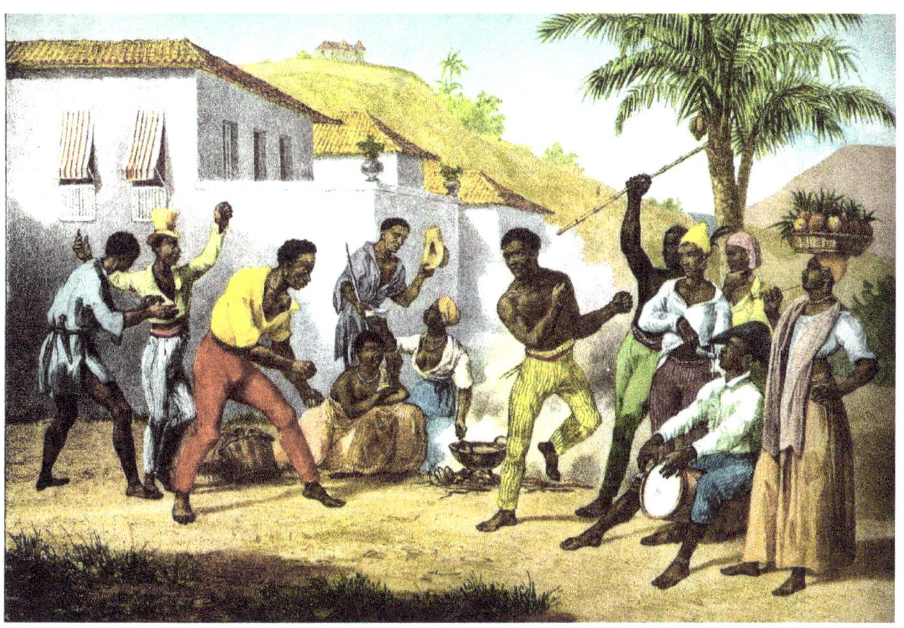

Capoeira or the Dance of War (1825) by Johann Moritz Rugendas (1802–1858) published in 1835. The dance and music were incorporated in the system to disguise the fact that they were practicing fighting techniques
(Public domain / Wikimedia Commons)

Capoeira is a game, it is dance, it is fight, it is of war
and it is of peace, it is of culture, of music,
it is a portion of things.
Mestre Suassuna

The Culture of Slavery v the Culture of Resistance

> *Inde etiam habitus nostri honor et frequens toga; pau-*
> *latimque discessum ad delenimenta vitiorum, porticus et*
> *balinea et convivorum elegantiam. Idque apud imperitos*
> *humanitas vocabatur, cum pars servitutis esset*
>
> *(They adopted our dressing fashion, and begun wearing*
> *the togas; little by little they were drawn to touches such as*
> *colonnades, baths, and elegant talks. Because they didn't*
> *know better, they called it 'civilization,'*
> *when it was part of their slavery)*
> Tacitus

The general problem of culture today is its ability to facilitate and support negative aspects of society. Many important issues of contemporary life such as economic crises, repressive legislation, poverty, and climate chaos are exacerbated by the escapism, diversion and ignorance prevalent in our culture. Or worse still, culture is used to promote elite views of society regarding power and money, as well as imperialist agendas through negative depictions of targeted ethnic groups or countries.

In this, some would call a neo-feudalist age, we see echoes of an earlier feudalism with its abuse of power and wealth that the philosophers of the Enlightenment tried to deal with and rectify during the seventeenth and eighteenth centuries.

It was led by philosophers such as Cesare Beccaria, Denis Diderot, David Hume, Immanuel Kant, Gottfried Wilhelm Leibniz, John Locke, Montesquieu, Jean-Jacques Rousseau, Adam Smith, Hugo Grotius, Baruch Spinoza, and Voltaire. Their concerns about injustice, intolerance and autocracy led to the introduction of democratic values and institutions, and the creation of modern republics.

However, the Romanticist reaction emphasized inspiration, subjectivity, and the primacy of the individual. Romanticism became the basis of many cultural movements whose common feature has been anti-science and individualism.

The Romanticist influence can be seen in 'mainstream' mass culture and high culture in terms of its emphasis on formal experimentation or emotions over sociopolitical content. Romanticism stressed 'sensibility' or feeling, and tended to look inwards. It was a movement whose ideas have come to dominate much of culture today.

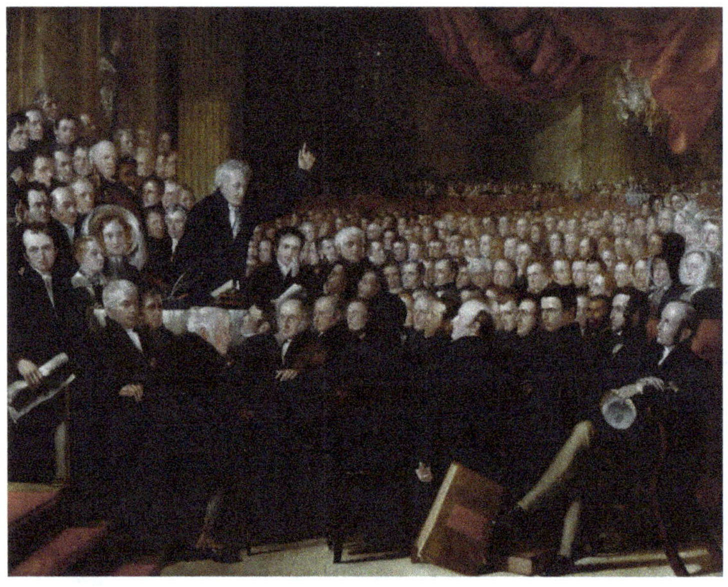

A painting of the 1840 Anti-Slavery Conference, *The Anti-Slavery Society Convention*, 1840, by Benjamin Robert Haydon (died 1846), given to the National Portrait Gallery, London in 1880 by the British and Foreign Anti-Slavery Society. Oil on canvas, 1841. 117 in. x 151 in. (2972 mm x 3836 mm). This monumental painting records the 1840 convention of the British and Foreign Anti-Slavery Society which was established to promote worldwide abolition
(Public domain / Wikimedia Commons)

Weighing scales, planets, and fractals

Romanticism is portrayed as having left and right socio-political aspects. If we picture a weighing scales with opposing ideas, for example, we can have in Romanticism the radical opposition to fascism (Romanticist Expressionism) on one side and the radical right of National Socialism on the other side. We live in a society where we are generally presented with the two-sides-to-everything (the bi-party system, good Nazis [only following orders] v the bad Nazis [gave the orders], this 'good' person v that 'bad' person, good cop v bad cop) but the reality is that they are usually different sides of the same coin. On these scales, the left and right aspects of Romanticist ideas are also two sides of the same coin, because what they both have in common is the Romanticist rejection of science and reason.

However, what if these weighing scales was standing on one side of an even bigger scale? On the other side of that bigger scales would be Enlightenment ideas. We rarely get to see the Enlightenment side of the larger scales.

Yet, on the big scales, on the Enlightenment side, we find progressive politics, the democratic opposition (who were the first to be put into the concentration camps in the 1930s), and the community workers, writers, and activists who work diligently today for change in the background. They are all squeezed out of the larger, dominant media-controlled picture.

The problem with this skewed picture is that understanding what is going on becomes as difficult to ascertain as the movements of the planets were to the ancients. The movements of the planets were perplexing in a geocentric (earth-centered) universe. Seeming to go in all sorts of strange directions, the ancient Greeks called the planets 'planeta' or 'wanderers'. It was only with the application of modern science, putting the sun at the center of a solar system, that the odd movements of the planets suddenly fell into place and made sense.[320] We have the same experience of 'revelation' or understanding when science is applied to the many different and difficult problems of history, philosophy and society itself.

---

[320] https://www.quora.com/Why-were-the-planets-given-a-name-that-means-wanderer

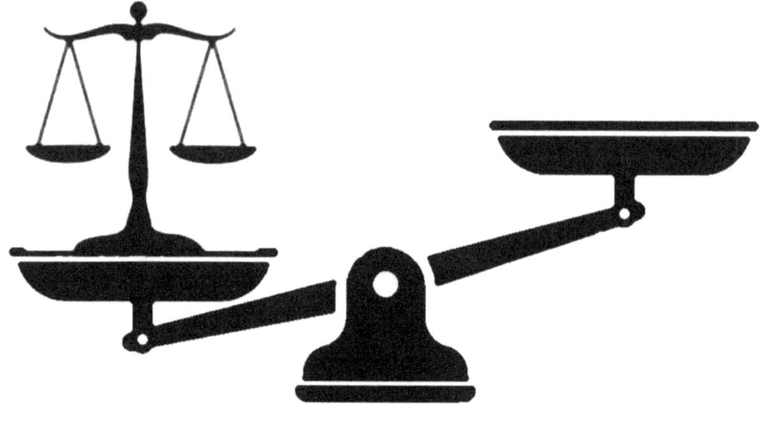

Little weighing scales on one side of an even bigger scales

The word 'science' comes from the Latin word 'scientia' meaning 'knowledge' and is a systematic exploration that allows us to develop knowledge in the form of testable explanations and predictions about the universe. The development of science has allowed us to determine what is truth and what is falsehood. Truth is defined as the property of being in accord with fact or reality and the application of science allows us to verify truth in a provable way.[321]

In this sense truth is like a fractal. Fractals are geometrical shapes that have a certain definite appearance. When we magnify a fractal, we see the same shape again. No matter how much we magnify the shape, the same geometrical patterns appear infinitely.[322] Truth is similar to a fractal in that whether the truth of something is held by one person, a group of people, a community or a nation its essence remains the same on a micro or macro level.

The heliocentric view of the universe remains true even if only one person believes or many believe, even in the face of powerful forces. For example, Galileo's championing of heliocentrism led him to be investigated by the Roman Inquisition in 1615, where he was

---

[321] https://en.wikipedia.org/wiki/Science
[322] https://en.wikipedia.org/wiki/Fractal

found guilty of heresy and spent the rest of his life under house arrest. The truth eventually came out and Galileo was pardoned by the Roman Catholic church 359 years later.[323]

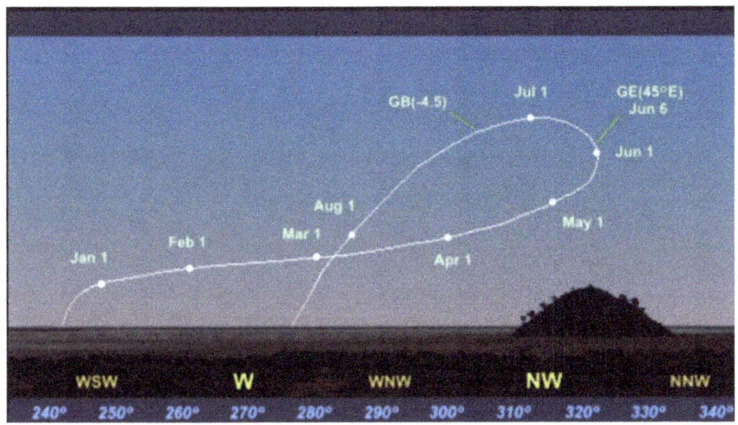

"Planets appear to go in one direction, take a looping turn, and then go in the opposite direction. This appears because of the differences of our orbits around the Sun. The Earth gets in an inside or outside track as we pass them causing a planet to look as if it had backed up and changed direction. They wander around the sky"
James Smith
(https://www.quora.com/Why-were-the-planets-given-a-name-that-means-wanderer)

Contradictions and falsehoods

It has often been said that the truth will set you free. We live in a society of contradictions and falsehoods where lies, cheating and deception contradict reality. However, many refuse to see the truths of modern society, while others are actively involved in creating the deceptions that maintain the status quo. We know that people are 'unfree' and we accept many different levels of this condition: captivity, imprisonment, suppression, dependency, restrictions, enslavement, oppression.

We may even see this condition as applying to others and not to ourselves. But if we examine closely and truthfully our own position in the societal hierarchy we may recognize our own powerlessness:

---

[323] https://en.wikipedia.org/wiki/Galileo_Galilei

the contradiction between our view of ourselves and the reality of our situation. Although we vote and we recognize the social contract by rendering taxes to the state, the fact is that very little of substance changes and generally things seem to get worse.

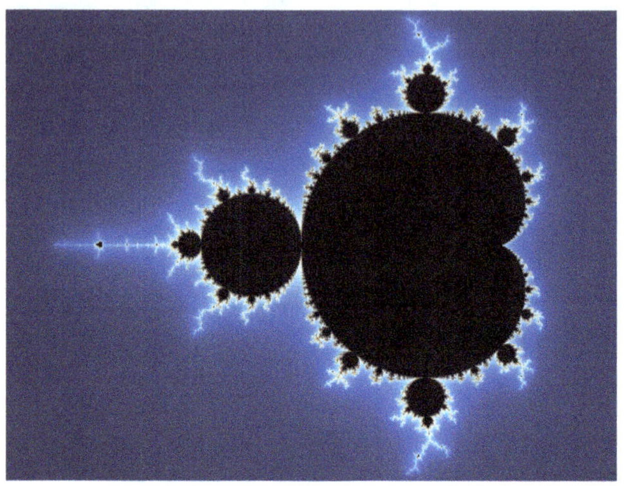

'Fractals appear the same at different levels, as illustrated in successive magnifications of the Mandelbrot set. Fractals exhibit similar patterns at increasingly small scales called self-similarity, also known as expanding symmetry or unfolding symmetry'
(Created by Wolfgang Beyer / program Ultra Fractal 3.
/ CC BY-SA 3.0 / Wikimedia Commons)

As I have written elsewhere, the fact is that we are triply exploited: we are taxed on wages, alienated from wealth created (profits), and we pay interest on the money borrowed from the wealthy to pay for the capital and current expenditure needed for the maintenance of society and to fill in the gap created by the wealthy in the first place.[324]

How is this system of exploitation maintained? Aside from the obvious threat of imprisonment for nonpayment of taxes, and the existence of police and army to enforce the laws of the state: the most influential, and sometimes most subtle tool, is through culture.

---

[324] https://www.globalresearch.ca/austerity-is-a-scam-crisis-legislation-and-dodgy-debt-repayment-schemes/5322437

The culture of slavery

Culture has a long history of use and abuse, from the bread and circuses of Roman times to the social media of today. In modern society mass culture helps to maintain this system of exploitation and keeps people in general from questioning their position in the societal hierarchy. The middle-classes are lulled into thinking they are free because of better wages making for an easier life, while the working-class work ever harder to achieve the advantages of the middle-class: higher education, higher status, higher wages. (It has been suggested that the middle class are essentially 'working-class people with huge debts' e.g. large mortgages.)

However, in general, people work in a globalized system of exploitation in states that support and maintain it thus making wage slaves of the 99 per cent.

The traditional definition of slavery is 'someone forbidden to quit their service for another person and is treated like property.' Modern slavery takes on different forms such as human trafficking, debt bondage, and forced labour:

Experts have calculated that roughly 13 million people were captured and sold as slaves between the 15th and 19th centuries; today, an estimated 40.3 million people – more than three times the figure during the transatlantic slave trade – are living in some form of modern slavery, according to the latest figures published by the UN's International Labour Organization (ILO) and the Walk Free Foundation. Women and girls comprise 71% of all modern slavery victims. Children make up 25% and account for 10 million of all the slaves worldwide.[325]

While these are the most extreme cases in modern society, the majority of workers have no control over the wealth they produce:

one of the defining features of the employment relationship

---

[325] 'One in 200 people is a slave. Why? Slavery affects more than 40 million people worldwide – more than at any other time in history', Kate Hodal. See: https://www.theguardian.com/news/2019/feb/25/modern-slavery-trafficking-persons-one-in-200

in all capitalist countries is that the worker's will is, by law, 'subordinate' to the employers. The employer has the right, within broad bounds, to define the nature of the task, who performs it, and how. This shows up in all kinds of surveillance, control, and submission — also known as maximizing productivity and extracting profit.[326]

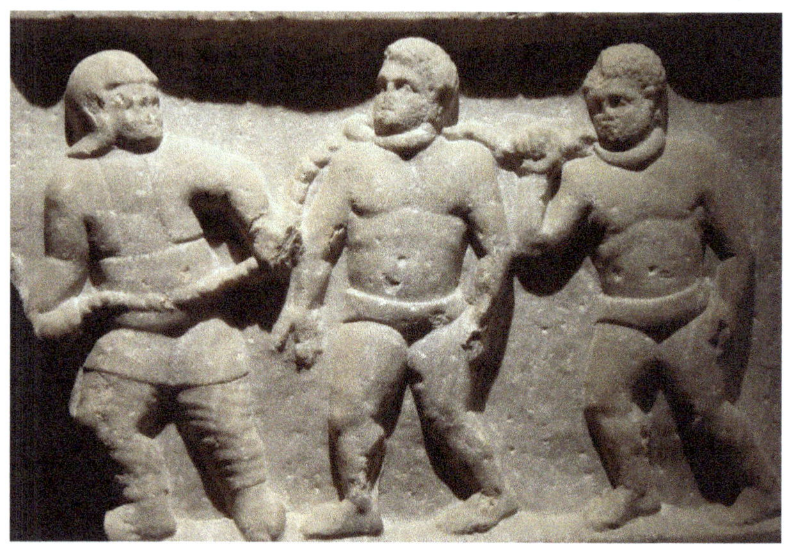

Slaves in chains during the period of Roman rule at Smyrna (present-day İzmir), 200 CE
(Ashmolean Museum / CC BY-SA 2.0 / Wikimedia Commons)

The investors and the shareholders benefit the most, while the employees receive wages of varying levels according to the demand for their particular skillset.

We are encouraged to accept this way of life and there are plenty of different state methods and forces to make sure that we do. However, culture is an important tool of soft power, in particular, mass culture.

The role of mass culture is absolutely essential for the creation, maintenance, and perpetuation of a broad acceptance of the ever-changing forms of technological 'progress' and geopolitical shifts

---

[326] 'Bernie Sanders Was Right to Talk About Wage Slavery. We Should Talk About It, Too', Alex Gourevitch. See: https://www.jacobinmag.com/2020/01/wage-slavery-bernie-sanders-labor

in modern capitalist societies, particularly as the global financial crisis (corporate and national debt) deepens.

Culture on three levels

To do this, modern mass culture operates on three different levels. The first level is creating acceptance, through diversion and escapism and turning people into passive consumers. Secondly, through the overt representation of elite ideology. Thirdly, and more controversially, through covert manipulation of mass culture to benefit the agenda of elites.

In the first case, consumption becomes inseparable from the ideas of enjoyment and fun. Earlier twentieth century theorists of the Frankfurt School saw consumers as essentially passive but later theoreticians such as Baudrillard saw consumption as an unconscious social conditioning, consuming culture to achieve social mobility by showing awareness of the latest trends in mass culture.[327]

Secondly, overt representation of elite ideology is evident in mass culture that glorifies the upper classes, and promotes racism and militarist imperialism. In particular, mass culture depicting historical and contemporary events is portrayed from an elite perspective.

Thirdly, conscious manipulation of the masses using psychological means, and more controversially, predictive programming. In the 1930s, Edward Bernays was a pioneer in the public relations industry using psychology and other social sciences to design public persuasion campaigns. Bernays wrote:

> If we understand the mechanism and motives of the group mind, is it not possible to control and regiment the masses according to our will without their knowing about it? The recent practice of propaganda has proved that it is possible, at least up to a certain point and within certain limits.[328]

---

[327] https://en.wikipedia.org/wiki/Popular_culture
[328] https://en.wikipedia.org/wiki/Edward_Bernays

An interesting science-fiction film on this theme is *They Live* (1988), an American action thriller written and directed by John Carpenter that "follows an unnamed drifter who discovers through special sunglasses that the ruling class are aliens concealing their appearance and manipulating people to consume, breed, and conform to the status quo via subliminal messages in mass media."[329] The glasses reveal a black and white world with words like 'conform', 'obey', and 'consume' in the place of the usual advertisements.

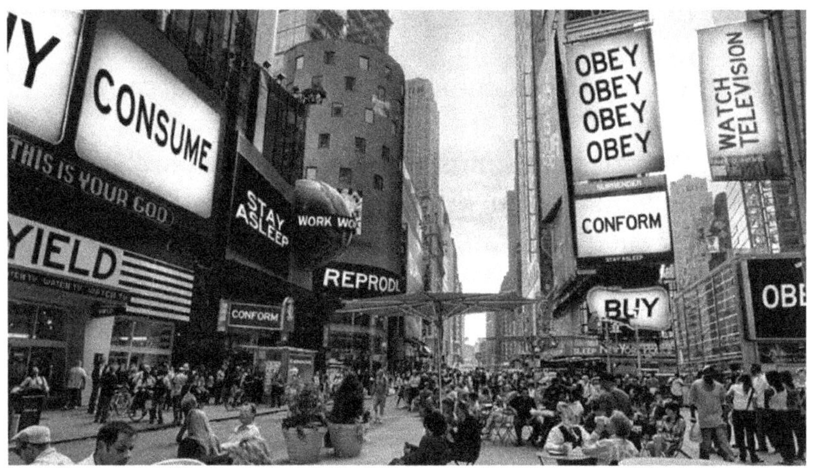

They Live (1988) by John Carpenter, based on the 1963 short story 'Eight O'Clock in the Morning'
(https://en.wikipedia.org/wiki/They_Live)
'For Adorno and Horkheimer, the culture industry creates false needs to keep us purchasing products we do not actually need by manipulating our psychological impulses and desires'
(https://www.shalonvantine.com/secondasfarce/2020/2/21/adorno-and-the-culture-industry)

Another form of mass manipulation is the concept of predictive programming. Predictive Programming is the theory "that the government or other higher-ups are using fictional movies or books as a mass mind control tool to make the population more accepting of planned future events."[330] It is by its nature hard to prove yet the many extraordinary coincidences between events depicted in mass

---

[329] https://en.wikipedia.org/wiki/They_Live
[330] https://u.osu.edu/vanzandt/2018/04/18/predictive-programming/

culture and later actual events is, at the very least, disconcerting. For example, the film *The Manchurian Candidate*[331] depicting the son of a prominent U.S. political family who is brainwashed into being an unwitting assassin for a Communist conspiracy, was released in 1962, a year before the assassination of J. F. Kennedy in 1963 by Lee Harvey Oswald, an emotionally disturbed 'communist sympathizer' who declared his innocence and believed he was being used as a 'patsy'.[332]

Thus, these three levels of cultural manipulation allow elites to control how the past, the present, and the future is depicted in mass culture, according to national and geopolitical agendas.

Cultural producers

In their defense, the role of cultural producers has never been easy, and the more money or support that is needed for a cultural project, the harder it is to maintain an independent position. While with modern production methods and technology it is easier to produce books, films and music independently of the major producers and distributors, in the past elite pressure, censorship, and imprisonment were common.

Pushkin, for example, in his *Ode to Liberty*, exclaimed with indignation:

> Unhappy nation! Everywhere
> Men suffer under whips and chains,
> And over all injustice reigns,
> And haughty peers abuse their power
> And sombre prejudice prevails.[333]

However, later during the time of Nicholas I, Pushkin changed and "adopted the theory of 'art for art's sake'":

According to the touching and very widespread legend, in

---

[331] https://en.wikipedia.org/wiki/The_Manchurian_Candidate_(1962_film)
[332] https://en.wikipedia.org/wiki/Lee_Harvey_Oswald
[333] https://www.marxists.org/archive/plekhanov/1912/art/ch01.htm

1826 Nicholas I graciously 'forgave' Pushkin the political 'errors of his youth,' and even became his magnanimous patron. But this is far from the truth. Nicholas and his right-hand man in affairs of this kind, Chief of Police Benkendorf, 'forgave' Pushkin nothing, and their 'patronage' took the form of a long series of intolerable humiliations. Benkendorf reported to Nicholas in 1827: 'After his interview with me, Pushkin spoke enthusiastically of Your Majesty in the English Club, and compelled his fellow diners to drink Your Majesty's health. He is a regular ne'er-do-well, but if we succeed in directing his pen and his tongue, it will be a good thing.' The last words in this quotation reveal the secret of the 'patronage' accorded to Pushkin. They wanted to make him a minstrel of the existing order of things. Nicholas I and Benkendorf had made it their aim to direct Pushkin's unruly muse into the channels of official morality.[334]

Pushkin's contemporaries, the French Romanticists, were also, with few exceptions, ardent believers in 'art for art's sake', the idea of the absolute autonomy of art with no other purpose than itself.

In the twentieth century, *Ars Gratia Artis* (Latin: 'Art for Art's Sake'), the renunciation of all political and social activity, would become the motto for the American media company Metro-Goldwyn-Mayer (formed in 1924), to designate art that is independent of political and social pressures.[335] Of course, while some believe that art should not be politicized, it can be argued that if art is not a social endeavor then it will be used as a commercial item only available to the rich, e.g. a profitable escapist product while simultaneously maintaining and promoting a conservative mindset.

However, by the 1930s any thoughts of art as a progressive tool in the USA were soon quashed by the HUAC (House Un-American Activities Committee), a body which was set up in 1938 to investigate alleged disloyalty and subversive activities on the part of private citizens, public employees, and any organizations with left wing sympathies.[336]

---

[334] https://www.marxists.org/archive/plekhanov/1912/art/ch01.htm

[335] https://en.wikipedia.org/wiki/Art_for_art%27s_sake

[336] https://en.wikipedia.org/wiki/House_Un-American_Activities_Committee

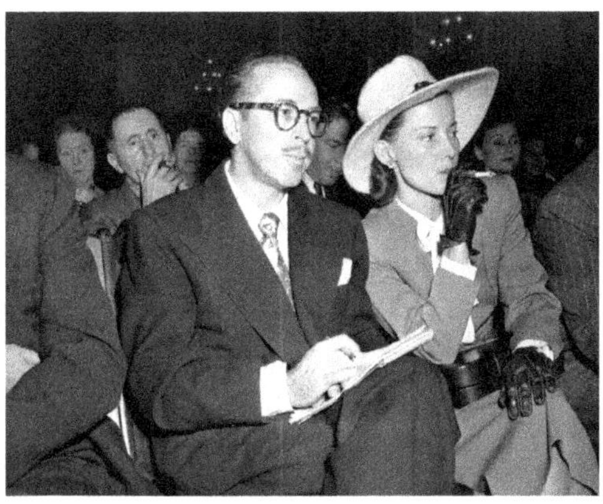

Dalton and Cleo Trumbo (1947 HUAC hearings)
James Dalton Trumbo (1905–1976) was an American screenwriter
who scripted many award-winning films, including *Roman Holiday*
(1953), *Exodus, Spartacus* (both 1960), and *Thirty Seconds Over Tokyo*
(1944). One of the Hollywood Ten, he refused to testify before the
House Un-American Activities Committee (HUAC) in 1947 during the
committee's investigation of alleged Communist influences
in the motion picture industry
(Public domain / Wikimedia Commons)

Dialectic of Enlightenment

Not long after, a theoretical analysis of consumerist mass culture
was published in a book by Theodor Adorno (1903–1969) and Max
Horkheimer (1895–1973) in 1947 entitled *Dialectic of Enlightenment* in which they coined the term the Culture Industry. For Adorno and Horkheimer "the mass-media entertainment industry and
commercialized popular culture, which they saw as primarily concerned with producing not only symbolic goods but also needs and
consumers, serving the ideological function of diversion, and thus
depoliticizing the working class."[337]

They believed that the production of culture had become like
a "a factory producing standardized cultural goods — films, radio
programmes, magazines, etc.— that are used to manipulate mass
society into passivity."[338]

[337] https://www.oxfordreference.com/view/10.1093/oi/authority.20110803095652757
[338] https://en.wikipedia.org/wiki/Culture_industry

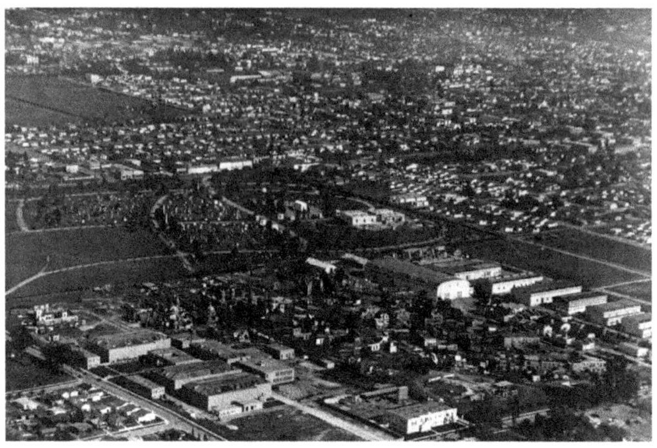

Hollywood movie studios, 1922
(Public domain / Wikimedia Commons)

More significantly, Adorno and Horkheimer also believed that the scientific thinking the Enlightenment philosophers had developed "led to the development of technologically sophisticated but oppressive and inhumane modes of governance."[339] Adorno and Horkheimer believed that because the rationalization of society had ultimately led to Fascism, science and rationalism provided little optimism for future progress and human freedom.

However, this view of the history of science and its relationship with human emancipation is, according to Jeffrey Herf in *'Dialectic of Enlightenment* Reconsidered'*, one that ignores many progressive movements and changes brought about by Enlightenment ideas, and that Horkheimer and Adorno's view of modern society and politics simply reduced modernity to technology, science, and bureaucracy. Herf outlines many of the events, institutions, laws, rights, treatments and other human benefits that Adorno and Horkheimer (and others) had ignored:

In Weber's sociology, Heidegger's philosophical ruminations, or *Dialectic of Enlightenment*, the panoply of ideas and events associated with the 1688 revolution in Britain, the moderate wing of the French Revolution, and the ideas and

---

[339] https://www.britannica.com/topic/Dialectic-of-Enlightenment

institutions that emerged from the American Revolution, and then from the victory of the North in the American Civil War, are simply absent. As a result of this paucity of historical specificity, Horkheimer and Adorno's view of modernity during World War II was a very German caricature that did not include ideas about the extension of citizenship, British antislavery, American abolitionism, feminism in Europe and the United States, and the rule of law. Theirs was modernity without liberal democratic ideas and institutions, the rule of law, and the freedom of speech, of assembly, of the press, and of religion or unbelief. [...] *Dialectic of Enlightenment* presented modern science as primarily an exercise in the domination of nature and of human beings. Theirs was a view of the history of the scientific revolution that left out Galileo's challenge to religious authoritarianism and Francis Bacon's liberating restatement of the role of evidence in resolving contentious issues. From reading Horkheimer and Adorno — as well as Heidegger and Baumann — one would conclude that modern science was first and foremost a source of control, and would have no idea of how modern medicine, unthinkable without the Enlightenment and the scientific revolution, had come into existence.[340]

Thus, Adorno and Horkheimer's view leaves us with an almost Nietzschian nihilism, that knowledge is impossible, and life is meaningless because to try and improve society will fail and ultimately only increase oppression, and ultimately misses the point that the Enlightenment philosophers were concerned with the prevalence of injustice in society, not technology and science. Without action, Nietzsche predicted a society of 'the last man', the "apathetic person or society who loses the ability to dream, to strive, and who become unwilling to take risks," and slave morality characterized by pessimism and cynicism. A society which has not only lost its 'will to power' but also its will to revolt.[341]

---

[340] Jeffrey Herf, '"Dialectic of Enlightenment" Reconsidered', Source: *New German Critique*, Fall 2012, No. 117, Special Issue for Anson Rabinbach (Fall 2012), pp. 81-89 Published by: Duke University Press [p84] Stable URL: https://www.jstor.org/stable/23357065

[341] https://en.wikipedia.org/wiki/Last_man

The culture of resistance

Throughout history, oppression has been met with resistance in many forms such as uprisings, rebellions, and insurrections. The resistance often starts with strikes, boycotts, and civil disobedience, leading to mass movements of people who ultimately reject the old system of governance and change it for a new system which can be anti-colonial, anti-imperialist or anti-capitalist. The rise of resistance seems to generally develop in three stages, each affecting culture in very different ways. These different stages could be called (1) criticism, (2) substitution and (3) implementation.

(1) Criticism

Resistance often begins as criticism of the policies or nature of government, or the state. This can be aesthetic or intellectual resistance appearing, for example, in various art forms. Critiques can be of an ideological nature, or simply highlight social problems and issues. Resistance can take the form of criticism of officially sanctioned culture through demonstrations and boycotting (the Irish refusal collectively to harvest the crops in the charge of land agent Captain Charles Boycott in 1880 as resistance to evictions).

It may also take a violent form, for example, the blowing up of colonial statues as happened to many statues in Ireland from the 1870s to 1966.[342] The blowing up of Nelson's Pillar in Dublin in 1966, for example, was celebrated subsequently in two different ballads which became immensely popular, an aesthetic critique arising out of a violent 'critique'.

On a formal level resistance can also be 'form-poor' as struggle without help from educated or trained professionals is left to amateurs.

---

[342] For a comprehensive list of attacks on public statues in Ireland see my blogpost 'Redrawing the Cultural Cityscape: The Destiny of Colonial Monuments in Ireland': http://gaelart.blogspot.com/2020/06/redrawing-cultural-cityscape-destiny-of.html

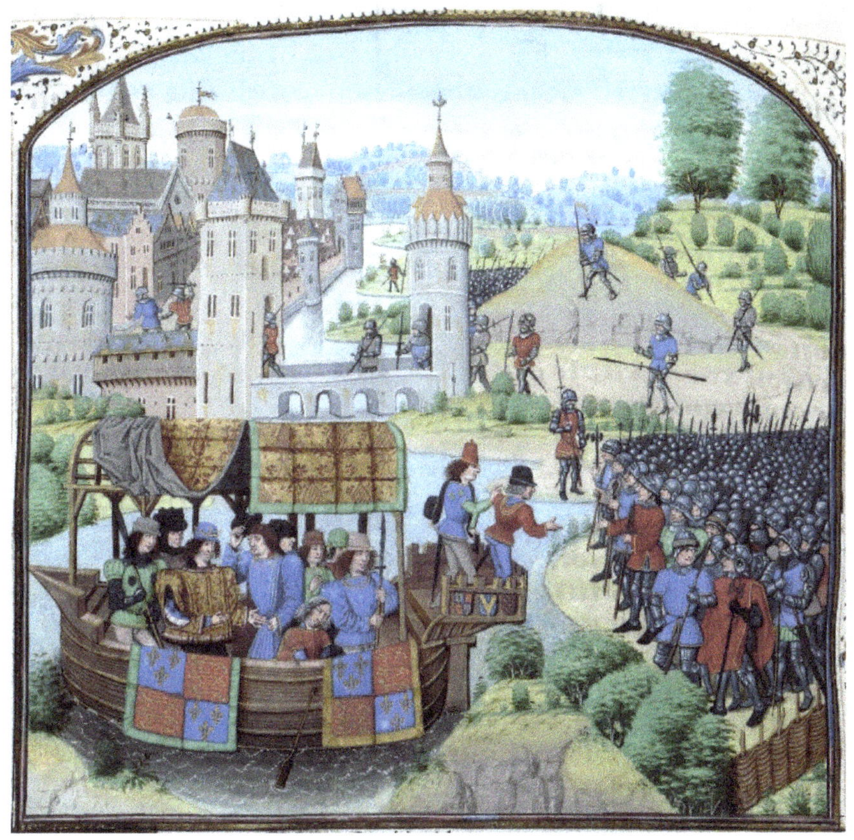

"Richard II meeting with the rebels of the Peasants' Revolt of 1381. The revolt had various causes, including the socio-economic and political tensions generated by the Black Death pandemic in the 1340s, the high taxes resulting from the conflict with France during the Hundred Years' War, and instability within the local leadership of London" (https://en.wikipedia.org/wiki/Peasants%27_Revolt) (Image: Jean Froissart / Public domain / Wikimedia Common)

(2) Substitution

Gradually, a new ideology, a different reading of history, a new set of artists and writers produce culture which eventually substitutes the old culture with a new culture as the movement gathers momentum (for example, when the Irish Republic unilaterally declared independence in 1919, the Dáil Courts or Republican Courts were set up, creating for the time being, a parallel - and popular - judicial system that frustrated the colonial power by undermining British rule in Ireland, and which continued until independence.[343]).

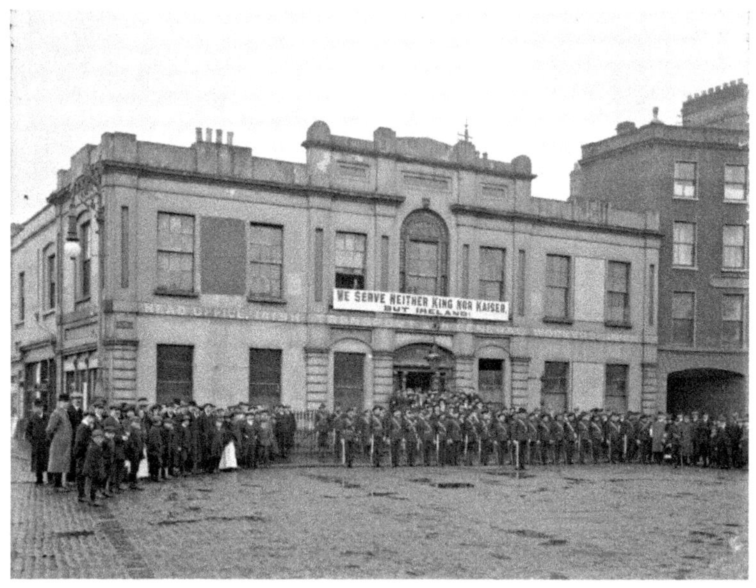

Irish Citizen Army group outside Liberty Hall. Group are lined up outside ITGWU HQ under a banner proclaiming "We serve neither King nor Kaiser, but Ireland!". Photo taken in early years of WWI
(National Library of Ireland on The Commons / Public domain / Wikimedia Commons)

The less costly forms like art, music, ballads, books etc. can become very popular and important elements of the resistance itself. The more expensive cultural forms are difficult to produce in the new culture, e.g., cinema, theatre, opera, TV etc., (unless of course if the format is changed like in community theatre substituting for state theatre). Digital equipment can be vastly cheaper to use for the making of movies for mass viewing assuming that the outlet for presentation, the internet, is not closed off through censorship.

---

[343] https://en.wikipedia.org/wiki/D%C3%A1il_Courts

(3) Implementation

The final stage is implementation, whereby popular resistance takes control of the state and is able to implement progressive culture as state policy. This is particularly important for the more costly art forms which also gain access to state finance and auditoriums. It allows movies, for example, to cover ignored themes such as histories of resistance, or to show past events from more radical perspectives than the previous elite mindset and agendas.

These different levels of cultural change: criticism, substitution, and implementation can be a long process or can all come together in a short span of time.

I have tried to show in my previous examination of ten different art-forms (art, music, theatre, opera, literature, poetry, cinema, architecture, TV, and dance) that since the Age of Enlightenment there has been a strong vein of radical ideas relating to social progress. Over the centuries radical culture has looked at the plight of the oppressed using different forms such as naturalism, realism, social realism, and working-class socialist realism.

The philosophers of the Enlightenment believed that advancements in science, technology, economic development and social organization would have global application. They also believed in the idea that empirical knowledge should be the basis of society and that with these ideas political and societal change would strengthen civilization itself. While social progressivism, as a political philosophy, is reformist in nature, it also has the potential to snowball into more radical action through discussion around questions as to who runs the state and ownership of the means of production.

The form and content of the culture of resistance has many aspects. Some emphasize change on the community level, developing the skills, community spirit, and artistic sensibilities of the community members whether they be producers, creators or observers.

An important element of this strategy for social change is encouraging critical thinking through participation in active dialogue. General themes for discussion have been, for example, gender equality, human rights, the environment and democracy.

Others have taken a more radical approach of examining human conflict and its sources. They look at human conflict from a social perspective and see society in terms of conflicting economic classes. By portraying economic classes in conflict, they hope to evolve or expand a working-class consciousness or at least an understanding of, and empathy with, oppressed groups. Radical artists, writers, composers etc. are encouraged to take a scientific approach and work against superstitions and blind practices. As radical cultural producers they try to present the truth and inspire wide-ranging social and political activism.

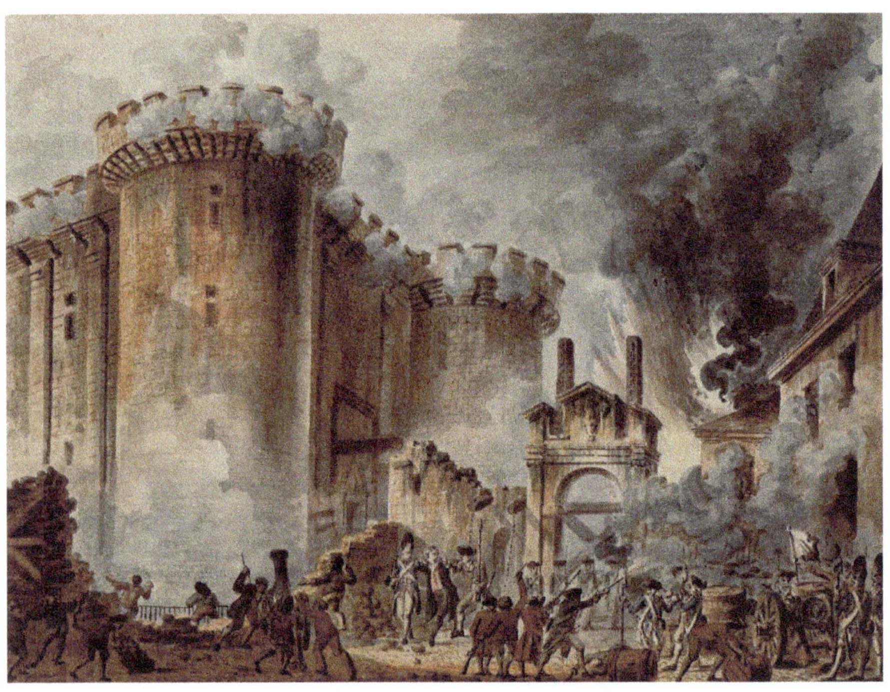

Prise de la Bastille (*Storming of The Bastille*) (1789)
by Jean-Pierre Houël (1735–1813)
(Public domain / Wikimedia Commons)

Modern resistance, often in digital form on the internet today, is now subject to a creeping censorship as Big Tech tries to slow down the efficacy of the internet at making widely available different perspectives on many different issues. At the same time, Big Tech tries to portray technological progress as social progress, and is at the forefront of liberal campaigns for individual rights at the expense of mass movements for collective or group rights.

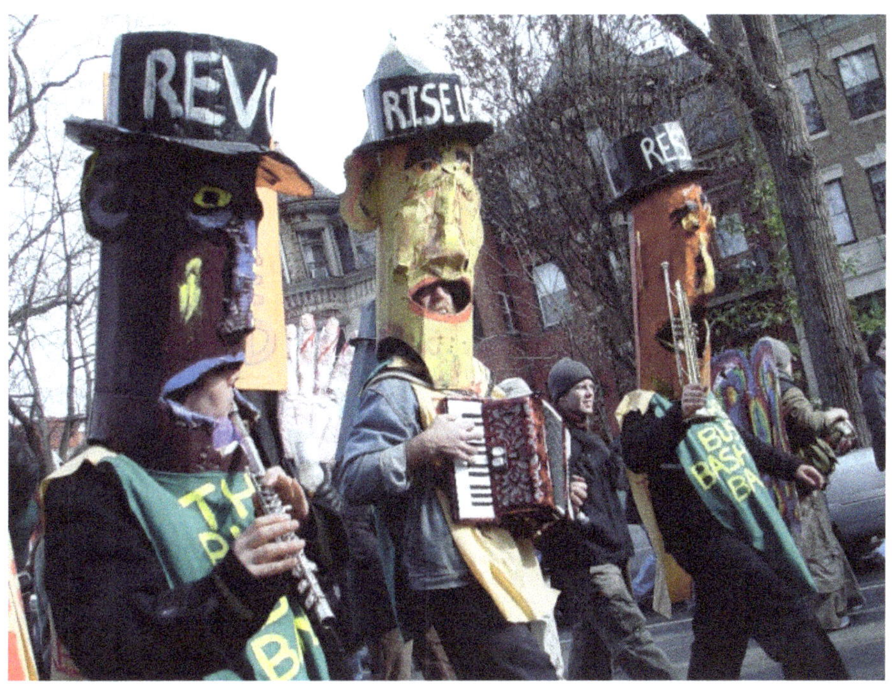

The Bash Bush Band musical protesters at Bush's 2nd inauguration, Washington DC (Revolt, Rise Up, Resist)
(Jonathan McIntosh / CC BY 2.0 / Wikimedia Commons)

Such group rights allow for organizations to speak for, and negotiate on behalf of trade unions, trade associations, specific ethnic groups, political parties, and nation-states.

However, internet censorship and the gradually increasing power of the state (through police, courts, and prisons) using current and new legislation will be able to continue unabated, that is, unless the slave culture that facilitates it is shaken off and a new culture of resistance is born.

Conclusion

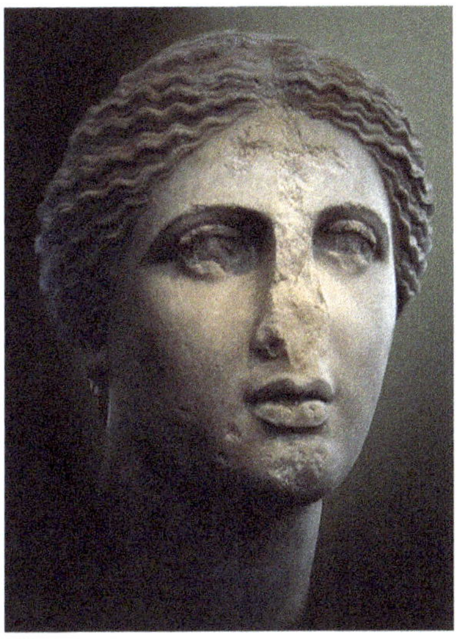

Head of Aphrodite, 1st century AD copy of an original by Praxiteles. The Christian cross on the chin and forehead was intended to "deconsecrate" a holy pagan artifact. Found in the Agora of Athens
(National Archaeological Museum of Athens / CC BY-SA 3.0 / Wikimedia Commons)

I stand four-square for reason, and object to what seems to me to be irrationality, whatever the source. If you are on my side in this, I must warn you that the army of the night has the advantage of overwhelming numbers, and, by its very nature, is immune to reason, so that it is entirely unlikely that you and I can win out. We will always remain a tiny and probably hopeless minority, but let us never tire of presenting our view, and of fighting the good fight for the right."
Isaac Asimov

The Power of Romanticism today:
21st Century Irrationalism

> *Christianity defeated and wiped out the old faith of the*
> *pagans. Then with great fervour and diligence it strove to*
> *cast out and utterly destroy every last possible occasion of*
> *sin; and in doing so it ruined or demolished all the mar-*
> *velous statues, besides the other sculptures, the pictures,*
> *mosaics and ornaments representing the false pagan gods;*
> *and as well as this it destroyed countless memorials and*
> *inscriptions left in honor of illustrious persons who had*
> *been commemorated by the genius of the ancient world in*
> *statues and other public monuments .... their tremendous*
> *zeal was responsible for inflicting severe damage on the*
> *practice of the arts, which then fell into total confusion.*
> Giorgio Vasari (1511-1574), *Lives of the Artists*

> *'Tis the temper of the hot and superstitious part of man-*
> *kind in matters of religion ever to be fond of mysteries, &*
> *for that reason to like best what they understand least.*
> Isaac Newton

The development and spread of Enlightenment ideas in the eighteenth century instituted new movements based on a scientific approach to the pursuit of happiness, sense evidence as the primary
source of knowledge, and which believed in progress, liberty, constitutional government and separation of church and state. However, while the growth of Romanticism in the nineteenth century was
a new movement emphasising the non-rational, or irrational, this

was not new. Irrationalism stressed feeling, will and instinct over or against reason and its influence stretched back through time to the early Greeks.

Here I will look at the relationship between science and irrationalism throughout history showing that at times rational investigation complemented irrational ideas, and at other times irrational ideas arose that conflicted with rational analysis. Early polytheistic society was less dogmatic in its attitude to science compared with Christian theology. Science slowly regained a foothold over the centuries and church ideology weakened. However, Romanticism took the place of the church as the main irrationalist ideology to hinder the growing influence of science in many different fields. Similarly, with Christian ideology, it was the conservative elites who advanced and benefited from the irrationalist ideas of Romanticism, using the various offshoots of Romanticism (Nationalism, Modernism, Postmodernism, Metamodernism etc.) to try and hold back the progressive development of societies towards genuine democracy and freedom, the essential ideas that originated in the Enlightenment. However, as globalised hegemonic culture today becomes ever more saturated with Romanticism - in parallel with Romanticist political movements - there is a real fear that another wave of extreme irrationalist ideas and violence could be provoked and sweep the world within a short period of time.

Early religion and rational investigation

In early societies the irrational ideas of polytheistic religion were aided by rational investigation that helped with human understanding of nature, for example, the Mesopotamians studied scientific subjects, like astronomy, that helped with their religious system. [344]

Astronomy was of utmost importance to some civilizations who left behind large artefacts (proto-observatories e.g. Newgrange in Ireland, Stonehenge in Great Britain, Angkor Wat in Cambodia, Abu Simbel in Egypt etc.) connected with the longest and shortest days

---

[344] https://en.wikipedia.org/wiki/Science

of the year.[345] This would have helped in determining the seasons and understanding the length of the year and when was the best time to plant crops. Early religion was polytheistic and rooted in nature, and which can still be seen today amongst the indigenous peoples of many countries. In Ancient Greece, worshipping the gods centred around fertility, childbirth, farming, harvest and death:

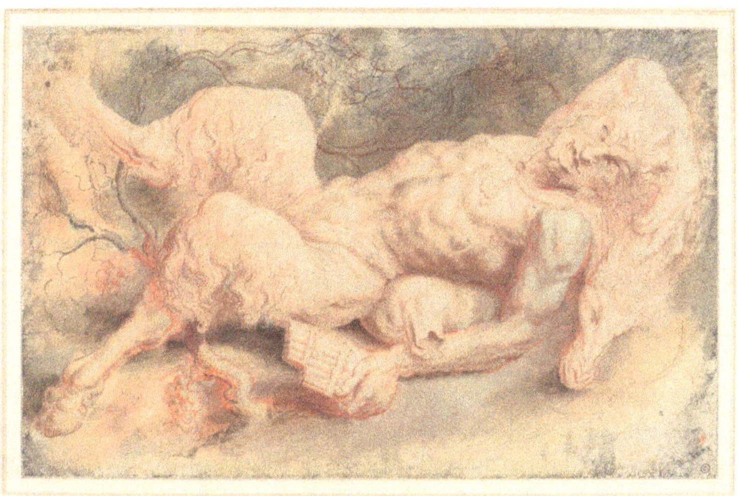

Pan Reclining (c. 1610) by Peter Paul Rubens (1577–1640), National Gallery of Art, Washington, USA. Pan is the god of the wild, shepherds and flocks, and connected to fertility and the season of spring. Pan's goatish image recalls conventional faun-like depictions of Satan
(National Gallery of Art / CC0 / Wikimedia Commons)

Peasants worshipped the omnipresent deities of the countryside, such as the Arcadian goat-god Pan, who prospered the flocks, and the nymphs (who, like Eileithyia, aided women in childbirth) who inhabited caves, springs (Naiads), trees (dryads and hamadryads), and the sea (Nereids). They also believed in nature spirits such as satyrs and sileni and equine Centaurs. Among the more-popular festivals were the rural Dionysia, which included a phallus pole; the Anthesteria, when new wine was broached and offerings were

---

[345] https://en.wikipedia.org/wiki/Astronomy

made to the dead; the Thalysia, a harvest celebration; the Thargelia, when a scapegoat (pharmakos) assumed the communal guilt; and the Pyanepsia, a bean feast in which boys collected offerings to hang on the eiresiōne ("wool pole").[346]

The desire to systematize the connection between nature and farming resulted in the many-century long scientific endeavour to create an accurate calendar. The Greek poet Hesiod, who lived around 700 BC developed the Works and Days calendar "in which the farmer was to regulate seasonal activities by the seasonal appearances and disappearances of the stars, as well as by the phases of the Moon which were held to be propitious or ominous."[347] Thus, the calendar would help people more accurately mark the seasons with celebrations and rituals that integrated their activity with the earth's cycles, as Helen Ellerbe explains:

The cycle of the year, at both the change of the four seasons as well as the height of each season, used to hold great importance. The winter solstice, the darkest day of the year, was a time of new birth. Often it was symbolized by the birth of an annual male fertility figure, a representation of the year's new sun. The height of the winter, midway between the winter solstice and the spring equinox, was a time to nurture that new life. Spring was about encouraging fertility, when the sun and earth would unite to later bring forth the abundance of the harvest and the bounty of the hunt. From the summer solstice through autumn the sun's energy transferred to the crops. The height of summer and the fall equinox were celebrations of the year's harvest and bounty. The end of the year when fields lay dormant and the earth seemed to die at the height of autumn was a time to honor the dead and release the past.[348]

From the later sixth century BCE onward, myths and gods were

---

[346] https://www.britannica.com/topic/Greek-religion/The-Archaic-period
[347] https://en.wikipedia.org/wiki/History_of_science_in_classical_antiquity
[348] Helen Ellerbe, *The Dark Side of Christian History* (1995) p145

subject to rational criticism on ethical or other grounds[349] as the early Greek philosophers such as Thales of Miletus and later Anaximander and Anaximenes tried to explain natural phenomena without relying on the supernatural.[350]

The rise of irrationalism

The spread of Christendom from the Middle East to Africa and Europe by 600 CE was to have huge consequences not only for polytheistic religions but also on burgeoning scientific exploration. The struggle to convert the Roman Empire to Christianity was perceived by Christians as a struggle between the forces of darkness and light, between God and Satan.[351]

As Christianity gained more and more power it worked to not only convert the polytheists to monotheism but also to eradicate scientific learning through attacks on books, libraries and the philosophers themselves. The only thing that mattered in life was worshipping god and any threat to the ideology and theology of Christianity, like, for example, Epicurean (341–270 BCE) atomic theory, was to be eradicated. Atomic theory stated that everything in the world was made by the collision and combination of atoms and not created by a divine being. Thus, according to Catherine Nixey:

> The intellectual consequences of this powerful [atomic] theory were summarized succinctly by the Christian apologist Minucius Felix. If everything in the universe has been 'formed by a fortuitous concourse of atoms, what God is the architect?' The obvious answer is: no god at all. No god magicked up mankind out of nothing, no divinity breathed life into us; and, when we die, our atoms are simply reabsorbed into this great sea of stuff. 'No thing is ever by divine power produced from nothing,' wrote Lucretius in his great poem,

---

[349] https://www.britannica.com/topic/Greek-religion/The-Archaic-period

[350] https://en.wikipedia.org/wiki/Science

[351] Catherine Nixey, *The Darkening Age: The Christian Destruction of the Classical World* (2017) p9

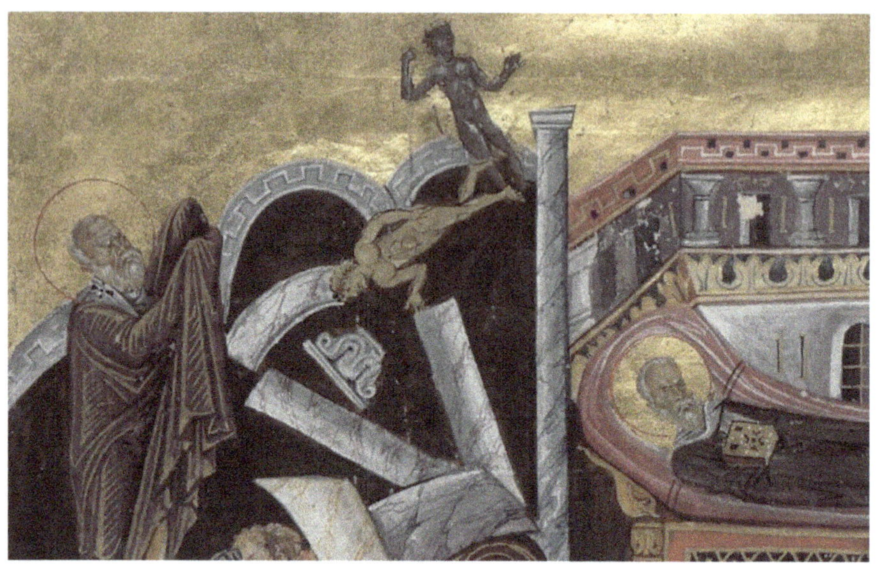

Depiction of Cornelius the Centurion, a gentile who converted to Christianity as related in the Acts of the Apostles. When forced to sacrifice to idols, he caused an earthquake that brought down the temple and its statues (*Menologion of Basil II*, 11th c. CE, in Vat.gr.1613 of the Vatican Library)
(Public domain / Wikimedia Commons)

On the Nature of Things, and 'no single thing returns to nothing'. Atomic theory thus neatly did away with the need for and possibility of Creation, Resurrection, the Last Judgement, Hell, Heaven, and the Creator God himself.[352]

While the classical philosophers had variously argued multiple positions on the existence of gods ("that there were countless gods; that there was one god; that there were no gods at all, or that you simply couldn't be sure"[353]), they were tolerated by the general polytheistic populace. This could be because the general population and the philosophers had the same aim in common: to understand nature.

---

[352] Catherine Nixey, *The Darkening Age: The Christian Destruction of the Classical World* (2017) p36

[353] Catherine Nixey, *The Darkening Age: The Christian Destruction of the Classical World* (2017) p147

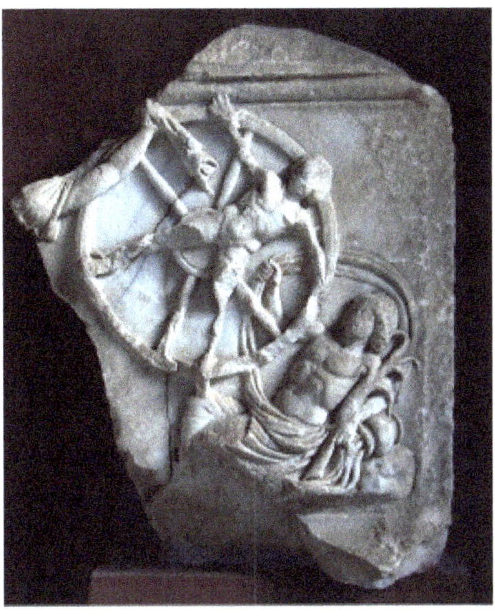

Marble relief from the first or second century showing the mythical transgressor Ixion being tortured on a spinning fiery wheel in Tartarus. Epicurus taught that stories of such punishment in the afterlife are ridiculous superstitions and that believing in them prevents people from attaining ataraxia ("tranquility")
(user:bgds / CC BY-SA 3.0 / Wikimedia Commons)

This was also because the Greeks saw their gods as being similar to themselves:

> it is important not to forget the fact, which Hannah Arendt stressed (quoting Herodotus), that whereas in other religions God is transcendent, beyond time and life and the universe, the Greek gods are *anthropophyeis*, i.e. have the same nature, not simply the same shape, as man. If therefore one takes into account the Greeks' absence of belief in supernatural God, their lack of belief in fixed and revealed truths and the consequent absence of given moral codes, one may assume that Greeks were, in a sense, atheists.[354]

In Christianity, irrationalism is founded on the idea that hu-

---

[354] https://www.democracynature.org/vol4/fotopoulos_irrationalism.htm

man reason cannot fully grasp the meaning of the human condition, and that God and evil coexist in a way that cannot be rationally explained. Therefore, only prayer and faith were necessary for salvation and all earthly necessities and desires were to be swept aside to focus on the promise of eternal life. The Christians attacked classical monuments and shrines, razed temples, burned books and sacred groves, imprisoned and executed 'idolaters'. As a result, according to Helen Ellerbe, "As the Church assumed leadership, activity in the fields of medicine, technology, science, education, history, art, and commerce all but collapsed. Europe entered the Dark Ages. Although the Church amassed immense wealth during these centuries, most of what defines civilization disappeared."[355]

The effect of the Church on classical learning was devastating. While a lot of classical literature was preserved over the centuries "it has been estimated that less than ten per cent of all classical literature has survived into the modern era. For Latin, the figure is even worse: it is estimated that only one hundredth of all Latin literature remains."[356] Instead of celebrating nature directly, people eventually prayed to the Christian "saints for good crops, rain and healthy children almost as pagans once prayed to specific gods assigned to oversee agriculture or fertility."[357]

Christian eschatology (study concerned with the ultimate destiny of the individual soul and the entire created order) and the idea of linear time took over from the people's strong connection with nature and the ever-changing seasons.

Although, according to David Ewing Duncan, in early medieval times the peasants still lived and died "in a continuous cycle of days and years that to them had no discernible past or future."[358] Old habits die hard and the church eventually had no choice but to incorporate polytheistic nature-based traditions of the solstice, the Nativity, Saturnalia, Yuletide, the Easter hare and Easter eggs into their own traditions over time.

---

[355] Helen Ellerbe, *The Dark Side of Christian History* (1995) p41

[356] Catherine Nixey, *The Darkening Age: The Christian Destruction of the Classical World* (2017) p166

[357] David Ewing Duncan, *The Calendar: The 5000-year Struggle to Align the Clock and the Heavens – and What Happened to the Missing Ten Days*, (2011) p142

[358] David Ewing Duncan, *The Calendar: The 5000-year Struggle to Align the Clock and the Heavens – and What Happened to the Missing Ten Days*, (2011) p137

TIME OF YEAR	PRE-CHRISTMAS OR PAGAN TRADITION	CHRISTIAN ADAPTATION
Winter Solstice	The feminine gives birth to the sun or a masculine fertility figure. Often celebrated with yule fires, processions of light, tree decorating.	Christmas Epiphany
Winter Season	A time of nurturing and honoring inspiration and creativity. Common practices involving festivals of light, wearing animal masks and skins in hopes of augmenting the coming year's supply.	Candlemas
Spring Equinox	The sun is resurrected and gains prominence over the night. Fertility celebrations involving symbols such as the egg and the prolific hare.	Easter
Spring season	The mating of the earth and sky from which will come the year's harvest. Often celebrated with maypole dancing, decorating with new foliage.	Pentecost Feast of the Ascension
Summer Solstice	The peak of the sun's light. Celebrated with large bonfires, burning fragrant herbs, decorating with flowers.	Feast of Saint John
Summer Season	The sun's energy transfers to the crops. Ritual blessings of the harvest, herbs, fields, mountains, and ocean. Making figures of dolls or grain.	Assumption Day
Fall Equinox	A time of gratitude for the harvest. Feasts and decorating with fall fruits, grains and vegetables.	Michaelmas Nativity of Mary
Fall Season	Acknowledgment of the year's completion. Honoring the dead, honoring and releasing the past.	All Soul's Day All Saint's Day

Chart of Pagan traditions and Christian adaptations
(The Dark Side of Christian History by Helen Ellerbe)

Science makes a comeback - the Renaissance

By the twelfth century things began to change. The intellectual revitalization of the Renaissance in Europe led to a new vigorous intellectual life. Universities were set up and Europeans gained access to scientific Arabic and Greek texts, including the works of Aristotle, Alhazen, and Averroes. There was a huge increase in the rate of inventions and economic growth. As Jean Gimpel writes in *The Medieval Machine*:

The Middle Ages was one of the great inventive eras of mankind. It should be known as the first industrial revolution in Europe. The scientists and engineers of that time were searching for alternative sources of energy to hydraulic power, wind power, and tidal energy. Between the tenth and the thirteenth centuries, western Europe experienced a technological boom. [...] Energy consumption increased considerably. Technological innovations brought about improvements in the efficiency of existing methods and also led to a successful search for new sources of energy. Many of the tasks formerly done by hand were now carried out by machines. Concurrently, there was a revolution in agricultural methods, which enabled farmers to produce enough food for an expanding population and provide a more varied diet. There was a marked increase in the general standard of living.[359]

The re-emergence of Aristotelian scientific ideas exerted pressure on the Catholic Church to synthesize Aristotelian philosophy with the principles of Christianity. Thomas Aquinas (1225 – 1274) believed that: "Faith and reason, while distinct but related, are the two primary tools for processing the data of theology. Thomas believed both were necessary—or, rather, that the confluence of both was necessary—for one to obtain true knowledge of God." Aquinas combined Greek philosophy and Christian doctrine "by suggesting that rational thinking and the study of nature, like revelation, were valid ways to understand truths pertaining to God."[360] Therefore, the general attitude of the church was bleak. As Peter Gay noted:

Pagan learning, then, was a slave, precious booty, or secret enemy information – all metaphors implying that it was invaluable and indispensable without being respectable. As antique thinker as Augustine defended the use of the classics for religious purposes only. No wonder that the philosophes, who liked their classics neat, could find no virtue in such procedures.[361]

Like the pagan festivals, scientific or rational thinking was incorporated into Christian thinking mainly to bolster Christian theology and not as ends in themselves.

---

[359] Jean Gimpel, *The Medieval Machine: The Industrial Revolution of the Middle Ages* (1986) pviii/ix

[360] https://en.wikipedia.org/wiki/Thomas_Aquinas

[361] Peter Gay, *The Enlightenment: Science of Freedom*, Vol 2 (1995) p221

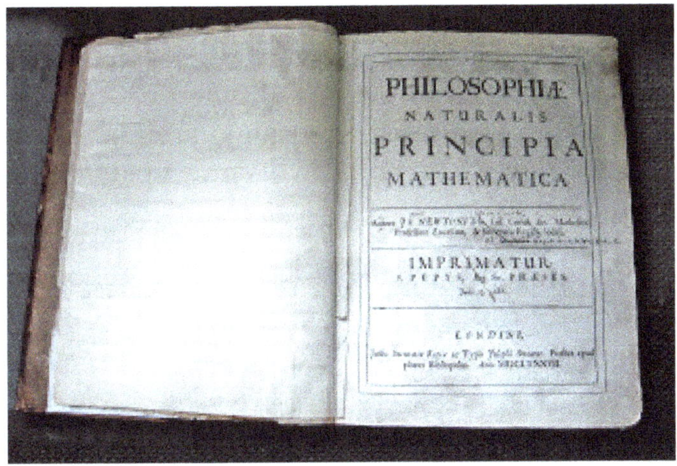

Isaac Newton's (1642–1726/27) copy of *Principia* from 1687. Newton made seminal contributions to classical mechanics, gravity, and optics. Newton also shares credit with Gottfried Leibniz for the development of calculus
(Andrew Dunn / CC BY-SA 2.0 / Wikimedia Commons)

The influence of the Renaissance was long lasting and allowed for the growth of scientific communities which by the sixteenth century produced profound results. The Scientific Revolution is believed to have been initiated by the publication in 1543 of Nicolaus Copernicus' *De revolutionibus orbium coelestium* (*On the Revolutions of the Heavenly Spheres*) and ended in 1632 with publication of Galileo's *Dialogue Concerning the Two Chief World Systems*. It was a process that started with the recovery of what was left of the knowledge of the ancients and was completed by "the 'grand synthesis' of Isaac Newton's 1687 *Principia*.[362] This work formulated the laws of motion and universal gravitation, thereby completing the synthesis of a new cosmology." Indeed, as James Gleick writes in *Isaac Newton*:

Greek mathematics had almost vanished; for centuries, only Islamic mathematicians had kept it alive, meanwhile inventing abstract methods of problem solving called algebra. Now

---

[362] https://en.wikipedia.org/wiki/Scientific_Revolution

Europe became a special case: a region where people were using books and mail and a single language, Latin, to span tribal divisions across hundreds of miles; and where they were, self-consciously, receiving communications from a culture that had flourished and then disintegrated more than a thousand years before.[363]

The Scientific Revolution progressed into the Age of Enlightenment (or the Age of Reason) which became the main intellectual and philosophical movement in Europe during the seventeenth and eighteenth centuries and covered a range of ideas "centered on the pursuit of happiness, sovereignty of reason and the evidence of the senses as the primary sources of knowledge and advanced ideals such as liberty, progress, toleration, fraternity, constitutional government and separation of church and state."[364]

The Romanticist reaction

The revolutionary significance of such progressive ideas was not lost on the wealthy who discussed universal ideas of freedom, equality, and fraternity but soon limited them to their own class. They reacted to progressivism by looking back to medieval times and society (to a non-threatening peasant class) as an ideal, hoping to divert or divide the developing new revolutionary working class. They rejected collectivist ideals and emphasised emotion and individualism. Romanticist ideas had a profound negative effect on the liberatory and progressive aspects of the arts, and Romanticist thinkers influenced liberalism, conservatism, and nationalism. In contrast to the usually social art of the Enlightenment, Romanticists were distrustful of the human world, emphasised a belief in spiritual freedom, individual creativity, the artist's own unique, (often dark) inner vision, ultimately melting away the very notion of objective truth.[365]

---

[363] James Gleick, *Isaac Newton* (2004) p34

[364] https://en.wikipedia.org/wiki/Age_of_Enlightenment

[365] https://en.wikipedia.org/wiki/Romanticism

Philosophers like Arthur Schopenhauer, Friedrich Nietzsche and Søren Kierkegaard emphasised the idea that the world of rationalism was deceptive and ill-equipped to grasp the 'essence' of things.

The rise of Romanticist irrationalism in the twentieth century led to the Nationalist conflicts of the First Word War and the aggressive Fascism of the Second World War. Since then irrationalism has been a more subtle part of many social and political movements. Takis Fotopoulos, for example, has discussed two types of irrationalism: 'old' and 'new' irrationalism. The 'old' irrationalism which has flourished since the Second World War "has taken various forms ranging from the revival, in some cases, of the old religions (Christianity, Islam etc) up to the expansion of various irrational trends (mysticism, spiritualism, astrology, esoterism, neopaganism, 'New Age' etc) which, especially in the West, threaten old religions."[366]

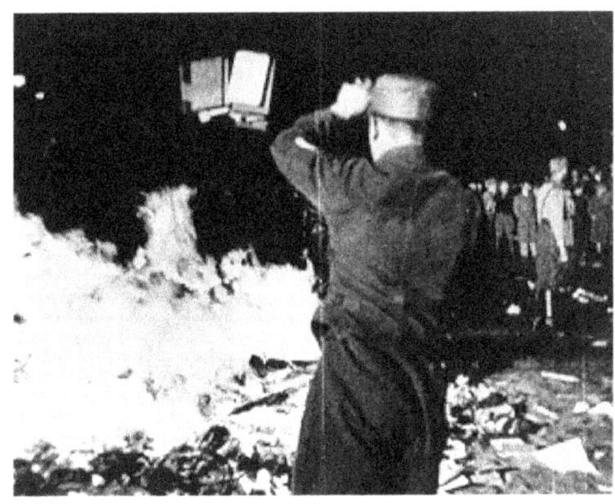

Book burning in Berlin, May 1933
(Public domain / Wikimedia Commons)

Fotopoulos describes three aspects of the 'new' irrationalism in terms of (1) the universalisation of the market/growth economy, (2) the ecological crisis, and (3) the collapse of 'development' in the South. At first, he writes: "at the cultural level, the liberalization and de-regulation of markets have contributed significantly to the present cultural homogenization, which led to an irrational reaction, in the form of the rise of various fundamentalisms [and], at the ideo-

---

[366] https://www.democracynature.org/vol4/fotopoulos_irrationalism.htm

logical level, the emergence of the neoliberal consensus was associated with the rise of postmodernism [a form of Romanticism]."

Secondly, he sees the ecological crisis in terms of "the 'instrumental' or 'pragmatic' approaches versus the 'spiritual' ones". For example, he believes "the deep ecology approach considers the present non-sustainable development as a *cultural* rather than as an institutional issue, as a matter of *values* rather than as the inevitable outcome of the rise of the market economy, with its grow-or-die dynamic, which is to blame for the present growth economy [my emphasis]."

Thirdly, this led to collapse of 'development' in the South:

> Under these circumstances, the return to tradition and, particularly, to religion seemed very appealing to the impoverished people in the South, whose communities and economic self-reliance were being destroyed by the internationalized market/growth economy. Particularly so, when religion was seen as a moral code preaching equality of all men before God set against the injustices of the market/growth economy. Similarly, the return to spirituality looked as the only way to match an imported materialism which was associated with a distorted consumer society, i.e. one that was not even capable of delivering the goods to the majority of the population, as in the North.[367]

Thus, the influence of irrationalism in society today is very broad and deep, and affects so many people and movements negatively. It pervades culture, society and politics. I have argued that the emotion in Enlightenment ideas was based on a genuine desire to end injustice, unlike the self-serving emotion in Romanticist ideas: like the difference between a good friend, and a friend who is only affable when it suits them.

This distinction is demonstrated in the chameleon-like nature of Romanticism which reacts to any progressive ideas or movements by appearing either as a radical opposite while it soaks up dissent (e.g. promoting medieval crafts in opposition to modern industry),

---

[367] https://www.democracynature.org/vol4/fotopoulos_irrationalism.htm

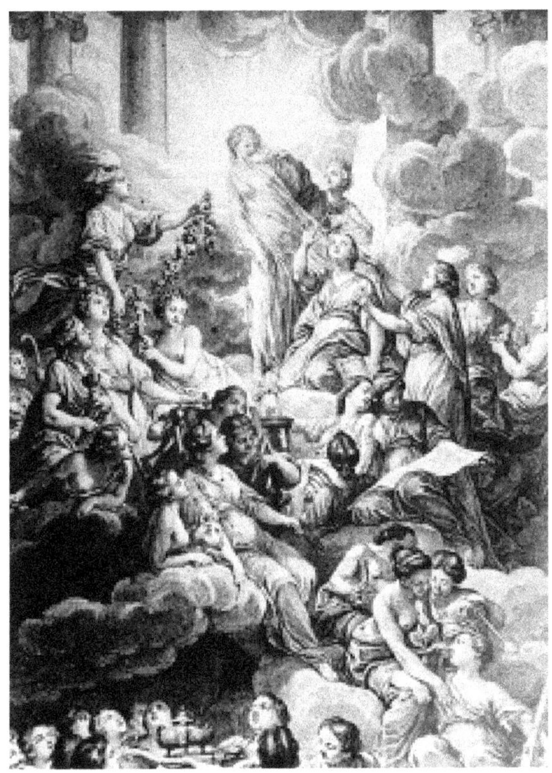

Extract from the frontispiece of the *Encyclopédie* (1772). It was drawn by Charles-Nicolas Cochin and engraved by Bonaventure-Louis Prévost. The work is laden with symbolism: The figure in the centre represents truth—surrounded by bright light (the central symbol of the Enlightenment). Two other figures on the right, reason and philosophy, are tearing the veil from truth
(Public domain / Wikimedia Commons)

or, by appearing progressive when it copies the form while substituting in an opposite content (e.g. the monotheistic Church incorporating polytheistic nature-based traditions of the solstice, the Nativity, Saturnalia, Yuletide, Easter etc. for the benefit of Christianity rather than nature, not to mention modern usage of mass media and the internet). This means that the insidious nature of irrationalism must be constantly exposed and dealt with before it develops its own momentum again and leads to the kind of socio-political disasters we have seen in the past.

However, the importance of the legacy of the Enlightenment is not so much its support for and development of science, but how particular philosophers used that scientific learning to fight against injustice (an older legacy of many centuries of enslavement, exploitation and oppression). The idea that knowledge would not just make one aware of how exploitation and oppression worked, but would develop into ideas and practices that could eventually bring such exploitation and oppression to an end was the truly revolutionary legacy of the Enlightenment movement.

Bibliography

Books and journals

Adorno, T. (2006) *The Culture Industry*, London: Routledge.

Anderson, E. N., 'German Romanticism as an Ideology of Cultural Crisis', p301-312. *Journal of the History of Ideas*, Jun., 1941, Vol. 2, No. 3 (Jun., 1941). University of Pennsylvania Press. (URL: http://www.jstor.com/stable/2707133).

Ang, I. (1991) *Watching Dallas: Soap Opera and the Melodramatic Imagination*, London: Routledge.

Barnard, F. M. (2010) *Herder on Social and Political Culture*, Cambridge: Cambridge.

Beccaria, C. (1872) *An Essay on Crimes and Punishments* [1764], (URL: https://files.libertyfund.org/files/2193/Beccaria_1476_EBk_v6.0.pdf).

Berlin, I. (1961) *The Age of Enlightenment*: The 18th Century Philosophers, selected, with Introduction and Commentary, New York: Mentor.

Berlin, I. (2013) *The Roots of Romanticism*, Princeton: Princeton.

Betz, A. (1982) *Hanns Eisler: Political Musician*, trans Bill Hopkins, Cambridge: Cambridge.

Blanning, T. (2010) *The Romantic Revolution*, London: Phoenix.

Blanning, T. (2008) *The Triumph of Music*: Composers, Musicians and Their Audiences, 1700 to the Present, London: Penguin.

Blechman, M. (ed.), (1999) *Revolutionary Romanticism*: A Drunken Boat Anthology, San Francisco: City Lights.

Boal, A. (1998) *Theatre of the Oppressed*, London: Pluto.

Boucher, G. and **Martyn Lloyd, H**. (eds.), (2018) *Rethinking the Enlightenment: Between History, Philosophy, and Politics*, Lanham: Lexington.

Bronner, S. E. (2004) *Reclaiming the Enlightenment: Towards a Politics of Radical Engagement*, New York: Columbia.

Butler, M. (1981) *Romantics, Rebels and Reactionaries: English Literature and its Background 1760-1830*, Oxford: Oxford.

Clark, K. (1973) *The Romantic Rebellion: Romantic Versus Classic Art*, London: John Murray.

Cronin, M. (2016) *Eco-Translation: Translation and Ecology in the Age of the Anthropocene* (New Perspectives in Translation and Interpreting Studies), London: Routledge.

Denby, D. J. (2006) *Sentimental Narrative and the Social Order in France 1760-1820* (Cambridge Studies in French), Cambridge: Cambridge.

Denby, D. J., 'Individual, universal, national: a French revolutionary trilogy?' (*Studies on Voltaire and the Eighteenth Century*, 335, Voltaire Foundation, 1996).

Denby, D., 'Herder: culture, anthropology and the Enlightenment', *History of the Human Sciences* Vol. 18 No. 1. © 2005 Sage Publications (London, Thousand Oaks, CA and New Delhi).

Duncan, D. E. (1999) *The Calendar: The 5000-year Struggle to Align the Clock and the Heavens – and What Happened to the Missing Ten Days,* London: Fourth Estate.

Ellerbe, H. (1995) *The Dark Side of Christian History,* Windermere: Morningstar and Lark.

Evans, R J. (2000) *In Defence of History,* London: Granta.

Fichte, J. G. (1922) *Addresses to the German Nation* [1808], trans. R.F. Jones and G.H. Turnbull, Chicago and London: Open Court, (URL https://en.wikisource.org/wiki/Addresses_to_the_German_Nation/Front_matter).

Frazer, M. L. (2012) *The Enlightenment of Sympathy*: *Justice and the Moral Sentiments in the Eighteenth Century and Today,* Oxford: Oxford.

Furst, L. R. and **Skrine, P. N.** (1978) *Naturalism,* London: Methuen.

Furst, L. R. (1978) *Romanticism,* London: Methuen.

Gay, P. (1995) *The Enlightenment: The Rise of Modern Paganism,* Vol 1, New York: W.W. Norton.

Gay, P. (1996) *The Enlightenment: Science of Freedom,* Vol 2, New York: W.W. Norton.

Gay, P. (2015) *Why the Romantics Matter* (Why X Matters Series), New Haven: Yale.

Gibbons, L. (2003) *Edmund Burke and Ireland,* Cambridge: Cambridge.

Gimpel, J. (1986) *The Medieval Machine: The Industrial Revolution of the Middle Ages,* Harmondsworth: Penguin.

Gleick, J. (2004) *Isaac Newton,* London: Harper Perennial.

Grabs, M. (ed.) (1999) *Hanns Eisler: A Rebel in Music: Selected Writings by Hanns Eisler,* London: Kahn and Averill.

Grant, D. (1981) *Realism,* London: Methuen.

Greer, T. H. (1972) *A Brief History of Western Man,* New York: Harcourt, Brace, Jovanovich.

Hampson, N. (1990) *The Enlightenment: An evaluation of its assumptions, attitudes and values,* London: Penguin.

Harlow, B. (1987) *Resistance Literature,* London: Methuen.

Hauser, A. (1958) *The Social History of Art,* 4 Vols., New York: Vintage.

Heinberg, R. (1995) *Memories and Visions of Paradise: Exploring the Universal Myth of a Lost Golden Age,* Wheaton: Quest.

Heine, H. (1887) *The Romantic School and Other Essays,* (URL https://www.gutenberg.org/files/37478/37478-h/37478-h.htm).

Herf, J. (2008) *Reactionary Modernism: Technology, culture, and politics in Weimar and the Third Reich,* Cambridge: Cambridge.

Herf, J., '"Dialectic of Enlightenment" Reconsidered', *New German Critique,* Fall 2012, No. 117, Special Issue for Anson Rabinbach (Fall 2012), Duke University Press, (URL: https://www.jstor.org/stable/23357065).

Herman, A. (2003) *The Scottish Enlightenment: The Scots' Invention of the Modern World,* London: Fourth Estate.

Holmes, R. (2009) *The Age of Wonder: How the Romantic Generation Discovered the Beauty and Terror of Science*, London: Harper.

Honour, H. (1991) *Neo-Classicism*, London: Penguin.

Horkheimer, M. and **Adorno, T.** (2002) *Dialectic of Enlightenment Philosophical Fragments,* Stanford: Stanford (URL https://monoskop.org/images/2/27/Horkheimer_Max_Adorno_Theodor_W_Dialectic_of_Enlightenment_Philosophical_Fragments.pdf).

Hutcheson, F. (1726, 2004) *An Inquiry into the Original of our Ideas of Beauty and Virtue* (https://oll.libertyfund.org/title/leidhold-an-inquiry-into-the-original-of-our-ideas-of-beauty-and-virtue-1726-2004)

Israel, J. (2010) *A Revolution of the Mind: Radical Enlightenment and the Intellectual Origins of Modern Democracy*, Princeton: Princeton.

Kant, I. "What is Enlightenment?" "An Answer to the Question: What is Enlightenment?" (1784), (URL https://resources.saylor.org/wwwresources/archived/site/wp-content/uploads/2011/02/What-is-Enlightenment.pdf).

Kennedy, E. (1989) *A Cultural History of the French Revolution,* New Haven: Yale.

Kramnick, I. (ed.) (1995) *The Portable Enlightenment Reader*, New York Penguin.

Levey, M. (1991) *Early Renaissance*, London: Penguin.

Löwy, M. and **Sayre, R.** (2001) *Romanticism Against the Tide of Modernity*, translated by Catherine Porter, Durham: Duke.

Mackenzie, H. (2009) *The Man of Feeling*, Oxford: Oxford.

Marx, K. and **Engels, F.** (1978) *On Literature and Art*, Moscow, Progress Publishers.

McBride, J. (1992) *Frank Capra: The Catastrophe of Success*, New York: Simon and Schuster.

Murphy, R. (1999) *Theorizing the Avant-Garde: Modernism, Expressionism, and the Problem of Postmodernity*, Cambridge, Cambridge.

Nadler, S. (2014) *A Book Forged in Hell: Spinoza's Scandalous Treatise and the Birth of the Secular Age*, Princeton: Princeton.

Nixey, C. (2018) *The Darkening Age: The Christian Destruction of the Classical World*, London: Pan.

Nochlin, L. (1983) *Realism*, Harmondsworth: Penguin.

O'Connor, E. and **Teehan, V.** (2009) *Sean Keating: In Focus*, Limerick: Hunt Museum.

Ó Croidheáin, C. (2006) *Language from Below: The Irish Language, Ideology and Power in 20th Century Ireland*, Oxford: Peter Lang.

Pagden, A. (2015) *The Enlightenment: And Why it Still Matters*, Oxford: Oxford.

Pallasmaa, J. (1996) *The Eyes of the Skin: Architecture and the Senses*, Chichester: Wiley.

Pinker, S. (2018) *Enlightenment Now: The Case for Reason, Science, Humanism, and Progress,* UK: Allen Lane.

Porter, R. (2001) *Enlightenment: Britain and the Creation of the Modern World*, London: Penguin.

Praz, M. (1970) *The Romantic Agony*, London: Oxford.

Prettejohn, E. (2005) *Beauty and Art*, Oxford: Oxford.

Robertson, J. (2015) *The Enlightenment: A Very Short Introduction* (Very Short Introductions), Oxford: Oxford.

Rosenblum, R. (1974) *Transformations in Late Eighteenth Century Art*, Princeton: Princeton.

Ross, A. (2009) *The Rest is Noise: Listening to the Twentieth Century*, London: Harper Perennial.

Rousseau, J-J. and **Herder, J. G.** (1968) *On the Origin of Language: Two Essays by Jean-Jacques Rousseau and Johann Gottfried Herder*, Chicago: University of Chicago Press.

Rousseau, J-J. (1994) *Discourse on Inequality*, Oxford: Oxford.

Russell, B. (1984) *A History of Western Philosophy*, London: Unwin.

Saunders, F. S. (1999) *The Cultural Cold War: The CIA and the World of Arts and Letters*, New York: New Press.

Secretan, D. (1973) *Classicism*, London: Methuen.

Shaftesbury, A. Ashley Cooper Third Earl Of (2001) *Characteristics of Men, Manners, Opinions, Times* [1711], (URL https://oll.libertyfund.org/title/shaftesbury-characteristicks-of-men-manners-opinions-times-3-vols).

Shi, D. E. (1996) *Facing Facts: Realism in American Thought and Culture 1850-1920*, New York: Oxford.

Snowman, D. (2010) *The Gilded Stage: A Social History of Opera*, London: Atlantic.

Solnit, R. (2014) *Wanderlust: A History of Walking*, London: Granta.

Solomon, R. C. (1995) *A Passion for Justice: Emotions and the Origins of the Social Contract*, Lanham: Rowman.

Spencer, V., 'In Defense of Herder on Cultural Diversity and Interaction', *The Review of Politics*, Winter, 2007, Vol. 69, No. 1 (Winter, 2007), Cambridge: Cambridge.

Strathern, P. (2005) *The Medici: Godfathers of the Renaissance*, London: Pimlico.

Till, N. (1993) *Mozart and the Enlightenment: Truth, Virtue and Beauty in Mozart's Operas*, London: Faber and Faber.

Weber, E. (1979) *Peasants into Frenchmen: The Modernization of Rural France, 1870-1914*, London: Chatto & Windus.

Wheen, F. (2004) *How Mumbo Jumbo Conquered the World*, London: Harper Perennial.

White, D. A. (2008) *Siqueiros: Biography of a Revolutionary Artist*, Booksurge.com.

Wolfe, T. (1987) *The Painted Word*, Toronto: Bantam.

Wu, D. (ed.), (2006) *A Companion to Romanticism*, Oxford: Blackwell.

Index

Enlightenment is mankind's exit from its self-incurred immaturity. Immaturity is the inability to make use of one's own understanding without the guidance of another. *Self-incurred* is this inability if its cause lies not in the lack of understanding but rather in the lack of the resolution and the courage to use it without the guidance of another. *Sapere aude!* Have the courage to use your *own* understanding! is thus the motto of enlightenment.

Immanuel Kant
An Answer to the Question: What Is Enlightenment?